RENEGADES

BORN IN THE USA

BRUCE
SPRINGSTEEN

RENEG

BORN IN THE USA

NEW YORK

BARACK OBAMA

GADES

DREAMS · MYTHS · MUSIC

CROWN

Here everybody has a neighbor,
everybody has a friend

Everybody has a reason to begin again

My father said "Son, we're lucky in this town
it's a beautiful place to be born

It just wraps its arms around you,
Nobody crowds you, nobody goes it alone.

You know that flag flying over the courthouse
Means certain things are set in stone

Who we are, what we'll do and what we won't"

It's gonna be a long walk home

–BRUCE SPRINGSTEEN,
"LONG WALK HOME"

We are one people, all of us pledging allegiance to the stars and stripes, all of us defending the United States of America. . . . Do we participate in a politics of cynicism or do we participate in a politics of hope? . . .

I'm not talking about blind optimism here—the almost willful ignorance that thinks unemployment will go away if we just don't think about it, or the health care crisis will solve itself if we just ignore it. That's not what I'm talking about. I'm talking about something more substantial. It's the hope of slaves sitting around a fire singing freedom songs. The hope of immigrants setting out for distant shores. The hope of a young naval lieutenant bravely patrolling the Mekong Delta. The hope of a millworker's son who dares to defy the odds. The hope of a skinny kid with a funny name who believes that America has a place for him, too.

Hope in the face of difficulty. Hope in the face of uncertainty. The audacity of hope! In the end, that is God's greatest gift to us, the bedrock of this nation. A belief in things not seen. A belief that there are better days ahead.

—BARACK OBAMA,
KEYNOTE ADDRESS,
2004 DEMOCRATIC NATIONAL CONVENTION

CONTENTS

3

AMAZING GRACE

4

AMERICAN SKIN

7

8

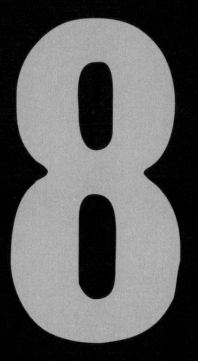

A FEARLESS LOVE

THE RISING

INTRODUCTION

Good conversations don't follow a script. Like a good song, they're full of surprises, improvisations, detours. They may be grounded in a specific time and place, reflecting your current state of mind and the current state of the world. But the best conversations also have a timeless quality, taking you back into the realm of memory, propelling you forward toward your hopes and dreams. Sharing stories reminds you that you're not alone—and maybe helps you understand yourself a little bit better.

When Bruce and I first sat down in the summer of 2020 to record *Renegades: Born in the USA*, we didn't know how our conversations would turn out. What I did know was that Bruce was a great storyteller, a bard of the American experience—and that we both had a lot on our minds, including some fundamental questions about the troubling turn our country had taken. A historic pandemic showed no signs of abating. Americans everywhere were out of work. Millions had just taken to the streets to protest the murder of George Floyd, and the then occupant of the White House seemed intent not on bringing people together but on tearing down some of the basic values and institutional foundations of our democracy.

Almost a year later, the world looks a shade brighter. Thanks to amazing scientific advances and the tireless efforts of countless health workers on the front lines, the pandemic has receded (though not ended) and the economy is experiencing a steady if uneven recovery. George Floyd's killer has been convicted and sentenced, and my friend and former vice president, Joe Biden, is president of the United States.

But for all the change we've experienced as a nation and in our own lives since Bruce and I first sat down together for our recording sessions, the underlying conditions that animated our conversation haven't gone away. America remains more polarized than at any time we can remember—not just around issues like policing, climate change, taxes, and immigration, but over the very definitions of faith and family, on what constitutes justice, and whose voices deserve to be heard. We still grapple, in ways large and small, with the legacy of slavery and Jim Crow and the scourge of racism. The chasm between rich and poor continues to grow, with too many families struggling to get by. Even a violent attack on the US Capitol—a blow to our democratic order that was broadcast in real time for all the world to see—is subject to dispute, with a big chunk of the country either pretending it didn't happen or suggesting that the anger of the mob was somehow justified.

That's why the conversations Bruce and I had in 2020 feel as urgent today as they did back then. They represent our ongoing effort to figure out how it is that we got here, and how we can tell a more unifying story that starts to close the gap between America's ideals and its reality.

We didn't come up with any simple formulas for resolving America's ongoing conflicts. As different as our backgrounds are, as much as we've tried in our work to give voice to the thousands of people whom we've met along the way, neither Bruce nor I can claim to capture all the divergent perspectives and attitudes that make up this big, raucous country of ours.

If nothing else, we tried to show that it's possible to approach tough issues with compassion, humor, and conviction, but also a big dose of humility. And in fact, since the podcast was released, both of us have heard from folks from every state and every walk of life who've reached out to say that something in what they heard resonated with them, whether it was the imprint our fathers left on us; the awkwardness, sadness, anger, and occasional moments of grace that have arisen as we navigate America's racial divide; or the joy and redemption that our respective families have given us. People told us that listening to us talk made them think about their own childhoods. Their own dads. Their own hometowns.

They also asked Bruce and me questions, wanting to know a little more about the stories we told—which is what led to this book. In the pages that follow, you can read our conversations in full. But you'll also find the text of speeches, personal photos, and handwritten song lyrics that track some of the moments described in the podcast and that serve as markers along the crisscrossing highways and byways that each of us has traveled.

Our greatest wish is that our conversations inspire you to go out and start one of your own—with a friend, family member, coworker, or someone you know only in passing. Someone whose life intersects with yours but whose story you've never really heard. We're betting that if you listen hard enough, with an open heart, you'll feel encouraged. Because at a time when it's easy to talk past each other, or just restrict our conversations to those who look or think or pray like we do, the future depends on our ability to recognize how we're all a part of the American story—and that we can write a new and better chapter together.

—PRESIDENT BARACK OBAMA

When President Obama suggested we do a podcast together, my first thought was, *Okay, I'm a high school graduate from Freehold, New Jersey, who plays the guitar. . . . What's wrong with this picture?* Patti said, "Are you insane?! Do it! People would love to hear your conversations!" The president and I had spent some time together since we met on the campaign trail in '08. That time included some long, telling conversations. These were the kind of talks where you speak from the heart and walk away with a real understanding of the way your friend thinks and feels. You have a picture of the way he sees himself and his world. So I took Patti's advice and followed the president's generous lead, and before we knew it we were sitting in my New Jersey studio (which the E Street Band had recently vacated), riffing off each other like good musicians.

We started at the start: growing up, our similarities, our differences. Hawaii, New Jersey . . . pretty different; absentee fathers . . . pretty similar. We then let the conversation expand as life itself does. We explored the way you start to put together an identity, from a pose, a photo, a piece of music, a movie, a cultural hero. We examined the way you struggle to find your strengths, your potency, your manhood. We delved into how that shapes your art, your politics, and the way you are going to live your life. It was all about life and how it is lived, the world as it stands and the efforts we have made to shape that world, me through my music and Barack through his politics, into the kind of place we feel it could be.

There were serious conversations about the fate of the country, the fortunes of its citizens, and the destructive, ugly, corrupt forces at play that would like to take it all down. This is a time of vigilance when who we are is being seriously tested. Hard conversations about who we are and who we want to become can perhaps serve as a small guiding map for some of our fellow citizens. We found a lot in common. The president is funny and an easy guy to be around. He'll go out of his way to make you feel comfortable, as he did for me so that I might have the confidence to sit across the table from him. At the end of the day we recognized our similarities in the moral shape of our lives. It was the presence of a promise, a code we strive to live by. Honesty, fidelity, a forthrightness about who we are and what our goals and ideas are, a dedication to the American idea and an abiding love for the country that made us. We are both creatures stamped BORN IN THE USA. There is no other country that could have concocted the mix that makes a Barack Obama or a Bruce Springsteen, so our allegiance to its institutions, its dreams, and its ambitions remains unyielding. It's why we're here. Guided by our families, our deep friendships, and the moral compass inherent in our nation's history, we press forward, guarding the best of us while retaining a compassionate eye for the struggles of our still young nation.

As I've said, these are treacherous times with much at stake—with everything at stake. This is a time for serious consideration of who we want to be and what kind of country we will leave our children. Will we let slip through our hands the best of us or will we turn united to face the fire? Within this book you won't find the answers to those questions, but you will find a couple of seekers doing their best to get us to ask better questions. Safe journey, Mr. President, and thanks for picking up a fellow traveler and having me along for the ride.

—BRUCE SPRINGSTEEN

OUR UNLIKELY FRIENDSHIP

1

As it did for many people, the year 2020 stirred up a whole lot of emotions in me. For three years, I'd witnessed a country that seemed to be getting angrier and more divided with each passing day. Then came a historic pandemic, along with a slipshod government response that rained hardship and loss on millions and forced all of us to consider what's really important in life. How did we get here? How could we find our way back to a more unifying American story?

That topic came to dominate so many of my conversations last year—with Michelle, with my daughters, and with friends. And one of the friends was Mr. Bruce Springsteen.

On the surface, Bruce and I don't have a lot in common. He's a white guy from a small town in Jersey. I'm a Black guy of mixed race born in Hawaii with a childhood that took me around the world. He's a rock 'n' roll icon. I'm . . . not as cool. And, as I like to remind Bruce every chance I get, he's more than a decade older than me. Though he looks damn good.

But over the years, what we've found is that we've got a shared sensibility. About work, about family, and about America. In our own ways, Bruce and I have been on parallel journeys trying to understand this country that's given us both so much. Trying to chronicle the stories of its people. Looking for a way to connect our own individual searches for meaning and truth and community with the larger story of America.

And what we discovered during these conversations was that we still share a fundamental belief in the American ideal. Not as an airbrushed, cheap fiction or as an act of nostalgia that ignores all the ways that we've fallen short of that ideal, but as a compass for the hard work that lies before each of us as citizens to make this place and the world more equal, more just, and more free.

Plus, Bruce just had some great stories.

So we added a participant to our conversations: a microphone. And over the course of a few days at the converted farmhouse and property that Bruce shares with his amazing wife, Patti, along with a few horses, a whole bunch of dogs, and a thousand guitars—all just a few miles from where he grew up—we talked.

CHAPTER
— 1 —

BRUCE SPRINGSTEEN: A question: How do you like to be addressed?

PRESIDENT OBAMA: Barack, man. Come on, dude.

BRUCE SPRINGSTEEN: Just checking! I want to get it right.

PRESIDENT OBAMA: So we're sitting here in the great state of New Jersey with one of New Jersey's prodigal sons. . . .

BRUCE SPRINGSTEEN: That's about right.

PRESIDENT OBAMA: The Boss, my friend: Bruce Springsteen. And we're in a studio—just to paint a picture here, we've got . . . How many guitars you got up in here?

BRUCE SPRINGSTEEN: We're looking at the house of a thousand guitars right now. . . .

PRESIDENT OBAMA: I haven't counted them all. But there are guitars everywhere. There is a ukulele, a banjo. . . .

BRUCE SPRINGSTEEN: So if we get moved to make music, we—

PRESIDENT OBAMA: I've been known to sing.

BRUCE SPRINGSTEEN: —we got the instruments at hand.

PRESIDENT OBAMA: It's good to see you, my friend. What brings us here today are conversations we've had over the years. Both of us had to be storytellers. We *had* to tell our own stories, and they became a part of a larger American narrative. The story we told resonated.

I was trying to remember the first time we actually met, and it probably was in 2008. During the campaign.

BRUCE SPRINGSTEEN: That's right.

PRESIDENT OBAMA: You came to do a concert with us in Ohio. Your family was with you and I remember thinking, "He's very low-key, even maybe a little bit shy." And I liked that in you. So I thought, "I hope I get a chance to talk to him at some point." But because it was in the middle of the campaign, we were rushing around. So, you know, we had a nice chat, but it wasn't like we had a deep conversation.

BRUCE SPRINGSTEEN: No.

OPPOSITE, TOP: Along with Jay-Z and Bruce Springsteen, dozens of musicians performed and recorded in support of Barack Obama's 2008 presidential campaign, including Arcade Fire, P Diddy, Stevie Wonder, Jeff Tweedy, John Legend, Moby, Common, The Decemberists, Roger Waters, Patti Smith, Pearl Jam, Joan Baez, Michael Stipe, and Usher. In October 2008, the official 2008 campaign soundtrack, titled *Yes We Can*, was released. **OPPOSITE, BOTTOM:** Ticket for the Change Rocks campaign rally in Philadelphia, 2008. **FOLLOWING:** Finishing the night on the Darkness tour, 1978.

FIRST NAME _____ MI _____

LAST NAME _____

EMAIL _____

CELL PHONE _____ HOME PHONE _____

ADDRESS _____

CITY _____ ZIP CODE _____

☐ I WANT TO RECEIVE CAMPAIGN TEXT UPDATES
☐ I NEED TO REGISTER TO VOTE
☐ PLEASE SEND ME MORE INFORMATION ABOUT BARACK OBAMA
☐ I WILL VOLUNTEER ON ELECTION DAY, NOV. 4TH

VOTEFORCHANGE.COM

CHANGE ROCKS
with **BRUCE SPRINGSTEEN**

SATURDAY, OCTOBER 4TH

GATES OPEN *at* 2:00 PM
SHOW STARTS *at* 3:30 PM

BENJAMIN FRANKLIN PARKWAY
BETWEEN 20TH AND 22ND STREETS
PHILADELPHIA, PA

FREE & OPEN TO ALL PENNSYLVANIA RESIDENTS & STUDENTS
For info, visit PA.BARACKOBAMA.COM/SPRINGSTEEN

PAID FOR BY OBAMA FOR AMERICA

PRESIDENT OBAMA: There was also the time in New York when you and Billy Joel got up onstage and you guys did a whole concert. That was the first time I saw how much you were working out in the middle of your shows. You were jumping up and down on a piano. You were drenched, man. You were soaked. And I thought, "That man, he might hurt himself out there." But I had been a fan from afar for a long time. And we had started playing some of your music at our rallies. And then we just reached out and said, "Hey, would you be willing to do something?"

BRUCE SPRINGSTEEN: I had wonderful experiences playing those rallies and those appearances with you. Because you gave me something that I've never been able to give myself. And that was the diversity that was in the audience. I was playing to white faces and Black faces, old people and young people. And that's the audience that I always dreamed of for my band. One of the nicest events I had ever performed at was when Jay-Z and I played in Columbus. I think I played "Promised Land."

It was a fabulous audience. All kinds of people—working-class people, old folks, and young folks. A lot of folks who didn't know me from the man in the moon, probably hearing me maybe for the first time.

PRESIDENT OBAMA: But the same was true for Jay-Z. I guarantee there were a bunch of elderly white folks in that crowd who had not heard a Jay-Z song in their lives. And I had to tell him, "Change a few lyrics here, brother." We need the family version of some of his stuff.

BRUCE SPRINGSTEEN: It was the first time I met him . . . great guy. I only played three or four songs, but it was a deeply thrilling performance. This is the audience of my dreams, the audience I imagined playing for.

Plus, there is so much of the language of my writing that comes out of Christian faith, out of gospel, out of the Bible. There was a commonality of language that filtered across cultural lines.

PRESIDENT OBAMA: Right, folks feel it. Which is why when you do something like "The Rising"—with a choir in the back—or "Promised Land" . . . you might have been a preacher, Bruce. You might have missed your calling.

BRUCE SPRINGSTEEN: It was a gift to be able to be there. I have a lot of great memories of playing those rallies. I had watched you ever since you were a senator. You came up on my screen and I thought, "Yeah, that's the language I want to speak, that

Promised Land

On a rattlesnake speedway in the Utah desert
Willi Lee collats his money & drives back ~~home~~ heads back into town
ridii thags Saoba ob get a drink -radio up
  loud so Willy Lee dont have to think
About workin all day in his daddy's garage
"   drivin all night chasin some mirage
that vanishes soon as you get it in your hands

    blow away the dreams that tear you apart
    "   "   "   "   " break your heart
    " everythi done stot and got the faith
        to stand too

C'ertain things come easy when your face down
        in the dirt
you think you can give it all away & it wont
        hurt
did your eyes go blind your blood runs cold you feel
        so weak you susst wanna explode
explode
reach out across this desolation
take out the walls

Willie Lee rode thrugh the desert & was crowned king
made love to angels with burnig wings
sley burnd his hands burnd his eyes burnd his
    heart with dreams of lies

    out in the desert you cant hear a thing

    I wanna go out tonight & find out what
            I got
    I wanna scream out loud in somebodys face

On a rattlesnake speedway in the Utah desert / I pick up my money and head back into town / Driving 'cross the Waynesboro county line / I got the radio on and I'm just killing time / Working all day in my daddy's garage / Driving all night chasing some mirage / Pretty soon, little girl, I'm gonna take charge / The dogs on Main Street howl / 'Cause they understand / If I could take one moment into my hands / Mister, I ain't a boy, no I'm a man / And I believe in a promised land / I've done my best to live the right way / I get up every morning and go to work each day / But your eyes go blind and your blood runs cold / Sometimes I feel so weak I just want to explode / Explode and tear this whole town apart / Take a knife and cut this pain from my heart / Find somebody itching for something to start / There's a dark cloud rising from the desert floor / I packed my bags and I'm heading straight into the storm / Gonna be a twister to blow everything down / That ain't got the faith to stand its ground / Blow away the dreams that tear you apart / Blow away the dreams that break your heart / Blow away the lies that leave you nothing but lost and brokenhearted

—FROM DARKNESS ON THE EDGE OF TOWN (1978)

I am *trying* to speak." I felt an enormous internal commonality with your vision of the country.

PRESIDENT OBAMA: It felt like we were striving for the same thing. In our own mediums in our own different ways. So when you talk about that straddling between these two places—"Here's where I want the country to be and here's where it is." I've got to be rooted in where it is. But I want to push and nudge folks to where it could be.

BRUCE SPRINGSTEEN: Yeah. In our little corner of what we do, we are working on the same building.

PRESIDENT OBAMA: That's exactly right. And we had a number of those interactions over the years: you performed at the inaugural concert, came by the White House; I run for reelection, you do some more stuff.

BRUCE SPRINGSTEEN: We had a nice dinner or two.

PRESIDENT OBAMA: We had a great dinner at the White House where we sang—

BRUCE SPRINGSTEEN: I played the piano, and you sang.

PRESIDENT OBAMA: Well, I don't know about that. But we all sang some Broadway tunes. And some Motown. And some classics.

BRUCE SPRINGSTEEN: That's right.

PRESIDENT OBAMA: And there were libations involved. And then I said, "Well, he's not as shy as I thought, he just has to loosen up a little bit."

BRUCE SPRINGSTEEN: I don't know if I would say it's true for most people in my business, but the shyness is not unusual. If you weren't quiet, you wouldn't have so desperately searched for a way to speak. The reason you have so desperately pursued your work and your language and your voice is because you haven't had one. And once you realize that, you feel the pain of being somewhat voiceless.

PRESIDENT OBAMA: And so the performance then becomes the tool, the mechanism—

BRUCE SPRINGSTEEN: It becomes the mechanism from which you express the entirety of your life—your entire philosophy and code for living—and that was how it came to me. And I felt, previous to that, I was pretty invisible, and there was a lot of pain in that invisibility.

PRESIDENT OBAMA: And see, the kind of thing that you just said here is how we became friends. Because after a few drinks, and maybe in between songs, you'd say something like that, and I'd say, "Aw, that makes sense to me." Those are some deep waters. And I think that we just grew to trust each other and have those kinds of conversations on an ongoing basis, and once I left the White House we were able to spend more time together. And, turns out, we're just a little simpatico.

BRUCE SPRINGSTEEN: I felt really at home around you.

PRESIDENT OBAMA: And the other part of it was Michelle and Patti hit it off. And Michelle was very pleased about the insights you had about your failings as a man. After we would leave a dinner, or a party, or a conversation, she'd say, "You see how Bruce understands his shortcomings and has come to terms with them—"

BRUCE SPRINGSTEEN: Ha! Sorry about that.

PRESIDENT OBAMA: "—in a way that you have not? You should spend some more time with Bruce. Because he's put in the work." And so there was also a little of the sense that I needed to get coached in how to be a proper husband.

BRUCE SPRINGSTEEN: It's been my pleasure.

PRESIDENT OBAMA: I tried to explain: "Look, he's ten years older than me. He's been through some of this stuff. I'm still in

> THE REASON YOU HAVE SO DESPERATELY PURSUED YOUR WORK AND YOUR LANGUAGE AND YOUR VOICE IS BECAUSE YOU HAVEN'T HAD ONE. . . . YOU FEEL THE PAIN OF BEING SOMEWHAT VOICELESS.
>
> —BRUCE SPRINGSTEEN

ABOVE: A night at Camp David, 2015. **OPPOSITE:** Celebrating change, 2008.

training mode." But despite the fact that we come from such different places and obviously had different career paths, the same issues that you struggle with have been issues I've struggled with. The same joys and doubts. There's a lot of overlap.

BRUCE SPRINGSTEEN: Well, the political comes from the personal.

PRESIDENT OBAMA: If a musician is looking for a way to channel and work through pain, demons, personal questions, so is a politician when getting into public life.

BRUCE SPRINGSTEEN: But you gotta have two things going, which is very difficult. One, you've got to have the egotism—

PRESIDENT OBAMA: The megalomania—

BRUCE SPRINGSTEEN: The megalomania to believe that you have a voice that is worth being heard by the whole world. Yet on the other hand, you've got to have the tremendous empathy for other people.

PRESIDENT OBAMA: It's a hard trick to pull off. You start off with ego, but then at some point you become a vessel for people's hopes and dreams. You just become a conduit. We're talking today just after I delivered the eulogy for my friend John Lewis, one of the giants of the civil rights movement and somebody who was probably as responsible as anyone for making America a better, freer, more generous place, and making our democracy live up to its promise. The first time I met John, he came to speak at Harvard, where I was at law school. After he spoke, I came up to him and said, "You are one of my heroes. You helped me find my sense of who I at least wanted to be in this huge, complicated, contentious, multiracial, multiethnic, multireligious place called America."

Because when I got into politics, I didn't say to myself that I wanted to be president. It was a journey. How do I reconcile all the different parts of me? How do I belong?

BRUCE SPRINGSTEEN: To come at it like that is coming at it as an outsider. . . .

PRESIDENT OBAMA: This is going to be interesting, because I'm going to have to figure out why you thought you were

> MICHELLE WAS VERY PLEASED ABOUT THE INSIGHTS YOU HAD ABOUT YOUR FAILINGS AS A MAN. . . . SHE'D SAY, . . . "YOU SHOULD SPEND SOME MORE TIME WITH BRUCE. BECAUSE HE'S PUT IN THE WORK." AND SO THERE WAS ALSO A LITTLE OF THE SENSE THAT I NEEDED TO GET COACHED IN HOW TO BE A PROPER HUSBAND.
>
> —PRESIDENT OBAMA

an outsider. I know why *I* was an outsider. A nice Jersey boy doesn't have to be an outsider. You know what I mean?

BRUCE SPRINGSTEEN: I don't think it's something that you choose! I think it's something that is innate. I had a very, very strange upbringing. You know, I grew up in a small town, very provincial. The great town of Freehold, New Jersey.

PRESIDENT OBAMA: Population?

BRUCE SPRINGSTEEN: Around ten thousand. Sixteen hundred of whom worked at the Karagheusian Rug Mill, including my dad. My mom was the main breadwinner. My father worked when he could, but he was pretty mentally ill. Since he was quite young, he'd suffered from schizophrenia, which we didn't understand at the time, but it made life at home very difficult and it made holding on to any kind of job very difficult. So our house was different from others, I'd say.

PRESIDENT OBAMA: My upbringing on the surface looks completely different.

BRUCE SPRINGSTEEN: Right.

PRESIDENT OBAMA: I'm born in Hawaii—Hawaii's a long ways from Freehold, New Jersey.

BRUCE SPRINGSTEEN: It's a long way from everywhere!

PRESIDENT OBAMA: Yeah, in the middle of the Pacific. And I am the product of a mom from Kansas: a teenager when she had me, and a college student who had met my father, who was an African student at the University of Hawaii. Now, my grandparents are basically Scots-Irish. And the Irish were outsiders for a long time.

BRUCE SPRINGSTEEN: Yeah. My grandparents were old-school Irish people. And they were very provincial: quite backward, country people. We all lived in one house: my parents, my grandparents, and myself.

OPPOSITE: Law school days, Cambridge, MA, circa 1991. Barack Obama had just had his bandages taken off after breaking his nose playing basketball.

PRESIDENT OBAMA: Grandparents on your dad's side or mom's side?

BRUCE SPRINGSTEEN: My grandparents on my dad's side. I was brought up from the Irish side of my family, and they were just as eccentric as American Irish could be. And they started me off when I was a very young child on simply being different from everybody else.

PRESIDENT OBAMA: Yeah. I tell a story about how my grandfather used to take me to the beach, where he'd play checkers and he'd drink beers. I still have memories of that little bottle of Primo beer that had King Kamehameha's picture on the front of it. The tourists would come up and they'd see me, when I'm like three, four, five years old, and they'd say, "Is he Hawaiian?" My grandfather would say, "Yeah, he's the great-grandson of King Kamehameha," and they'd be taking pictures.

BRUCE SPRINGSTEEN: I like that.

PRESIDENT OBAMA: It's a nice story in the sense that my grandfather enjoyed pulling the wool over their eyes. But it's also a story about the fact that I wasn't easily identifiable. I felt like an outsider. There was visible proof that I wasn't like everybody else.

BRUCE SPRINGSTEEN: And what city were you in?

PRESIDENT OBAMA: Honolulu, Hawaii, which is this little jewel in the middle of the ocean that is made up of all these immigrants who come from all these different places. You've got Japanese and Chinese, Portuguese who've come over as seamen, and you've got the native Hawaiians, who, like many indigenous peoples, find themselves decimated by disease. And so there is a base culture that's beautiful and powerful. But as a kid I'm looking around and none of these people really look like me.

BRUCE SPRINGSTEEN: My initial memories of Freehold were pretty Norman Rockwell–ish. As a child in a small town, you're immersed in it: Memorial Day parades, VFW marches, American Legion, the flags. When I was a kid, they gave you one of those tiny flags at the Memorial Day parade and you waved it. And I think I felt a sense of belonging to something that was very special, a sense that we were a blessed country in some way. There had been a great war. We won. We fought

for the freedom of others. We risked American lives in other lands. We were the good guys. My father was a truck driver at the Battle of the Bulge. And there was that feeling that of all the countries of the world, God looked down especially favorably on the United States. As a child, that had a deep impact and was unforgettable.

But my grandparents, they allowed me freedoms that children really shouldn't have, because my grandmother had lost her daughter, my father's sister, in a traffic accident at five years old. There was a gas station on the corner of McLean Street, two blocks from where we all lived. She was there on a tricycle and was run over by a truck. I was the next child that came along, the redemptive child. I was given complete license to do whatever I wanted to do.

PRESIDENT OBAMA: So what were you doing, man? I mean, you were just tearing up, tearing up Freehold? Just running rampant?

BRUCE SPRINGSTEEN: Exactly! At five years old.

PRESIDENT OBAMA: Up and down the streets? Terrorizing the population—

BRUCE SPRINGSTEEN: I was given so much license. I was getting up later than all the other kids. I was going to bed later than all the other kids. I didn't fit in. I did . . . not . . . like . . . the rules. If you're a kid like me and school presents to you a set of rules, you're not prepared for them. I said, "OK, what do I want to do?" And it wasn't until I discovered music and found a way to process my own identity, and to find a way to speak and to have some impact on how to be heard, that I began to feel at home where I lived.

PRESIDENT OBAMA: When I heard your music, I caught that sense of emotional displacement, and it was a reminder that, in a lot of ways, in America we all have started off in some fashion as outsiders. What was the makeup of Freehold?

ABOVE: Splashing around, Hawaii, 1966. **OPPOSITE** (clockwise from top left): President Obama's mother, Ann Dunham, and her mother, Madelyn Dunham, circa 1958; Obama's grandfather, Stanley Dunham, and the "great-grandson of King Kamehameha," Hawaii, 1966; early portrait, Hawaii, circa 1961; Obama and his mother at her college graduation, Hawaii, circa 1967; Obama and his first set of wheels, Hawaii, circa 1964; Obama's father, Barack Obama Sr., during his college years, Hawaii, circa 1960; Ann Dunham, in college, circa 1960; (center) Obama's maternal grandparents, Stanley and Madelyn Dunham, California, circa 1945.

My HomeTown

I was 8 yrs old + runnin with a dime in my hand
        into the bus top to pick up a paper for my
                old man
I'd sit on his lap in that big ol' Buick and steer
            as we drove through town
he'd tussel my hair and say son take a good
            look around. this is your hometown

In 65 Tension was runnin high at my high school
there was a lotta fights tween the black and white
            there was nothin you could do
2 cars at a light on a Saturday night in the
            backseat there was a gun
words were passed in a shotgun blast
        troubled times had come
            to my hometown

Now Main streets whitewashed windows + vacant
                stores
seems like there ain't nobody (wants to)
        comin down here no more
they're closin down the textile mill cross the tracks
    (railroad) texas tracks
        foreman says these jobs are goin boys
            and they ain't comin back
                to your hometown

Last night me and Kate we layed in bed talkin bout
    gettin out packin up our bags maybe headin
we   south   I'm 35
& got a boy of our own now last night I ~~teach him~~
~~down~~ ~~town~~ sittin up behind the wheel and
        said son take a good look now
                this is your hometown

MY HOMETOWN

I was eight years old and running with a dime in my hand / Into the bus stop to pick up a paper for my old man / I'd sit on his lap in that big old Buick and steer as we drove through town / He'd tousle my hair and say son take a good look around this is your hometown / This is your hometown / This is your hometown / This is your hometown / In '65 tension was running high at my high school / There was a lot of fights between the black and white / There was nothing you could do / Two cars at a light on a Saturday night in the back seat there was a gun / Words were passed in a shotgun blast / Troubled times had come to my hometown / My hometown / My hometown / My hometown / Now Main Street's whitewashed windows and vacant stores / Seems like there ain't nobody wants to come down here no more / They're closing down the textile mill across the railroad tracks / Foreman says these jobs are going boys and they ain't coming back to your hometown / Your hometown / Your hometown / Your hometown / Last night me and Kate we laid in bed / talking about getting out / Packing up our bags maybe heading south / I'm thirty-five we got a boy of our own now / Last night I sat him up behind the wheel and said son take a good look around / This is your hometown

—FROM BORN IN THE U.S.A. (1984)

APR . 65

BRUCE SPRINGSTEEN: The shore was a lot of Irish/Italians and then the African Americans from the South, who were bused up every summer to work in the potato fields outside of town. So I grew up in a bit of an integrated neighborhood. I had Black friends when I was really young. But there were a lot of rules.

PRESIDENT OBAMA: Whose house you go to . . .

BRUCE SPRINGSTEEN: That's right, and who you can't have in your house.

PRESIDENT OBAMA: Right.

BRUCE SPRINGSTEEN: And whose house you shouldn't be in.

PRESIDENT OBAMA: That's before you even start talking about dating or—

BRUCE SPRINGSTEEN: That's right. You're a child on your bicycle. And you're aware of all of these unspoken rules. Freehold was your typical small, provincial, redneck, racist little American 1950s town. It was a town that suffered a lot of racial strife in the late sixties. The day of the Newark riots there was rioting in Freehold, a little town of around ten thousand people. They brought in the state troopers, and there was a state of emergency.

PRESIDENT OBAMA: How old were you at that point?

BRUCE SPRINGSTEEN: I was seventeen, in high school.

PRESIDENT OBAMA: You talk about *redneck*. That term has a particular set of connotations, you know, in the same way that in the African American community we can say certain things about ourselves. You've got to feel a certain comfort and love for a community to be able to describe it in terms like that. An outsider says that, you might get into a fight.

BRUCE SPRINGSTEEN: Of course!

PRESIDENT OBAMA: How do you think about that?

BRUCE SPRINGSTEEN: Well, these were the people I loved, with all of their limitations, all of their blessings, all of their curses, all

of their dreams, all of their nightmares. And that was like a lot of other small American towns in the 1950s and it's where I grew up.

I wrote "My Hometown" in 1984. It was a revisitation of my life as a young child. The town that I'd grown up in was really having a tough time. When I was a kid, there were three factories: 3M, Brockway Glass, Karagheusian Rug Mill. Everybody worked in town in one of those factories. Now they were leaving. When you went down our little main street you saw boarded-up businesses.

The event that started the race rioting that we had in town at the time was a shooting at a stoplight. A car full of white kids with a shotgun firing into a car full of Black kids. A friend of mine lost his eye. And then the town's just shutting down. The song was just something that came out, you know.

By the late seventies and the eighties I knew this is what I wanted my subject matter to be, this was who I was going to be and what I was going to write about. This is what made sense to me. I wanted to stay home. I wanted to live here. I wanted to be sort of surrounded by the people that I knew and tell my and their story.

There's a generational element to "My Hometown" because there's a boy sitting on his father's lap, and this father's saying, "This is your hometown and everything in it."

PRESIDENT OBAMA: Good and bad.

BRUCE SPRINGSTEEN: That's right. You are a part of the general flow of history, and as such what is happening and what has happened is partly your responsibility. You are tied in, historically, to the good and the bad things that have happened,

PREVIOUS (PAGE 18): Bruce Springsteen taking a swing in Freehold, 1965. **PREVIOUS (PAGE 19):** The teenage years, circa 1963. **ABOVE:** Beginning in the late nineteenth century, summer harvests brought migrant farmworkers, many of them poor white immigrants and Black southerners, to New Jersey. They spent winters in Florida, working the citrus groves, then moved north, harvesting potatoes and other crops with little to no labor protections. **OPPOSITE** (clockwise from top left): For the first half of the twentieth century, the Karagheusian Rug Mill defined Freehold, NJ. If you lived in Freehold and didn't work there, you had a relative who did. Founded in the early 1900s by two immigrant brothers fleeing persecution in their home country of Armenia, the mill provided its world-renowned carpeting for the newly built Radio City Music Hall; Bruce's parents, Douglas and Adele Springsteen, on their wedding day; Bruce and his sister Pamela, circa 1953; Bruce's maternal grandparents, Antonio Zerilli and Adelina Sorrentino, on their wedding day; Bruce's paternal grandfather, Frederick Springsteen, in front of his shop in Freehold circa 1935; Bruce's family, including his paternal grandparents. Bruce is in the front, lying on the floor, next to his cousin, mid-1950s. **FOLLOWING:** Of the more than 150 riots and rebellions that swept the country during the "long hot summer" of 1967, the five-day uprising in Newark was one of the deadliest. After a Black cab driver was brutally beaten by police and arrested, long-simmering tensions exploded. More than seven hundred people were injured, with twenty-six killed, and entire city blocks burned to the ground, forever altering the city.

not just in our little town, but in our country, and, as an active player in this moment in time, you have some power to acknowledge these things and perhaps do something about them in some small way.

I still love to sing the song today. It's more than an act of nostalgia. Everyone in the audience recognizes it. And people always sing that verse with me, "Mmmmyyyyyy hooommmetown." And the town they're talking about isn't Freehold, it's not Matawan, it's not Marlboro, it's not Washington, it's not friggin' Seattle. It's the whole thing. It's all of America, you know?

PRESIDENT OBAMA: Right.

BRUCE SPRINGSTEEN: It's a good song.

PRESIDENT OBAMA: It's a great song. So what happened in the immediate aftermath of these riots in Freehold? Because places like Newark, Detroit . . . they never really recover, right?

BRUCE SPRINGSTEEN: Asbury Park really suffered from its riots. And they were a long time coming and justified. The Black population of that town was totally underrepresented in the city government.

Asbury really didn't come back for a long, long time. It's obviously had a resurgence over the past ten years, but most of those issues still remain unresolved on the west side of town. So you would say, "How much did that really change? I'm not so sure."

In Freehold, what did I see get better? Not very much. Now, it was a much smaller event. Freehold's main street is three blocks.

PRESIDENT OBAMA: Some stores get torn up, some folks get arrested, but the guts of the town don't really get impacted that much. Did your family talk about it? Did you talk about it with your friends?

BRUCE SPRINGSTEEN: Less than talking about it, I was *experiencing* it. In high school there was a moment when my Black friends wouldn't speak to me. I said, "Hey . . . ," and my friend said, "I can't talk to you right now. . . ."

> YOU ARE TIED IN, HISTORICALLY, TO THE GOOD AND THE BAD THINGS THAT HAVE HAPPENED, NOT JUST IN OUR LITTLE TOWN, BUT IN OUR COUNTRY, AND, AS AN ACTIVE PLAYER IN THIS MOMENT IN TIME, YOU HAVE SOME POWER TO ACKNOWLEDGE THESE THINGS AND PERHAPS DO SOMETHING ABOUT THEM IN SOME SMALL WAY.
>
> —BRUCE SPRINGSTEEN

PRESIDENT OBAMA: It's interesting that he said "right now." He's sending you a signal: "Right now, you just—we need to let this lie."

BRUCE SPRINGSTEEN: That's right.

PRESIDENT OBAMA: Doesn't mean we can't have a conversation later.

BRUCE SPRINGSTEEN: But not today. Those tensions had become very real in '67, '68. Freehold Regional High School was a totally integrated high school, and it was filled with mostly working-class kids—maybe a few that were a little better off than that, but not so much. And there was a lot of flat-out fighting between white students and Black students. After grammar school, if people didn't want to send their children to integrated schools, they went to the Catholic high school.

PRESIDENT OBAMA: And that's true pretty much in cities all across the country.

BRUCE SPRINGSTEEN: My parents wanted me to go to a Catholic school, I think it was Trenton at the time. I said, "Trenton? I'm going to ride a freaking hour on the bus every day?"

PRESIDENT OBAMA: Plus you're not going to class anyway, so it didn't matter!

BRUCE SPRINGSTEEN: That's right!

PRESIDENT OBAMA: Because you're going to be a rock 'n' roll star! Which raises an interesting question. Right around this time you're starting to get serious about music, and it's shortly thereafter you start putting your bands together.

BRUCE SPRINGSTEEN: I pick the guitar up in 1964, and I'm playing it all through high school. You had the Rolling Stones and you had the Beatles, but very shortly you also had Sam & Dave and you had Motown, and you learned how to write from the great Motown songwriters.

OPPOSITE: During the summer of 1970, protests erupted in the small resort town of Asbury Park. Although the resorts had traditionally employed the town's Black residents, by 1970 jobs were mostly going to white teens from nearby towns. Local Black youth were fed up, and on the Fourth of July the unrest began. **FOLLOWING:** Sixteen-year-old Bruce Springsteen plays with his first band, the Castiles, at the Ferndock Surf Shop, Asbury Park, NJ, circa 1965.

PRESIDENT OBAMA: So if there aren't African American artists who are helping you to discover rock 'n' roll, there are certainly African American–*influenced* artists that are opening this door for you.

BRUCE SPRINGSTEEN: Absolutely. We had a band that used to play down on what was called Route 9, which was south of Freehold. You had to know some soul music because it was called "greaser territory." Greasers were the guys with three-quarter-length leathers, sharkskin suits, ties, hair slicked back, pointy black shoes, nylon see-through socks. All of it taken from the Black community. When you went south on Route 9 you had to be able to play soul music and doo-wop music or else you wouldn't survive on a Friday and Saturday night.

As a young musician, you were immersed in the African American culture that inspired the music that you loved. It was very strange because the Black kids in my high school were both envied and at the same time they suffered tremendous prejudice.

PRESIDENT OBAMA: What were they envied for?

BRUCE SPRINGSTEEN: The young guys, the way they *dressed* . . .

PRESIDENT OBAMA: They looked sharp.

BRUCE SPRINGSTEEN: We used to go to Springwood Avenue to this place called Fisch's. That was where those clothes were. It was a strange imbalance between envy and prejudice that was difficult to sort through.

PRESIDENT OBAMA: It makes me think of Spike Lee's movie *Do the Right Thing*.

BRUCE SPRINGSTEEN: Great picture.

PRESIDENT OBAMA: Great picture. One of the protagonists, a guy named Mookie, he's working for this Italian guy and his sons who are trying to run a small business, a little pizza joint. And one of the sons, Vito, is a sweet kid, loves the African American community that they're serving. And the older one, Pino, is cynical and more blatantly racist. And at one point, Mookie, who despite not working real hard is insightful about the neighborhood he's living in, he starts asking the racist older brother some questions:

MOOKIE: Pino, who's your
favorite basketball player?
PINO: Magic Johnson.
MOOKIE: Who's your favorite
movie star?
PINO: Eddie Murphy.
MOOKIE: Who's your favorite
rock star? Prince.
PINO: Wrong, Bruce.
MOOKIE: Prince.
PINO: BRRRUUUUUUCCCCE.

Then he says something like, "So why is it that you're always using the N-word? When all these folks are Black, and you're always talking about how much you love them." And I always thought that was such a brilliant and simple way to capture something that's always been true and complicated about America, which is this notion of "Black folks are the other." They are demeaned, they are discriminated against, and yet the culture is constantly appropriating and regurgitating and processing the style that arises out of being an outsider and knowing the blues, and having suffered these scars, and having to live on mother wit and make stuff up out of nothing. And rock 'n' roll is a part of that process.

I'm wondering whether as a teenager that's something that you're even processing, or do you just think, "You know what? This music's cool, and I like it, and it moves me in some way."

BRUCE SPRINGSTEEN: I think that if you were a teenager in the sixties, you were processing all this intensely. You couldn't be a teenager in the sixties and not be aware that race was the fundamental issue of the day. In America, we have loved Black people and brown people when they're entertaining us, but when they want to live next door to us, we remain a tribal society. It's part of the tragedy that continues, obviously, to this day. And . . . I don't think it's ever been a more essential subject than it is at this very moment. . . . I think, "Why is it so hard to talk about race? Why am I . . . why am I pausing here?"

ABOVE: Sam Moore and Dave Prater brought the sounds of the Black gospel church into the pop mainstream. Their biggest hits included "Soul Man" and "Hold On, I'm Comin'."
OPPOSITE: Released in 1989, Spike Lee's iconic film *Do the Right Thing* depicts racial tension and violence between Black and Italian American characters in a Brooklyn neighborhood during the course of one long, hot summer day.

To talk about race, you have to talk about your differences. To talk about race, you have to talk about, to some degree, deconstructing the myth of the melting pot, which has never fundamentally been true. To admit that a big part of our history has been plunderous and violent and rigged against people of color. We're ashamed of our collective guilt. We would have to admit and to grieve for what's been done. We would have to acknowledge our own daily complicity, and to acknowledge that we are tied to the history of racism.

PRESIDENT OBAMA: Of a great wrong.

BRUCE SPRINGSTEEN: Yeah. Those are all hard things for people to do.

PRESIDENT OBAMA: The interesting thing for me has been how, in part because my upbringing was so unusual, I had to figure this stuff out. But it wasn't right in my grill on a day-to-day basis in the same way. There were no riots in Hawaii. There was no other side of town where Blacks had to live. So I'm absorbing this, and I'm experiencing my share of day-to-day ignorance and slights.

I played tennis. I'm eleven, twelve years old, and I still remember, they used to put the seedings up for the tournaments that you'd play in. And I was not a great player but I was good enough to be in some tournaments, and I remember running my finger down to see where my name was on the seeding, and the tennis pro, who was basically the coach of the tennis team at this high school, he says, "Better be careful. You might rub off on the chart and make it dirty." I turned to him and I said, *"What did you say?"* It was an interesting moment of being an eleven- or twelve-year-old talking to a grown man, and watching him process and calculate what he should do. And then he said, "I'm just joking."

BRUCE SPRINGSTEEN: Who were your friends at this time?

PRESIDENT OBAMA: My best friends ended up being a bunch of misfits and outsiders themselves. Kids like . . . *you*—who were, maybe, a little bit emotionally displaced. I realize that my best friends in high school, who are—to this day—some of my best

friends, all of them came from broken homes. All of them, economically, were at the lower end of the totem pole relative to the other kids in the school. And one of the unifying things was basketball. We all became huge basketball fanatics, and sports became the place where a Black kid and white kid could meet on equal terms and be part of a community that wasn't free of race, but was an arena in which issues of who's up, who's down—status, you know— all that it came down to was who could play.

BRUCE SPRINGSTEEN: Where did your mom fit in all of this?

PRESIDENT OBAMA: She infused me with a basic sense of who I was and why I was blessed to have this beautiful brown skin and to be part of this grand tradition. And some of it, she romanticized. She was the last of the great liberal humanists. She was a naturally kind and generous person, but she inherited enough of the rebel spirit. She would bring me these kids' versions of the biographies of Muhammad Ali and Arthur Ashe. I think instinctually she understood, "I need to inoculate him early against what might be coming." And so I was loved, cherished, and special, and being Black was something to be proud of and to be cherished and special. And, in fact, the very struggles that Blacks in America were going through were part of what made Black folks special. Because they had, in some ways, been fortified by suffering. And they had experienced cruelty, and as a consequence could help all of us transcend that.

We started the conversation talking about us both, in some ways, feeling like outsiders, and part of my politics, part of a lot of the speeches I've made in the past, has always been to claim America as a place where you don't have to look a certain way, you don't have to come from a certain family, you don't have to have a certain religious background. You just have to have fidelity to a creed—a belief.

Folks sometimes ask me what's one of my favorite speeches of the speeches I've given, and it may be the speech I gave on the fiftieth anniversary of the march across the Edmund Pettus Bridge, starting in Selma.

> I WAS LOVED, CHERISHED, AND SPECIAL, AND BEING BLACK WAS SOMETHING TO BE PROUD OF AND TO BE CHERISHED AND SPECIAL. AND, IN FACT, THE VERY STRUGGLES THAT BLACKS IN AMERICA WERE GOING THROUGH WERE PART OF WHAT MADE BLACK FOLKS SPECIAL. BECAUSE THEY HAD, IN SOME WAYS, BEEN FORTIFIED BY SUFFERING.
>
> —PRESIDENT OBAMA

OPPOSITE: Barack Obama celebrating a state championship win with his Punahou High School teammates, 1979. **ABOVE:** Obama with his mother at his graduation, 1979.

It was at a time when you were seeing this ramp-up of criticism. Not just of me, but of progressives as "un-American" or "not real Americans." I thought it was a good moment to capture a different idea of America. I was down in Selma with John Lewis—and, by the way, George W. Bush, and a whole bunch of folks—celebrating this moment in our history. You have on one side outsiders: Black students and maids and laborers and busboys. And on the other side: the power of the state. There's a standoff, this historic clash of two ideas of America. On one side, you've got the idea that "No, America is just for certain people who have to be and look a certain way." And on the other side, led by this twenty-five-year-old kid in a trench coat and a knapsack, this idea of "America's for everybody."

In fact, what makes America "America" is all the outsiders and all the misfits and the folks who try to make something out of nothing. So that became the theme of my speech.

BRUCE SPRINGSTEEN: That's a great speech.

PRESIDENT OBAMA: It's the better idea of America: the idea that we take all comers, that everybody's gonna get a shot—those who came here as outcasts, outsiders, the discarded and the scorned. That here you're supposed to be able to overcome all that and make something new. That is the idea of America as it can be. That's what John fought for. That's what you sing about, and that's what those kids out there are organizing for.

BRUCE SPRINGSTEEN: Amen.

TOP LEFT: John Lewis making history, March 1965. The son of Alabama sharecroppers, Lewis was a congressman and an activist whose life and career closely tracked the Civil Rights Movement. He was one of the thirteen original Freedom Riders, a founding member of the Student Nonviolent Coordinating Committee (SNCC), and one of the organizers of the March on Washington for Jobs and Freedom in 1963. **TOP RIGHT:** He joined the US House of Representatives on January 3, 1987, and served seventeen terms until his death in 2020. Lewis was awarded the Presidential Medal of Freedom in 2011. **BOTTOM LEFT:** Martin Luther King Jr. marching and singing, March 1967.

REMARKS BY THE PRESIDENT AT THE FIFTIETH ANNIVERSARY OF THE SELMA-TO-MONTGOMERY MARCHES

EDMUND PETTUS BRIDGE

SELMA, ALABAMA

2:17 P.M. CST

DRAFT 3/6/15 1130pm
Keenan
6-4698 desk | 503-5633 mobile

Remarks of President Barack Obama
Selma, Alabama
March 7, 2015

It is a rare honor in this life to follow one of your heroes. And John Lewis is one of my heroes.

Now, I have to imagine that when a younger John Lewis woke up that morning fifty years ago and made his way to Brown Chapel, heroics were not on his mind. A day like this was not on his mind. Young folks with bedrolls and backpacks were milling about. Veterans of the movement trained newcomers in the tactics of non-violence; the right way to protect yourself when attacked. A doctor described what tear gas does to the body while marchers scribbled down instructions for contacting their loved ones. The air was thick with doubt, anticipation, and fear. But it all lifted with the final verse of the final hymn they sung:
— *They comforted themselves*

No matter what may be the test, God will take care of you;
Lean, weary one, upon His breast, God will take care of you.

Then, his knapsack stocked with an apple, a toothbrush, a book on government – all you need for a night behind bars – John Lewis led them out of the church on a mission to change America.

President Bush and Mrs. Bush, Governor Bentley, Members of Congress, Mayor Evans, Reverend Strong, friends and fellow Americans:

There are places, and moments in America where *his* nation's destiny has been decided. Many are sites of war – Concord and Lexington, Appomattox and Gettysburg. Others are sites that symbolize the daring spirit of the American character – Independence Hall and Seneca Falls, Kitty Hawk and Cape Canaveral.

Selma is such a place.

In one afternoon fifty years ago, so much of our turbulent history – the stain of slavery and anguish of civil war; the yoke of segregation and tyranny of Jim Crow; the nightmare of four little girls in Birmingham, and the dream of a King *a Baptist preacher* – met on this bridge. *dead*

It was not a clash of armies, but a clash of wills; a contest to determine the meaning of America.

And because of men and women like John Lewis, Joseph Lowery, Hosea Williams, Amelia Boynton, Diane Nash, Ralph Abernathy, C.T. Vivian, Andrew Young, Fred Shuttlesworth, Dr. King, and so many more, the idea of a <u>just</u> America, a <u>fair</u> America, an <u>inclusive</u> America, a <u>generous</u> America – that idea ultimately triumphed.

As is true across the landscape of American history, we cannot examine this moment in isolation. The march on Selma was part of a broader campaign that spanned generations; the leaders of that day part of a long line of quiet heroes.

We gather here to celebrate them. We gather here to honor the courage of ordinary Americans willing to endure billy clubs and the chastening rod; tear gas and the trampling hoof; men and women who despite the gush of blood and splintered bone would stay true to their North Star and keep marching toward justice.

They did as Scripture instructed: "Rejoice in hope, be patient in tribulation, be constant in prayer." And in the days to come, they went back again and again. When the trumpet call sounded for more to join, the people came – black and white, young and old, Christian and Jew, waving the same American flag and singing the same anthems full of faith and hope. A white newsman, Bill Plante, who covered the marches then and who is with us here today, quipped at the time that the growing number of white people lowered the quality of the singing. To those who marched, though, those old gospel songs must have never sounded so sweet.

In time, their chorus would reach President Johnson. And he would send them protection, echoing their call for the nation and the world to hear:

"We shall overcome."

What enormous faith ~~they~~ [these men and women] had. Faith in God – but also faith in America.

The Americans who crossed this bridge were not ~~war heroes~~ [held no officials office, physically imposing]. But they gave courage to millions. They ~~were not~~ elected ~~leaders~~. But they led a nation. They marched as Americans who had endured hundreds of years of brutal violence, and countless daily indignities – but they didn't seek special treatment, just the equal treatment promised to them almost 200 years before.

What they did here will reverberate through the ages, never to be undone. Not because the change they won was preordained; not because their victory was complete; but because they proved that nonviolent change is <u>possible</u>; that love and hope can conquer hate.

As we commemorate their achievement, we are well-served to remember that many in power condemned rather than praised them. [Back then,] They were called Communists, half-breeds, rabble-rousers, sexual and moral degenerates, and worse – everything but the name their parents gave them. Their faith was questioned. Their lives were threatened. Their patriotism was challenged.

And yet, what could be more American than what happened ~~right here~~ [in this place]?

What could more profoundly vindicate the idea of America than ~~ordinary~~ [plain and humble] people – the unsung, the downtrodden, the dreamers not of high station, not born to wealth or privilege, not of one religious tradition but many – coming together to shape their country's course?

What greater expression of faith in the American experiment than this; what greater form of patriotism is there; than the belief that America is <u>not</u> yet finished, that we are <u>strong</u> enough to be self-critical, that each successive generation can look upon our imperfections and decide that it is in our power to remake this nation to more closely align with our highest ideals?

<u>That's</u> why Selma is not some outlier in the American experience. <u>That's</u> why it's not just a museum or static monument to behold from a distance. It is instead the manifestation of a creed written into our founding documents:

"We the People…in order to form a more perfect union."

"We hold these truths to be self-evident, that all men are created equal."

These are not just words. They are a living thing, a call to action, a roadmap for citizenship and an insistence in the capacity of free men and women to shape our own destiny. For founders like Franklin and Jefferson, for leaders like Lincoln and FDR, the success of our experiment in self-government rested on engaging all our citizens in this work. That's what we celebrate here in Selma. That's what this movement was all about, one leg in our long journey toward freedom.

The American instinct that led these young men and women to pick up the torch and cross this bridge is the same instinct that moved patriots to choose revolution over tyranny. It's the same instinct that drew immigrants from across oceans and the Rio Grande; the same instinct that led women to reach for the ballot and workers to organize against an unjust status quo; the same instinct that ~~inspired us~~ to plant a flag at Iwo Jima and on the surface of the Moon.

It's the idea held by generations of citizens who believed that America is a constant work in progress; who believed that loving this country requires more than singing its praises or avoiding discomfiting truths. It requires the occasional disruption, the willingness to speak ~~truth to power~~ and shake up the status quo.

That's what makes us unique, ~~That's what~~ cements our reputation as a beacon of opportunity. Young people behind the Iron Curtain would see Selma and eventually tear down a wall. Young people in Soweto would hear Bobby Kennedy talk about ripples of hope and eventually banish the scourge of apartheid. From Burma to Venezuela to Tunisia, young people today draw strength from ~~an example – this~~ example – a place where the powerless ~~can~~ change the world's greatest superpower, and push their leaders to ~~create~~ freedom ~~and liberty where they didn't fully exist~~. They saw that idea made real in Selma, Alabama. They saw it made real in America.

Because of campaigns like this, a Voting Rights Act was passed. Political, economic, and social barriers came down, and the change these men and women wrought is visible here today: African-Americans who run boardrooms, who sit on the federal bench, who serve in elected office from small towns to big cities; from the Congressional Black Caucus to the Oval Office.

Because of what they did, the doors of opportunity swung open not just for African-Americans, but for every American. Women marched through those doors. Latinos marched through those doors. Asian-Americans, gay Americans, and Americans with disabilities came through those doors. Their endeavors gave the entire South the chance to rise again, not by reasserting the past, but by transcending the past. What a glorious thing, Dr. King would say.

What a solemn debt we owe.

Which leads us to ask, just how might we repay that debt?

First and foremost, we have to recognize that one day's commemoration, no matter how special, is not enough. If Selma taught us anything, it's that our work is never done – the American experiment in self-government gives work and purpose to each generation.

It teaches us, too, that action requires us to slough off cynicism. When it comes to the pursuit of justice, we can afford neither complacency nor despair.

Just this week, I was asked whether I thought the Department of Justice's Ferguson report shows that, when it comes to race, nothing has changed in this country. I understand the question, for the report's narrative was woefully familiar. It evoked the kind of abuse and disregard for citizens that spawned the Civil Rights Movement. But I cautioned against suggesting that this was proof nothing's changed. Ferguson may not be unique, but it's ~~not~~ *no longer* endemic; and before the Civil Rights Movement, it was. *— or sanctioned by law and custom*

who was virtue have been assigned to the secretarial pool

We do a disservice to the cause of justice by intimating that bias and discrimination are immutable, or that racial division is inherent to America. If you think nothing's changed in the past fifty years, ask somebody who lived through Selma whether nothing's changed. Ask the female CEO ~~or the woman who blazed a trail for her~~ if nothing's changed. Ask your gay friend if it's easier to be out and proud in America now than it was thirty years ago. To deny this progress – _our_ progress – would be to rob us of our own agency; our responsibility to ~~do~~ what we can to make America better. *depends on our actions, our efforts, our attitudes*

the race is not yet won · finished · upon

Of course, an even more common mistake is to suggest that racism is banished, that the work that drew men and women to Selma is ~~done~~, and that whatever racial tensions remain are a consequence of those seeking to play the "race card" for their own purposes. We don't need the Ferguson report to know that's not true. We just need to open our eyes, and ears, and hearts, to know that this nation's racial history still casts its long shadow ~~on~~ *over* us. We know the march is not yet ~~done~~ *over*, and that ~~traveling those next steps~~ require admitting as much. "We are capable of bearing a great burden," James Baldwin wrote, "once we discover that the burden is reality and arrive where reality is." *— the great good · reaching that blessed destination where we are all truly judged by the content of our character*

and · whites. Not · blacks · all and not just some

This is work for all ~~of us~~, not just some ~~of us~~. Not just ~~blacks or~~ just ~~whites~~. All of us. If we want to honor the courage of those who marched that day, then we will have to ~~take~~ possession ~~of~~ their moral imagination. ~~We will~~ *need to* feel, as they did, the fierce urgency of now. ~~We~~ *All of us need* ~~have~~ to recognize, as they did, that change ~~is up to us~~ – that no matter how hard it may seem, laws can be passed, and consciences can be stirred, and consensus can be built.

With such effort · All of us · all of us are called

~~Together~~, we can make sure our criminal justice system serves ~~everybody.~~ ~~We can recognize that all of us have a part to play in~~ addressing unfair sentencing and overcrowded prisons, that rob us of too many boys before they become men, and too many men who could be good dads. *all and not just some · and the stunted circumstances*

Together, we can raise the level of mutual trust that policing is built on – the idea that police officers are members of the communities they risk their lives to protect, and citizens just want the same thing young people here marched for – the protection of the law.

With effort · roll back · and

~~Together~~, we can ~~recommit ourselves to eradicating~~ poverty and the roadblocks to opportunity. Americans don't accept a free ride for anyone, nor do we believe in equality of outcomes. But we do expect equal opportunity. ~~We can strive to~~ make sure _every_ child gets an education suitable to this new century, one that expands ~~their~~ imaginations and lifts their sights. We can make sure every worker has a fair wage, a real voice, ~~and~~ sturdier rungs on that ladder into the middle class.

and

and if we really mean it, if were willing to to sacrifice for it, then were · every person willing to work has the dignity of a job, and 4

with effort,

And together, we can protect ~~that essential right,~~ the foundation stone of our democracy for which so many marched across this bridge – the right to vote. Right now, there are ~~new~~ laws across this country designed to make it harder for people to vote. *As we speak, more of such laws are being proposed.* Meanwhile, the Voting Rights Act, the culmination of so much ~~of this movement,~~ the product of so much sacrifice, stands weakened, its reauthorization subject to partisan rancor. *— blood and sweat and tears* *in the face of wanton violence*

How can that be? The Voting Rights Act was one of the crowning achievements of our democracy, the result of Republican and Democratic effort. President Bush signed its renewal when he was in office. More than 100 Members of Congress have come here today to honor people who were willing to die for the right ~~to vote~~. If we want to honor this day, let those hundred, and ~~the other 300,~~ pledge to make it their mission to reauthorize the law this year. *go back to Washington* *and together,*

Of course, our democracy is not the task of Congress alone, *it protects* *or the courts, or ~~even~~ the President* If every new voter suppression law was struck down today, we'd still have one of the lowest voting rates among free peoples. Fifty years ago, registering to vote here in Selma and much of the South meant guessing the number of jellybeans in a jar or bubbles on a bar of soap. It meant risking your dignity, and sometimes, your life. What is our excuse? How do we so casually discard the right for which so many fought? How do we so fully give away our power, our voice, in ~~this democracy~~? *today* *chudet?* *— shaping America's future*

Fellow marchers, so much has changed in fifty years. We've endured war, and fashioned peace. We've seen technological wonders that touch our ~~very~~ lives, and take for granted ~~convenience~~ *or* our parents might scarcely imagine. But what has not changed is the imperative of citizenship, that willingness of a 26-year-old ~~grandson,~~ a Unitarian minister, ~~and~~ a young mother of five, to decide they loved this country so much that they'd ~~give up their lives~~ to realize its promise. *or* *every aspect of* *rich everything*

That's what it means to love America. That's what it means to believe in America. That's what it means when we say America is exceptional.

For we were born of change. We broke the old aristocracies, declaring ourselves entitled not by bloodline, but endowed by our Creator with certain unalienable rights. ~~He created us equal – a self-evident truth that, until America happened, was never self-executing.~~ We secure our rights and responsibilities through a system of self-government, of and by and for the people. That's why we argue and fight with so much passion and conviction. That's why, for such a young nation, we are so big and bold and diverse and full of ~~complex~~ contradictions, because we know our efforts matter. We know America is what we make of it.

We are Lewis and Clark and Sacajawea – pioneers who braved the unfamiliar, followed by a stampede of farmers and miners, entrepreneurs and hucksters. That's our spirit.

then implausible

We are Teddy Roosevelt, who charged up that hill with the Rough Riders, and invited Booker T. Washington to dinner to hear his ~~radical~~ vision of things to come. That's what we do.

and then come

We are Sojourner Truth and Fannie Lou Hamer, women who ~~can~~ *could* do as much as any man, and we're Susan B. Anthony, who shook the system 'til the law made that true. That's our character.

We're the immigrants who stowed away on ships to reach these shores, and the dreamers who cross the Rio Grande because they want their kids to know a better life. That's ~~why we exist~~. *— how we came to be*

We're the ~~unacknowledged~~ slaves who built the White House and the ~~Southern~~ economy of the South, and we're the countless laborers who laid rail, raised skyscrapers, and organized for workers' rights.

We're the fresh-faced GIs who fought to liberate a continent, and we're the Tuskegee Airmen, Navajo code-talkers, and Japanese-Americans who fought ~~alongside them~~ for this country even as their own liberty had been denied.

We are the huddled masses yearning to breathe free – Holocaust survivors, Soviet defectors, the Lost Boys of Africa.

We are the gay Americans whose blood ran on the streets of San Francisco and New York, just as blood ran down this bridge.

We are storytellers, writers, poets, and artists who abhor unfairness, ~~puncture~~ and despise hypocrisy, and tell truths that need to be told.

We are the inventors of jazz and the blues, bluegrass and country, hip-hop and rock and roll, our very own sounds with all the sweet sorrow and ~~awesome~~ dangerous joy of freedom.

We are Jackie Robinson, ~~tearing down barriers,~~ enduring scorn and spiked cleats and stealing home plate in the World Series anyway.

We are the people Langston Hughes wrote of, who "build our temples for tomorrow, strong as we know how."

We are the people Emerson wrote of, "who for truth and honor's sake stand fast and suffer long;" who are "never too tired, so long as we can see far enough." That's what America is. Not ~~some~~ stock ~~photos~~ or revised ~~histories~~ or ~~narrow definitions~~ cramped feeble attempts to define some as ~~We are Americans.~~ more real. We respect the past, but we don't pine for it. We don't fear the future; we grab for it. America is not some fragile thing; ~~we're~~ boisterous and full of energy, perpetually young in spirit. That's why some~~body~~one like John Lewis at the ripe age of 25 could lead ~~this~~ a mighty march. That's what the young people here today and listening all across the country ~~have to understand~~. You are America. Unconstrained by habits and convention. Unencumbered by what is, and ready to seize what ought to be. For everywhere in this country, there are first steps to be taken, and ground to cover, and bridges to be crossed. And it is you, the young and fearless at heart, the most diverse and educated generation in our history, who we are waiting to follow.

Because Selma shows us that America is not the project of any one person.

Because the single most powerful word in our democracy is the word "We." We The People. We Shall Overcome. ~~Yes We Can.~~ It is owned by no one. It belongs to everyone. What a glorious task we are given, to continually try to improve this great nation of ours.

Fifty years from Bloody Sunday, our march is not yet finished. But we are getting closer. Two hundred and thirty-nine years after this nation's founding, our union is not yet perfect. But we are getting closer. Our job's easier because somebody already got us through that first mile. Somebody already got us over that bridge. When it feels that the road's is too hard, ~~or~~ the torch

6

"WE HONOR THOSE WHO WALKED SO WE COULD RUN. WE MUST RUN SO OUR CHILDREN SOAR."

feels too heavy ~~to hold high~~ *we've been passed*, we will remember these ~~earlier~~ *early* travelers, ~~we will~~ *and* draw strength from their example, and ~~we will~~ hold firmly the words of Isaiah: *the prophet*

"Those who hope in the Lord will renew their strength. They will soar on wings like eagles. They will run and not grow weary. They will walk and not be faint."

We honor those who walked so we could run. We must run so our children soar. And we will not grow weary. For we believe in ~~God's~~ *the* power *of an awesome God*, and we believe in America, ~~and we know we are not yet done.~~

May ~~God~~ *He* bless those warriors of justice no longer with us, and may He bless ~~the United States of America~~ *our precious ~~nation~~ ~~that~~ our United States.* *the promise of*

THE
AMERICAN
STORY

What does it mean to be an American? The stories and habits of mind that bind us together as a people.

For most Americans growing up in the fifties, the answers were pretty simple. We were hardworking and freedom loving. Rugged individualists with a can-do spirit. We opened up the frontier and built mighty industries and allowed everybody to get their piece of the American Dream. We were on the right side of history, having defeated Hitler and liberated Europe. We now stood sentinel against a godless, totalitarian communism—to make the world safe for democracy. We watched the same TV shows and listened to the same radio programs. We loved Westerns and baseball, hot dogs and apple pie, fast cars and Fourth of July parades.

That's the story we told ourselves, anyway. But it wasn't the whole story. It left a bunch of stuff out, whether it was the continuing discrimination against brown and Black people or all the ways that women were expected to stay in their place, or some of the ugly realities of our foreign policy during the Cold War. Bruce and I came of age as young people were challenging a lot of America's most cherished myths about itself. The result was a growing bitter divide in the country. A political and culture war that in a lot of ways we're still fighting today.

But before we got into the heavy stuff, Bruce and I decided to enjoy something Americans have long shared: our love affair with the open road. I got behind the wheel of the vintage Corvette that Bruce keeps in his barn. And we went for a little joyride. One that didn't make my Secret Service detail all that happy . . .

PRESIDENT OBAMA: Uh-oh.

BRUCE SPRINGSTEEN: That's all right, you're all right. Just give it some gas.

PRESIDENT OBAMA: Come on, Bruce.

BRUCE SPRINGSTEEN: Yeah, gas.

PRESIDENT OBAMA: There we go.

BRUCE SPRINGSTEEN: And as you pull it back, give it a little juice.

PRESIDENT OBAMA: Come on!

BRUCE SPRINGSTEEN: *AHHHHH HAAAAAAA!*

PRESIDENT OBAMA: It's time for us to *go!*

BRUCE SPRINGSTEEN: Do we have to stay on the farm or can we go off the farm?

PRESIDENT OBAMA: Can I go off the farm? I know the Secret Service is scrambling right now. So how far are we from the ocean?

BRUCE SPRINGSTEEN: Twenty minutes. I used to hitchhike every day from Freehold—twenty miles.

PRESIDENT OBAMA: How's the beach?

BRUCE SPRINGSTEEN: Oh, it's not Hawaii.

PRESIDENT OBAMA: But it is sandy?

BRUCE SPRINGSTEEN: Jersey Shore. Sandy.
    How's that baby feel?

PRESIDENT OBAMA: Feels actually really nice.

BRUCE SPRINGSTEEN: Take your left right here. This baby drives good.

PRESIDENT OBAMA: It's smooth, man. Smoother than I expected. Yeah, the Secret Service is following me now. I'm in trouble, but you know what? There are times where you just got to do—

BRUCE SPRINGSTEEN: You gotta do what you gotta do.

PRESIDENT OBAMA: You got to do something, man.

(President Obama and Bruce Springsteen re-enter the studio.)

So a theme in a lot of your songs, a theme in a lot of rock 'n' roll, is this idea of the open road and traveling toward the horizon, maybe not knowing where it is that you're going. And that's tied to ideas of freedom and remaking yourself—shedding your

OPPOSITE: After taking a spin in Bruce's C1 Corvette convertible, Colts Neck, NJ, August 2020.

Well, there she sits buddy justa gleaming in the sun / There to greet a working man when his day is done / I'm gonna pack my pa and I'm gonna pack my aunt / I'm gonna take them down to the Cadillac Ranch / Eldorado fins, whitewalls and skirts / Rides just like a little bit of heaven here on earth / Well buddy when I die throw my body in the back / And drive me to the junkyard in my Cadillac / Cadillac, Cadillac / Long and dark, shiny and black / Open up your engines let 'em roar / Tearing up the highway like a big old dinosaur / James Dean in that Mercury '49 / Junior Johnson runnin' thru the woods of Caroline / Even Burt Reynolds in that black Trans-Am / All gonna meet down at the Cadillac Ranch / Cadillac, Cadillac / Long and dark, shiny and black / Open up them engines let 'em roar / Tearing up the highway like a big old dinosaur / Hey, little girlie in the blue jeans so tight / Drivin' alone through the Wisconsin night / You're my last love baby you're my last chance / Don't let 'em take me to the Cadillac Ranch / Cadillac, Cadillac / Long and dark, shiny and black / Pulled up to my house today / Came and took my little girl away

—FROM THE RIVER (1980)

skin, freeing yourself from your past and your constraints and engaging in the act of re-creation, self-invention.

BRUCE SPRINGSTEEN: Right. The act of driving the car is a direct, aggressive act upon the world, you know? But it's funny: I did not drive until I was twenty-four. Hitchhiked everywhere I went.

PRESIDENT OBAMA: You didn't think to yourself, "Man, I need to try to get some wheels"? Did you not have a license? Or you just didn't have a car?

BRUCE SPRINGSTEEN: I did not have a license and I did not know how to drive.

PRESIDENT OBAMA: Let me just say, it is a good thing that you ended up being a rock star. Because otherwise it seems to me like you're kind of a shy, you know, not-that-well-adjusted kid, man. I mean . . . I wasn't a big car guy but, shit, I was gonna get my license—

BRUCE SPRINGSTEEN: Not me!

PRESIDENT OBAMA: I was going so I could get out on the road.

BRUCE SPRINGSTEEN: I was out on the road with just me and my thumb. And for the ten years from when I was fourteen, I was still hitchhiking myself around. I had two albums out; I didn't have a car.

PRESIDENT OBAMA: What are you doing with girls, man?

BRUCE SPRINGSTEEN: They had cars! I mean, you have to understand I'm going all the way from Asbury Park to Sea Bright, or Freehold. It's a total of about fifteen miles, you know; I'm not going anywhere.

My first actual trip was in a '48 Chevy flatbed similar to the one that's in my garage over there. The band had three days to make it to a gig we had in Big Sur. To make it across the country in three days, you cannot stop driving. In that Chevy it was just me and another guy, and in Nashville we lost all the guys behind us who were in a station wagon with a mattress in the back, sleeping and resting and driving. Remember: There were no cell phones. We couldn't call somebody to find out where they were. Those days, when somebody was lost, that

On the road, circa 1982.

was it. You weren't going to hear from them again until you got to California, which was thousands of miles away.

The first nightfall came and my buddy said, "Hey, it's your turn."

"You're going to get us killed, man," I said. "I can't drive this freaking—I can't drive a car. I can't drive this freaking truck."

He says, "If we don't drive, we don't get there in time. If we don't get there in time, we don't get paid. If we don't get paid, we don't have any money because it's taken us all our money to get across the damn country."

So I got behind the wheel. Four-speed, manual-gearshift, big ol' '48 Chevy with all of our equipment piled in the back.

PRESIDENT OBAMA: How many times did you strip the gears?

BRUCE SPRINGSTEEN: Oh, *many*. All you'd hear was *erghhh, erghhh erghhh erghhh erghhh*.

So finally, I say, "Hey, man, I can't handle this." The guy says, "Wait a second, I got an idea." He gets in the driver's seat. He puts it into first. Gets us rolling. "Let's switch seats." We switch seats! I'm driving as long as the truck is going, now I can go from first to second to third.

And it worked. I could drive a hundred miles at a pop like that, you know? Because out in the middle of the country, you can do that! And that was how I learned how to drive. Now I got all these cars in this garage. You were just tearing up the highway in my Corvette! Back then I couldn't drive. I couldn't fix a car if it broke down. But I knew what they were about. I knew what they symbolized—

PRESIDENT OBAMA: Escape.

BRUCE SPRINGSTEEN: Right. I knew the statement they made. This was a moment when America still felt very, very big. And the road was romantic. In the fifties, sixties, seventies, people were going places, gas was cheap. My first lengthy road trips were as a twenty-year-old going across the country to California by truck or station wagon once a year to see my parents because they had moved out west. I couldn't fly to see them because no one could afford it. I couldn't call them on the phone because the phone bills got too big and we were living hand-to-mouth. So once a year I drove out to see them.

But I had been connected to the car for a long time. I say in my book that somebody told me once that the safest place in a storm was in a vehicle. In a thunder-and-lightning storm, I used to scream to get in the car. And all I know is, they put me in the car, and they'd have to drive until the storm stopped. And I wrote about cars for the rest of my life.

I was also very interested in writing music using classic American images and reinventing them for the seventies. In the sixties, it was the Beach Boys, Chuck Berry, cars and girls, cars and girls. I used those images, but I filled my songs with the dread that was in the air during the seventies. During the Vietnam War the country was no longer innocent. The country was no longer wide open. It was a new age of limits. There was a gas crisis and lines at the stations. So I presented all of my characters in the context of a new American age. How did they resonate? Much darker. Where were people going? They weren't sure where they were going. Who were they becoming? They weren't sure.

All of these ideas I had to place in those cars with my characters and try to get them to sort them out.

PRESIDENT OBAMA: For me, part of the essential aspect of being an American is getting out of where you are. Now, where I am is paradise—in Hawaii, right? But somehow I'm thinking, "Man, I gotta get out on the open road."

BRUCE SPRINGSTEEN: And you're on an island!

PRESIDENT OBAMA: The road only goes so far! I remember the first time that I visited the mainland. My mother and my grandmother decided it was time for me to see it. And so the two of them, me, and my then-two-year-old sister fly first to Seattle, which is where my mom had gone to high school. We take the Greyhound bus down to San Francisco, LA. Then take the train to Arizona. Then Kansas City up to Chicago. Then rent a car, go to Yellowstone.

My mother didn't drive. She didn't have a license. My grandmother drove, but she was starting to go a little blind. So I remember being put in the front seat at around twilight so that I could direct my grandmother properly as we were hitting some of these turns in the road.

The Stolen Car

So you better if you conscious tells you
you gotta get it before it gets you

your drivin a stolen car
& I dont belong to you at all
can I got far / you cant get away, you cant ever get far
you dont answer to law call from & get car /
                                                    but you never do

I wanna find me a little girl + settle down
                    by a someny creek
I wanna find a little house in a little town
        so I find a heart wild & strong
                                    the
and we make love till my heart cuts loose,
                                  breaks
if it was just a restlessness that was my
            disappear as (I) you grow old
but if feels like so much more than restlessness
                                                this
                    somethin young inside   forever cold
        & feel different down in my soul

so I pped down the highway no license no i.D.

your drivin stolen car   been behind the wheel of a
of tears begin to fall   stolen car

somebody else lives in that quiet little house now
+ that quiet little house sounds as empty as can be
but from inside nights still shinin

STOLEN CAR

I met a little girl and I settled down / In a little house out on the edge of town / We got married, and swore we'd never part / Then little by little we drifted from each other's heart / At first I thought it was just restlessness / That would fade as time went by and our love grew deep / In the end it was something more I guess / That tore us apart and made us weep / And I'm driving a stolen car / Down on Eldridge Avenue / Each night I wait to get caught / But I never do / She asked if I remembered the letters I wrote / When our love was young and bold / She said last night she read those letters / And they made her feel one hundred years old / And I'm driving a stolen car / On a pitch black night / And I'm telling myself I'm gonna be alright / But I ride by night and I travel in fear / That in this darkness I will disappear

—FROM THE RIVER (1980)

You were talking about the country being so big. I remember looking out of Greyhound buses and looking out of trains, and looking out of car windows at miles of corn or miles of desert, or miles of forest, or miles of mountains, and just thinking, "Man, *imagine* where you can go." You can go anywhere—and by implication you can do anything and be anybody. Right?

And on that first road trip, we'd stop at Howard Johnson's. All the excitement was about the ice machine. And your mom or your grandma springing for a can of soda. And if you were really lucky, a couple of them had a little pool in the back.

BRUCE SPRINGSTEEN: Loved it.

PRESIDENT OBAMA: And if there was a pool, that was . . .

BRUCE SPRINGSTEEN: Heaven on earth!

PRESIDENT OBAMA: That was it.

BRUCE SPRINGSTEEN: You were living.

PRESIDENT OBAMA: That was luxury.

This is '73, so this is in the middle of the Watergate hearings. Every night my mom would turn on a little black and white set that was in the motel. And we'd sit there and I'd be watching Sam Ervin and Danny Inouye. We were very proud because Danny Inouye was on the committee, and he was the senator from Hawaii. A World War II hero, only had one arm. And that probably was somewhat formative of my politics, right? Because my mother is saying the whole time, "What do you expect? Nixon was a McCarthyite!" But that set of memories of the trip I never lost. And it was consistent with my own sense that, as much as I loved Hawaii, I was going to have to go on some sort of journey in order to find out who I was.

I remember when I was in college, I got an old beat-up Fiat—terrible car. And I'd just go driving. It was broke in the shop probably once every two weeks, but it zipped around when it was working. Five-shift. And I remember it breaking down on highways between LA and San Francisco, and me having to hitchhike with truckers.

It's pouring down rain and you don't have a cell phone, you don't have any money. Maybe you've got a little bit of change and you've got to find a pay phone and see if you can get a friend in town to come pick you up, and you're trying to look around to see what street you're on. But at each juncture, there was always that sense of—which I do think is essentially American—you go on the road to discover, like Ulysses.

BRUCE SPRINGSTEEN: That's right. Your hegira. A trip to discover your soul.

PRESIDENT OBAMA: Another moment like that for me was when I accepted a job to become a community organizer in Chicago. This group of churches hires me for $13,000 a year, gives me $2,000 for a car, and I buy this small compact Honda Civic hatchback. I stuff all my stuff in it and I drive from New York to Chicago and I go through Ohio. I don't know anybody in Chicago at this point and I have no idea how I'm going to organize these church folks and steelworkers who have been laid off. I'm twenty-three and what do I know? I'm leaving New York City and all my friends and all that I've known.

Halfway into Ohio, I go into a small town and get to a motel. The guy who checks me in, I can tell he's lonely. He starts asking, "Where are you going? What are you doing?" And when I say, "Well, I'm going to go be a community organizer," he says, "Well, what the heck is that? Are you sure you want to do this with your life?"

I'm in the middle of nowhere, sitting in that motel room by myself, with all the doubts I'm having, going to someplace I don't know . . . and having that feeling of you don't know what's ahead.

BRUCE SPRINGSTEEN: Curious about the world.

ABOVE: In the 1960s and '70s, the Howard Johnson chain of motels and restaurants was the largest in the country, with more than one thousand locations. The ubiquitous roadside "motor lodges" were well-known for their huge outdoor advertising displays, which featured familiar trademarked characters like "Simple Simon and the Pieman" and an old-timey lamplighter. OPPOSITE, TOP: The Honolulu-born son of Japanese immigrant parents, Sen. Daniel K. Inouye (D-HI) was the first Japanese American elected to both the House and Senate and a distinguished World War II vet who lost his right arm in combat. He served on the Senate Watergate Committee and later gained national attention for his scathing criticism of the "shadowy Government" within the US military. OPPOSITE, BOTTOM: President Nixon resigning, August 8, 1974.

BARACK OBAMA'S SUMMER OF SEEING AMERICA

....
FLEW FROM
HAWAII
TO
SEATTLE
....

SEATTLE · 5 · 90 · 82 · PORTLAND · 80 · 5 · 80 · BOIS

DUG CLAMS IN

PUGET SOUND

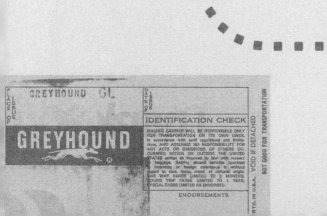

SACRAMENTO

SAN FRANCISCO

TOOK A GREYHOUND TO SF AND THEN ON TO LA (DISNEYLAND!)

VEGAS

15

LOS ANGELES

10

RENTED A CAR AND DROVE TO

YELLOWSTONE

(SAW A HERD OF BISON)

TOOK A TRAIN ACROSS THE

GREAT PLAINS

— TO —

KANSAS CITY

AND THEN UP TO THE

GREAT LAKES

— AND —

CHICAGO

WENT EAST
(BY GREYHOUND)
TO ARIZONA
(GRAND CANYON),
RODE HORSES
THROUGH A CREEK
AT THE BASE OF
CANYON DE CHELLY

PRESIDENT OBAMA: You're taking that adventure. I will say this: even in the moment there was that sense that the road offered, the sense of "I don't know what's around the bend. And I am excited to find out."

BRUCE SPRINGSTEEN: That's a great moment, man. It's a great moment, looking back.

PRESIDENT OBAMA: Even if I'm also a little scared, right? And that kind of feeling is hard to recapture. The road is full of surprises and adventures, but what's also true is that you get on it, and then at a certain point what you realize is "Yes, you can remake yourself. Yes, you can find yourself. But at the end of the day, you still have this longing for a *home*."

And the tension of America is this sense that we want to remake ourselves and reinvent ourselves and be free, but we also want a neighborhood and there's a loneliness to the road. The darker side is that drifter, existing in that unrooted, unmoored place.

BRUCE SPRINGSTEEN: And those were the icons that were being sold to us: Western heroes were lonely. They were never fathers, never husbands, always passing through.

PRESIDENT OBAMA: Yeah, those cowboys, Gary Cooper, Clint Eastwood—

BRUCE SPRINGSTEEN: Always passing through—

PRESIDENT OBAMA: *Shane. High Plains Drifter.*

BRUCE SPRINGSTEEN: The ultimate example of this is in John Ford's *The Searchers.*

You have John Wayne, who's a misanthrope. He has a series of violent skills that he can use to impact and preserve the community, but he can't join a community. There's this profound scene at the end where John Wayne finds Natalie Wood, brings her back to the family, the whole family runs inside the house, and the door closes. John Wayne is in the doorway and the door—and community itself—closes on him, and he is left walking off into the desert. That's the final shot of the film.

As a young man, I felt like this a lot, and I tried to live that out well into my thirties—until I was driving across the country with a friend of mine. We'd taken several trips, and I'd been across the country a bunch of times by now. Always

enjoyed it. I said, "If I had the blues, man, those miles could just roll those blues away, you know?"

But I got to California and I felt terrible. I felt like I wanted to get in the car and go back. But I knew if I did that I'd want to get in the car and come back again. I didn't want to stop moving, something felt really broken inside of me. And that's when I called a friend, Jon, and said, "I'm having some real problems." He got me a number. And I went into a gentleman's office in Beverly Hills or the Pacific Palisades—somewhere in LA. I looked at him. He was a little ol' man with white hair and a mustache. There was an empty chair. I sat down in it and I just broke out and cried for ten minutes.

It was these two chickens coming home to roost: the desire to, in theory, be free, but the deep need now, at my age, for roots, family, a real home, a spiritual home—the need to stop running, to make choices, to claim, "I'm going to be with you for my life. I'm going to live here during my life. I'm going to work this job during my life. And these are the things I'm committed to and I'm committing myself to: our love, our endeavors, our place." I ran into a moment in my life when I needed to make those choices in order to *live*.

My life changed on that day. Shortly thereafter I got married. It didn't work out the first time, but then I met Patti and built a home and realized, "Hey, I still go out there on the road. I hit the motorcycles out there once in a while, you know, a couple thousand miles, and come back."

I don't feel much like it anymore. Though you and I could jump in that Corvette and go to Route 66, but Michelle and Patti might kick our asses. Right?

PRESIDENT OBAMA: Yeah . . . I don't know how far we'd get. You know, look at that idea of being domesticated—it's something that Americans, particularly American men, are taught to resist. And I hear in your music this idea that—on the one hand—we want to break free of those communal constraints. Of small towns and rural communities, our neighborhood. Go to the big city or take the open road. Make it big. Flee the past.

> IT WAS THESE TWO CHICKENS COMING HOME TO ROOST: THE DESIRE TO, IN THEORY, BE FREE, BUT THE DEEP NEED NOW, AT MY AGE, FOR ROOTS, FAMILY, A REAL HOME, A SPIRITUAL HOME—THE NEED TO STOP RUNNING.
>
> —BRUCE SPRINGSTEEN

OPPOSITE: During the first five decades of the twentieth century, the Western was America's most popular film genre. Generally centered around a nomadic, horse-riding, gun-slinging cowboy—often played by actors such as John Wayne and Gary Cooper (inset)—the films stressed the lonesome harshness of the Wild West and depicted a tough brand of heroic masculinity.

Show folks that they shouldn't have counted us out. And that's one side. And on the other side, that's where family is.

BRUCE SPRINGSTEEN: I like to think of that as our noble argument. Where is the line between individualism and communalism—and where does it tilt at certain moments in our history? Where to put the emphasis? I started out innately as a populist. Maybe because of where I came from. And for me the people who made up America were the people who made up my neighborhood, from my little town.

PRESIDENT OBAMA: At some point, no matter how much self-invention you are doing, you have to plant a flag. And stand your ground and allow people to see you as you are, but also judge you in terms of how well you are living by that code that you've made for yourself. How much consistency can you show? Can you finish a task? Can you deliver on a commitment? All those things that, at the end of the day, are a different kind of satisfaction, but are what it means to grow up.

Because, you know, contrary to the song of a great American master, we're generally not born to run. Most of us are born to run a little bit and go back home.

BRUCE SPRINGSTEEN: That's right. You find the freedom in a life of limits, which is something I didn't believe in until I experienced it myself. I said I'm freer now than I was when I thought I was free. When you get to the point where you really want to find your freedom, you've got to find a place to stand and let them grow.

PRESIDENT OBAMA: For me, Chicago first became my home and then Michelle became an embodiment of that connection I had made to a place and a community. And the interesting thing is, by virtue of finding that place, I was then actually able to understand Hawaii as also my place. Because now I could see how all the various parts of me fit together.

One of the things we talk a lot about, Bruce, is this question: What is it that is essentially American? What's uniquely American? And you and I—you through your music, me through my politics—part of what we've been trying to do is to define a vision of this country and our part in it, our place in it.

Do you remember a moment when you just thought, consciously, "I'm an American, and that is part of my identity"?

Bruce Springsteen with the same C1 convertible that President Obama drove during these conversations and that appeared on the front cover of Springsteen's 2016 memoir, *Born to Run.*

BRUCE SPRINGSTEEN: I think my first recollection of it would be at eight a.m. every morning at St. Rose School.

Facing the flag. You've got your hand over your heart. That, I think, is when I first identified myself as, and thought there was a sacredness about, being an American.

PRESIDENT OBAMA: For me, another big moment was the space program.

And the reason it was especially important was because when the capsules land with those parachutes in the middle of the Pacific, they get brought to Hawaii. One of my earliest memories is sitting on my grandfather's shoulders with one of those little American flags. I guarantee you that we were probably so far back from where the capsule and the astronaut were. But my grandfather would be like, "Yeah! Neil Armstrong waved at you!" And I'm sure that wasn't the case, but your memory imprinted the thought "I'm a fellow countryman of that guy who was just in space."

BRUCE SPRINGSTEEN: Right.

PRESIDENT OBAMA: "That's what we do."

And then for me, the interesting thing was at six I go overseas. Ironically, one of the ways that I became strongly patriotic was being outside the country, because now I realize what we have. My mother would explain that in Indonesia where we're living, there is a military government, but in America you elect people, and everybody has a voice. Now, it was mythologized, it was idealized, how she portrayed it, but you start getting this idea that "All right, we are this experiment in democracy where everybody has got a voice and nobody is better than anybody and nobody is worse than anybody." And when you're living in a country—at the time, Indonesia, you still had scurvy and rickets and polio, and you try to explain to your friends over there, "You know, back in the States we take care of people." There was a sense of superiority.

BRUCE SPRINGSTEEN: Total exceptionalism. Yeah.

PRESIDENT OBAMA: And exceptionalism that got us in all kinds of trouble as a country, but, as a kid, it made you feel as if "I'm glad I was born under this flag."

BRUCE SPRINGSTEEN: As a child, you simply thought you were living in the greatest place on Earth. The first disturbance of that would've been the "duck and cover" drills.

PRESIDENT OBAMA: Yeah, I missed those.

BRUCE SPRINGSTEEN: The first sense of dread and paranoia. And I remember being thirteen during the Cuban Missile Crisis in 1962. And people were really scared.

PRESIDENT OBAMA: And they should've been, because—

BRUCE SPRINGSTEEN: The world was going to blow up.

PRESIDENT OBAMA: Let me tell you, when you look at the history of how that went down . . . that was a close call.

BRUCE SPRINGSTEEN: I became a real space program buff as I got older. But in 1969, I was a nineteen-year-old kid playing in a bar in Asbury Park the night that they landed on the moon. And we were like . . . "Fuck the moon landing, man."

PRESIDENT OBAMA: It's the Man!

BRUCE SPRINGSTEEN: It's a trick of the Man! And we don't want to have anything to do with it. At nine o'clock we're playing these fucking guitars and that's all there is to it. The place had about fifty people in it; twenty-five wanted to watch the moon landing on television—

PRESIDENT OBAMA: And twenty-five wanted the band to play.

BRUCE SPRINGSTEEN: So all we did was stand onstage. They had the little black and white TV. The moon landing would start. People would run up to the band and go, *Play some damn music, man!* And then we started to play and everybody would say, *"Shut the fuck up, boys!"* And finally, I had a bass player

ABOVE: In 1954, President Eisenhower (who had just recently been baptized as a Presbyterian) officially added the words *under God* to the Pledge of Allegiance. The impetus for the change was a mixture of anti-Communist Cold War sentiments and pressure from private groups like the Knights of Columbus and the Daughters of the American Revolution. OPPOSITE, TOP: A view of the moon landing, 1969. OPPOSITE, BOTTOM: The Apollo 14 astronauts' mobile quarantine facility as it is transported to Hickam Air Force Base on Oahu, February 17, 1971.

who was a bit of a techie and he said, "You guys are freaking rubes, man. I quit. I'm watching the moon landing."

PRESIDENT OBAMA: In the middle of the set?

BRUCE SPRINGSTEEN: In the middle of the set!

PRESIDENT OBAMA: And he was right.

BRUCE SPRINGSTEEN: And he was right! He walked off and that was the end of it, man. I look back on it now and realize that we were all idiots at the time, but it was funny.

PRESIDENT OBAMA: Here's where there's a little bit of a generational gap between the two of us, because I see the counterculture at the tail end. It's already kind of washing away. But '67 and '68, once you start getting the Vietnam protests and the civil rights movement, there's a big shift right there. How is that feeling to you?

BRUCE SPRINGSTEEN: I think there was a period of real disillusionment, you know? I was young—fifteen in '65, sixteen in '66. I felt like an outsider anyway because of the life that I'd chosen. But I was kind of a faux hippie. I wasn't really a hippie. I always kept one foot in a blue-collar world and one foot in a countercultural world, and I never truly belonged completely in either. But you did get a feeling that the system was fixed and prejudiced toward a lot of its citizens.

PRESIDENT OBAMA: Now you were of draft age—

BRUCE SPRINGSTEEN: I was.

PRESIDENT OBAMA: So what happened? Was there a draft number?

BRUCE SPRINGSTEEN: What happened to me was that my aunt pulled some strings and got me into a community college.

PRESIDENT OBAMA: Right. So you got a college deferment.

BRUCE SPRINGSTEEN: Then I met a guy in New York City who wanted to sign me to a record label deal. Nineteen. I thought I had died and went to heaven. He said, "You got to quit school if you're serious about this." I had no problem quitting school

whatsoever. Glad to. But if I do quit school, I'm going to be drafted.

"No worries," he says. "I have it completely fixed, you know. It's not a big deal."

I go home. I tell my parents, "I'm quitting school. Music is what I want to do with my life." They gave me their blessing, reluctantly, and I quit school, and, two or three months later, I got my draft notice in the mailbox. This would've been 1968.

PRESIDENT OBAMA: So this is just right in the thick of it.

BRUCE SPRINGSTEEN: Yeah. So I said, "I'll get my man on the line in New York." I was never able to get him on the phone again. Never answered another call of mine.

PRESIDENT OBAMA: Wow.

BRUCE SPRINGSTEEN: Believe it or not, me and two other guys from my band get drafted on the exact same day. All three of us are going on the bus to Newark. Bright and early we all meet in the parking lot outside of the Asbury Selective Service office. Everybody is lined up. It's about 80 percent young Black guys from Asbury Park, maybe 20 percent white guys who are young blue-collar guys, factory workers, just guys who weren't in college.

PRESIDENT OBAMA: The guys who get drafted.

BRUCE SPRINGSTEEN: That's right. Boom, we're all on the bus. We're going up. Some guys have got some tricks up their sleeves. One guy had a big body cast on that he confided to me was not completely authentic.

I know one thing and one thing only. I'm going to Newark and I'm coming home. Whatever that takes, that's what I'm going to do. For a variety of reasons: (1) I don't believe in the war and in 1968 not many people did anymore. (2) I'd seen my friends die. (3) I didn't want to die. So we get there and I pull out every trick I have in the book. I'm signing the papers and I'm *totally* screwing them up; as far as they know I am . . .

PRESIDENT OBAMA: Mentally deficient—

BRUCE SPRINGSTEEN: A gay, drug-taking—

OPPOSITE: Young Bruce Springsteen in his long-hair days, circa 1968. **ABOVE:** A peek inside Mission Control, 1969.

PRESIDENT OBAMA: You name it.

BRUCE SPRINGSTEEN: Guitar playing . . . and brain concussed, which I was. I had been in a terrible motorcycle accident about seven months before and I got a brain concussion.

PRESIDENT OBAMA: And at that point, these guys, they've seen every trick. It's not like you're original—

BRUCE SPRINGSTEEN: No.

PRESIDENT OBAMA: At nineteen you're not thinking of anything new that they haven't seen a hundred times.

BRUCE SPRINGSTEEN: So you go down a long hall. It's an empty hall. There's a guy at a desk. He looks up at you and says, "Sorry, Mr. Springsteen, you've been rejected from the armed services."

PRESIDENT OBAMA: Did you crack a smile or did you look sober and sad?

BRUCE SPRINGSTEEN: Very sober and sad. I said, "Oh."

And he said, "You can leave this way." So I left. I went out the door and it was me and a bunch of the guys that were on the bus. I don't know what they did, but they got out, too. And there was a party on the freaking street in Newark, New Jersey.

PRESIDENT OBAMA: What happened to the other guys in the band?

BRUCE SPRINGSTEEN: Everybody got out. I got out on the 4-F, which was for the concussion. The other guys got out on mental deferments for pulling stunts that were as outrageous or even more outrageous than what I was pulling. And these were the times, you know? I had no doubt that I was not going to go.

PRESIDENT OBAMA: The interesting thing for me was, there was not an active war as I'm entering into being a teenager. So controversies around Vietnam are not formative in my head.

I know them as history, but I didn't experience it. But by the time I became president, I think something very valuable had happened, which was a hard-learned lesson from Vietnam. By that time people understood we had done a disservice to veterans of Vietnam coming home by somehow taking it out on them. Bad decisions were being made in Washington and yet, suddenly, vets become stained with those bad decisions. The American public had come to recognize and revere the service of our troops, even those who were critical of certain aspects of US interventions. By the time I have the honor of being the commander in chief, I am in awe of our military and what they can accomplish. And what they can do, how they can take a twenty-year-old kid from a small Southern rural town and take an inner-city kid and they take a kid from Jersey and mold them into folks who are responsible for multibillion-dollar pieces of equipment and are commanding their fellow soldiers into unbelievable battles.

What you realize is, it is possible to revere the sacrifice, the courage, the bravery, the traditions of our military and at the same time say war is hell, and we haven't always made good decisions about the wars we fought. I use that just as an example of how I think about America. The fact that I can look squarely at all the mistakes and sins and cruelty and violence of the country and I can still say, "Yes that's true, and yet, look what is possible. Look how this thing has unfolded. Look at the beauty and the boldness and the achievement, even when the ideals are breached and betrayed. The ideals themselves are powerful and are beacons. And they're worth fighting for and preserving."

When I listen to you talking about the draft and Vietnam and you losing friends and the way the country was being torn apart around that war, I remember talking to friends who did go and come home and discover that they were called baby killers and spat on and they somehow became the objects of particularly young people's rejection of that war when in fact they were kids who were expressing their patriotism, duty.

BRUCE SPRINGSTEEN: A lot of the vets were ignored and mistreated for a long time as symbols of, quote, "the only war America has ever lost."

PRESIDENT OBAMA: And that, I think, was an important maturing of America: being able to distinguish between policies made by men in suits in Washington versus the professionalism and sacrifice and courage shown by those who actually fought.

BRUCE SPRINGSTEEN: This was a major thing. Vietnam was the first time in my remembered life that I felt the country had lost its way. Completely lost its way. Through the loss of my friends and my own experience, it was . . . the loss of innocence.

OPPOSITE: On December 1, 1969, a lottery drawing was held at Selective Service national headquarters in Washington, DC, to choose soldiers for the ongoing war in Vietnam in a more equitable fashion. The 366 plastic capsules contained birth dates for all men within the eighteen to twenty-five age range specified in Selective Service law and were drawn to determine the order of induction for 1970. By 1973, when the United States finally ended its involvement in the war in Vietnam after years of protests, the death toll of American military personnel topped 58,000.

AMAZING GRACE

3

What makes America exceptional isn't our wealth or size or skyscrapers or military power. It's the fact that America's the only nation in human history that's made up of people of every race, religion, and culture from every corner of the globe. And that we've had faith in our democracy, our common creed, to blend this hodgepodge of humanity into one people. Nothing symbolizes this truth more than our music.

It's the way that generations of Americans stitch together every imaginable tradition—from African rhythms to Irish ballads—to create something entirely new. Whether it was jazz or the blues, country or rock 'n' roll.

At the same time, our music's often been a mirror into the fault lines of American society, which are seen in what gets played and who gets paid, and heard in the songs of those who have been relegated to the margins of society and in the songs of those insisting that their truths finally be heard. It's got a power to reshape social attitudes and make connections between people when mere words—even in good speeches—aren't enough.

BRUCE SPRINGSTEEN: So you're in Hawaii, you're a teenager in the seventies. What is catching your ear as you are becoming interested in music . . . which, I would guess, is around fourteen?

PRESIDENT OBAMA: First album I bought with my own money: *Talking Book*, Stevie Wonder. I would sit with a banged-up, plasticky little old turntable. I got myself some headphones so my grandparents would not complain. And I would sing along to every Stevie Wonder song for hours.

Hawaii was a place where you had Top 40. Casey Kasem was on. Now, I'm ten, eleven years old. I'm listening to the radio and there's songs that I end up just getting really attached to . . . you got a ten-year-old saying, *Let's get it on. . . . Ahhhh baby!*

BOTH: *We're all sensitive people . . . with so much to give . . .*

PRESIDENT OBAMA: And my grandmother would hear and say, "*What* are you singing?" There was another song by Billy Paul, "Me and Mrs. Jones."

BRUCE SPRINGSTEEN: Huuuuuge.

PRESIDENT OBAMA: *Mrs. Jones, Mrs. Jones, Mrs. Jones. . . . We both know that it's wrong, but it's much too strong.* Eleven years old!

BRUCE SPRINGSTEEN: Ha!

PRESIDENT OBAMA: And Joni Mitchell came out with *Court and Spark*.

BRUCE SPRINGSTEEN: Beautiful record.

PRESIDENT OBAMA: *Help me, I . . .*

BOTH: *. . . think I'm falling in love with you.*

PRESIDENT OBAMA: So the interesting thing was that you had Top 40 and you had these crossover artists like Earth, Wind & Fire, but then there were other kinds of music that were much more . . . I won't say segregated, but identifiable as Black or white.

For instance, I loved the Ohio Players and Parliament. You might not find those records in some of my white friends' music library. Some of them might be into heavy metal, and if I get into a car with them and they turn that stuff all the way

OPPOSITE: President Obama's teenage musical tastes covered the popular music spectrum in the early to mid-1970s. Some of the era's most influential artists are responsible for his favorite albums and tracks, which included (clockwise from top left) Joni Mitchell's sixth studio album, *Court and Spark*, her most commercially and critically successful, which blended her folk sensibilities with pop and more experimental jazz sounds and structures (its first single, "Help Me," was Mitchell's only top 10 single on the Billboard Hot 100); Stevie Wonder's fifteenth studio album, *Talking Book*, which marked a significant turning point in his career, diverging from the Berry Gordy-influenced Motown sound and relying on the synthesizers heard on tracks like "Superstition" (*Talking Book* was also Wonder's most commercially popular album, topping the Billboard pop and R & B charts and earning him three Grammys); Marvin Gaye's eleventh studio album, *What's Going On*, which was a notable departure for the Motown star, featuring songs that would become the soundtrack for a generation shaped by anti-Vietnam protests and the Civil Rights Movement; and dance-floor hits like "Love Rollercoaster" and "Fire" by seventies funk band the Ohio Players, who were also notable for their distinctive, erotic album covers, especially the ones featuring model Pat Evans.

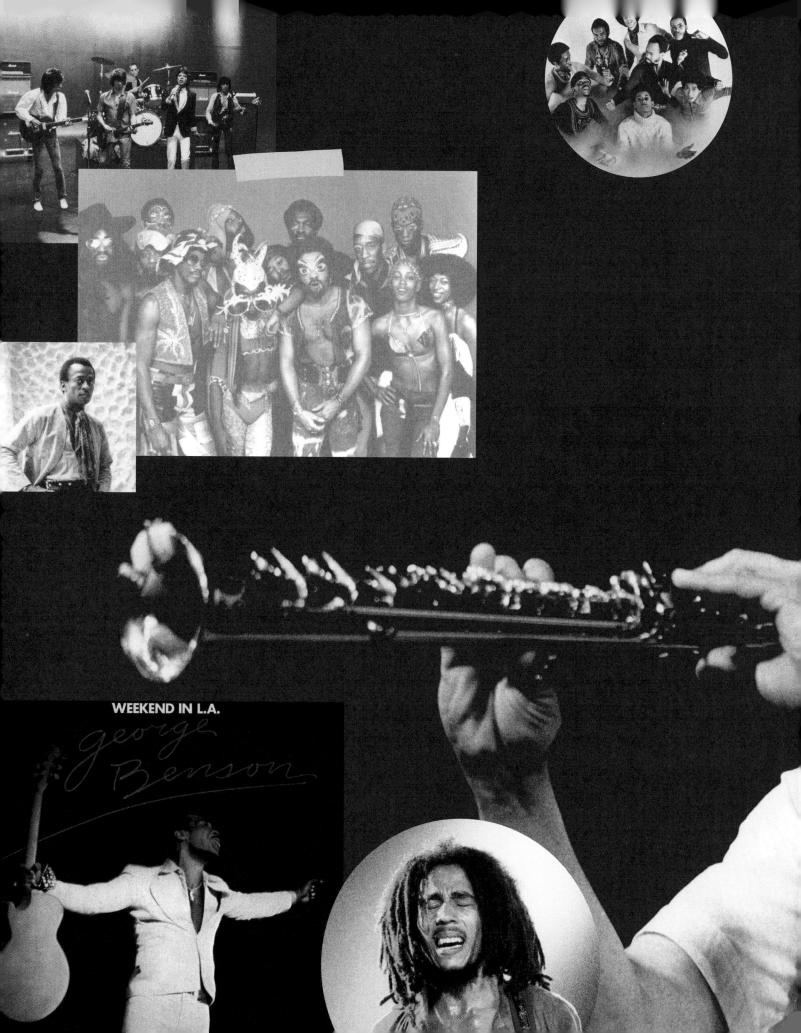

WEEKEND IN L.A.
george
Benson

up—you know, that could be a little painful for me. So even though Top 40 was integrated, at least in Hawaii, underneath, you could still see these distinctions between whose music was whose.

In my sophomore year in high school I veer away from just what's on the radio and start following these tangents. I go backward into rock 'n' roll and start listening to Dylan and the Stones, and Martin Scorsese's *The Last Waltz* comes out right around this time. I watch the Band and all the artists that are in that film and it shows all these strands in folk and soul and R & B and country and how these things get blended into rock 'n' roll. I start following all these streams and tributaries and rivers. It's also when I start listening to jazz in a serious way. My father had taken me to a jazz concert, but it did not connect at the time. Initially I'm listening to pop jazz—it would be what's now called smooth jazz. George Benson. He had that big record, "On Broadway."

BRUCE SPRINGSTEEN: Huge record.

PRESIDENT OBAMA: And Grover Washington Jr. had that song "Mister Magic." *Dunnnh dunnnah dunnnah.* And then in college, I get deep into Bob Marley. By that time my interest in jazz really starts. Miles Davis's *Kind of Blue,* John Coltrane's *My Favorite Things,* Mingus. Now I probably listen to more hip-hop by virtue of my daughters. That's oftentimes what's playing in the house.

BRUCE SPRINGSTEEN: My boys were different. My oldest son was into political punk music. Against Me! Tom Morello. Rise Against. And my youngest son was kind of into classical rock—Creedence Clearwater and Bob Dylan's early acoustic records. My daughter was into Top 40, so anything that was on Top 40 for a decade while I was driving her around, that's what I was going to listen to.

PRESIDENT OBAMA: But it's a great gift. To have your kids keep you on track.

Because then it goes both ways. Because my daughters will now listen to a Marvin Gaye album, you know? That's part of their childhood memories, listening to our records.

When you decided you were gonna be a rock 'n' roll star at the age of fifteen—

Grover Washington Jr.'s smooth saxophone sounds helped define the genre of smooth seventies jazz. His 1974 album *Mister Magic* topped the charts and had a major influence on other jazz-funk musicians of the seventies and eighties. Also chief among President Obama and Bruce Springsteen's influences—past and present—are (clockwise from top left): the Rolling Stones; Earth, Wind & Fire; Creedence Clearwater Revival; Bob Marley; George Benson; Miles Davis; and Parliament.

BILLBOARD TOP 40 — JUNE 5, 1971

1

ROLLING STONES
BROWN SUGAR
THE ROLLING STONES

2
DUNHILL
JOY TO THE WORLD
THREE DOG NIGHT

3
HOT WAX
WANT ADS
THE HONEY CONE

4
APPLE
IT DON'T COME EASY
RINGO STARR

5
A&M
RAINY DAYS AND MONDAYS
THE CARPENTERS

6
ATLANTIC
BRIDGE OVER TROUBLED WATER / A BRAND NEW ME
ARETHA FRANKLIN

7
MGM
SWEET -AND- INNOCENT
DONNY OSMOND OF THE OSMONDS

8

MOTOWN
NEVER CAN SAY GOODBYE
JACKSON 5

9
ODE
IT'S TOO LATE / I FEEL THE EARTH MOVE
CAROLE KING

10
BIG TREE
ME AND YOU AND A DOG NAMED BOO
LOBO

11
BELL
I'LL MEET YOU HALFWAY
THE PARTRIDGE FAMILY (STARRING SHIRLEY JONES AND FEATURING DAVID CASSIDY)

12
KAMA SUTRA
PUT YOUR HAND IN THE HAND
OCEAN

13
CAPITOL
I DON'T KNOW HOW TO LOVE HIM
HELEN REDDY

14
DECCA
SUPERSTAR
MURRAY HEAD AND THE TRINIDAD SINGERS

15
ATLANTIC
TREAT HER LIKE A LADY
CORNELIUS BROTHERS AND SISTER ROSE

16
STORMY FOREST
HERE COMES THE SUN
RICHIE HAVENS

17
SUNFLOWER
CHICK-A-BOOM (DON'T YA JES' LOVE IT)
DADDY DEWDROP

18
ELEKTRA
IF
BREAD

19
ELEKTRA
LOVE HER MADLY
THE DOORS

20
ATLANTIC
DON'T KNOCK MY LOVE (PART 1)
WILSON PICKETT

21

MOTOWN

NATHAN
JONES

THE SUPREMES

22

MGM

DOUBLE
LOVIN'

THE OSMONDS

23

TOP & BOTTOM

RIGHT ON THE
TIP OF MY
TONGUE

BRENDA AND THE
TABULATIONS

24

POLYDOR

STAY
AWHILE

THE BELLS

25

COLUMBIA

INDIAN
RESERVATION
(THE LAMENT
OF THE CHEROKEE
RESERVATION INDIAN)
THE RAIDERS

26

BRUNSWICK

(FOR GOD'S SAKE)
GIVE MORE
POWER
TO THE
PEOPLE

THE CHI-LITES

27

DECCA

WOODSTOCK

MATTHEWS
SOUTHERN COMFORT

28

RCA

WHEN
YOU'RE
HOT,
YOU'RE
HOT

JERRY REED

29

METROMEDIA

••• THE •••
DRUM

BOBBY SHERMAN

30

LIZARD

COOL
•AID•

PAUL HUMPHREY AND
HIS COOL AID CHEMISTS

31

DECCA

I DON'T KNOW
HOW TO
LOVE
HIM

YVONNE ELLIMAN

32

SCEPTER

TIMOTHY

THE BUOYS

33

CALLA

I LOVE YOU
FOR ALL
SEASONS

THE FUZZ

34

ATCO

TOAST AND
MARMALADE
FOR TEA

TIN TIN

35

ELEKTRA

THAT'S THE WAY
I'VE ALWAYS HEARD
IT SHOULD
BE

CARLY SIMON

36

INVICTUS

SHE'S NOT
JUST
ANOTHER
WOMAN

THE 8TH DAY

37

COLUMBIA

LOW-
DOWN

CHICAGO

38

SMOKEY ROBINSON
AND THE MIRACLES

TAMLA

I DON'T BLAME
YOU
AT ALL

39

MOTOWN

REACH OUT
I'LL BE
THERE

DIANA ROSS

40

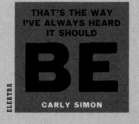

ALSTON

FUNKY
NASSAU
(PART 1)

THE BEGINNING
OF THE END

SETON HALL UNIVERSITY
PRESENTS
IN THE CENTER RING
NEW JERSEYS' OWN
BRUCE SPRINGSTEEN
ONE SHOW ONLY
APRIL 7, 1974
WALSH GYMNASIUM - 8:00 P.M.

★ ★ **Fun For The Whole Family** ★ ★

TICKETS 4.50 / 3.50 WITH STUDENT I.D.
ALSO APPEARING:
MISSY BIMBO, WILD BILLY, CRAZY JANEY, ZERO AND BLIND TERRY
WITH SPECIAL APPEARANCE BY SPANISH JOHNNY
NO ALCOHOL ALLOWED IN GYMNASIUM

BRUCE SPRINGSTEEN: Yeah.

PRESIDENT OBAMA: —or around there . . . it made sense to play the guitar.

BRUCE SPRINGSTEEN: Guitars were cheap. So that helped. My first guitar was eighteen dollars.

PRESIDENT OBAMA: Cheaper than a piano.

BRUCE SPRINGSTEEN: Much cheaper than a piano, much cheaper than the drums. I painted houses, tarred roofs, did some lawn work, saved up eighteen dollars, bought a cheap guitar at the Western Auto store in Freehold, New Jersey. My cousin Frankie was starting to play the guitar a little bit and he taught me a few chords and sent me home with a folk music book with all the chords in it. So for about a month or so I was strumming my way through folk music classics. You know, "Greensleeves" and "If I Had a Hammer." And, shortly after that, somebody taught me to play honky-tonk.

Then I started to learn some Beatles. I learned "Twist and Shout." You know . . . *Shake it up, baby!* I just started getting up in my room and closing the door, and just screaming my head off and strumming the guitar and standing in front of the mirror.

PRESIDENT OBAMA: Did your folks say anything? Like, "What are you yelling about?"

BRUCE SPRINGSTEEN: "Keep it down!" You know, the usual stuff.

PRESIDENT OBAMA: Yeah.

BRUCE SPRINGSTEEN: "Keep it down, man! Keep it down!" My mother was supportive. My father was like, "What . . . what's . . . what's going on now? What's this kid up to? I don't understand it."

And then I grew my hair and he *really* didn't understand. But it was the exact same course that thousands, if not millions, of other kids were taking at that exact same moment. So the miracle is there's a million kids who pick up a guitar.

A certain amount of those kids learn how to strum a few chords.

Certain amount of those kids learn how to play, play a few songs.

Few of those get into a little local band.

Few of those get into a little local band that makes a demo.

And then a few of those get into a little local band that makes a record.

And then a few of those get a local band that makes a record, and it sells a few copies.

And then even fewer of those make a record, get into a band where they have a short career.

And fewer of those get in, and they have a band where, like, they make somewhat of a regular living.

And then one night I was at the Rock & Roll Hall of Fame and I was standing between George Harrison and Mick Jagger singing something. And I said, "Okay, one of these kids is standing tonight between George Harrison and Mick Jagger."

Choosing music was both simple and complicated for me. It was the only thing I deeply desired to do. It was also an essential element in building an identity as a man, as an American, as a human being.

When I hold a guitar, I don't feel like I'm holding anything. It's just a part of my body, you know? It's just another appendage. When I strap it on, it feels like my natural state. And I also built a philosophy about performing: *I'm gonna give my best to bring out the best in you.*

And I'm going to send you home with a sense of community and a set of values that may sustain you past the concert. You know, I always make a joke, "I want to come out onstage and change your life." Except it's not really a joke. That is my purpose at night.

PRESIDENT OBAMA: It's your ministry.

BRUCE SPRINGSTEEN: Yes. I come out there at night and I believe that I can inspire you through hard work, the deep development of a philosophy, and the incorporation of spirituality. And that I can inspire you to develop those things within yourself. And if I can have some small piece in assisting you in doing those things, I've done my job. That is what I consider my job—as well as making you dance.

PRESIDENT OBAMA: I was about to say, you want people to have a good time, too.

OPPOSITE, TOP: A memento from one of Bruce's early gigs. A month later, in May 1974, he would begin work on his breakout album, *Born to Run.* **OPPOSITE, BOTTOM:** George Harrison, Bruce Springsteen, and Mick Jagger singing "I Saw Her Standing There" with the Rock Hall Jam Band at the Rock & Roll Hall of Fame induction ceremony, Cleveland, OH, January 1988. **ABOVE:** Bruce's first guitar.

GROWIN' UP

I stood stone-like at midnight suspended in my masquerade / I combed my hair till it was just right and commanded the night brigade / I was open to pain and crossed by the rain and I walked on a crooked crutch / I strolled all alone through a fallout zone and came out with my soul untouched / I hid in the clouded wrath of the crowd but when they said "Sit down" I stood up / Ooh-ooh, growin' up / The flag of piracy flew from my mast, my sails were set wing to wing / I had a jukebox graduate for first mate, she couldn't sail but she sure could sing / I pushed B-52 and bombed 'em with the blues with my gear set stubborn on standing / I broke all the rules, strafed my old high school, never once gave thought to landing / I hid in the clouded warmth of the crowd but when they said "Come down" I threw up / Ooh-ooh, growin' up / I took month-long vacations in the stratosphere and you know it's really hard to hold your breath / I swear I lost everything I ever loved or feared, I was the cosmic kid in full costume dress / Well, my feet they finally took root in the earth but I got me a nice little place in the stars / And I swear I found the key to the universe in the engine of an old parked car / I hid in the mother breast of the crowd but when they said "Pull down" I pulled up / Ooh-ooh, growin' up / Ooh-ooh, growin' up

—FROM GREETINGS FROM ASBURY PARK, N.J. (1973)

BRUCE SPRINGSTEEN: I am a song-and-dance man. I want you to laugh. I want you to have fun.

PRESIDENT OBAMA: Maybe forget your troubles for a while . . .

BRUCE SPRINGSTEEN: And if that's all you take from the show, that's plenty.

PRESIDENT OBAMA: Did you have that sense of purpose from the start? I mean, when you guys are playing little bars and clubs, you're just thinking, "I want to have a good set and people to come away saying, 'Aw, that band rocked.'"

BRUCE SPRINGSTEEN: I want a good set. I want to make my five dollars. I want them to think we are good—but increasingly I want them to think we're the best. I want to transmit a vicious joy and a voracious hunger for life.

PRESIDENT OBAMA: When do you start thinking in those terms? Or does it just start to happen as the crowds get bigger and you feel a greater responsibility to your audience?

BRUCE SPRINGSTEEN: I am doing it a lot longer before I think about it. The self-awareness came much later when I started to develop a philosophical point of view, which was my nature anyway as a human being. And I was interested in having a code. I believe every man has a code that he lives by. And that code guides us, protects us, delivers us. . . .

PRESIDENT OBAMA: Makes us feel bad when we break it.

BRUCE SPRINGSTEEN: That's right. All of my heroes, going back to the Western heroes, seemed to have a code of life.

I take my job seriously. I believe that I am involved in a ridiculous but noble profession, and that music had an impact on me, changed my life, changed who I thought I was, changed who I became. God has given me the opportunity to come out at night and to have that kind of impact on some individual in the crowd. If I can do that, that's worth being on the planet. That's something worth living for.

PRESIDENT OBAMA: How about your influences?

> YOU KNOW, I ALWAYS MAKE A JOKE, "I WANT TO COME OUT ONSTAGE AND CHANGE YOUR LIFE." EXCEPT IT'S NOT REALLY A JOKE. THAT IS MY PURPOSE AT NIGHT. . . . THAT IS WHAT I CONSIDER MY JOB—AS WELL AS MAKING YOU DANCE.
>
> —BRUCE SPRINGSTEEN

BRUCE SPRINGSTEEN: I was a creature of Top 40. First music I heard was my mother playing doo-wop and rhythm and blues on the radio in the morning when I was eight or nine years old. And then you had the other hits of the day, which were Beatle hits and Rolling Stone hits.

PRESIDENT OBAMA: And where does Dylan fit in?

BRUCE SPRINGSTEEN: Bob was funny. He had hits but he was pulling from some different tradition. He was pulling from Woody Guthrie. But I didn't know or learn anything about that till I was thirty. I never listened to Bob's early acoustic records.

PRESIDENT OBAMA: That's interesting.

BRUCE SPRINGSTEEN: I only listened to *Highway 61*, "Subterranean Homesick Blues." It wasn't until I got in my late twenties and thirties that I went back and heard his acoustic music. And then went back and heard Woody Guthrie.

Country music came later for me. I was looking for other solutions than rock music provided. Rock music was great music and there was some class anger in it and that agreed with me. But as you were getting older, it didn't address your adult problems—so I went to country music. Country music was great, incredible singing and playing, but it was rather fatalistic.

So I said, "Well, where is a music of hope?" Woody Guthrie and Bob Dylan were spelling out the hard world that you lived in, but they were also providing some transcendence and some actionable solutions to societal and your own personal problems. You could be active.

That drew my attention because I was now a relatively big rock star. I was interested in maintaining ties to my community. I was interested in giving voice to myself and folks in my community. I was also interested in being active to a certain degree, taking some of what I was earning, putting it

OPPOSITE: Bruce in "song-and-dance man" mode, with Clarence, on the 2005 Devils and Dust tour. FOLLOWING (PAGE 88): President and Michelle Obama greet the crowd at the inauguration on January 18, 2009. FOLLOWING (PAGE 89): President Lincoln looks on as Bruce plays for the estimated 400,000 people who filled the National Mall for "We Are One," a concert to celebrate the inauguration. It featured performances from top acts like Beyoncé, Stevie Wonder, Mary J. Blige, James Taylor, Jon Bon Jovi, and Pete Seeger, as well as readings from American historical documents and literature. After an opening passage read by actor Denzel Washington, Bruce kicked off the concert with a performance of "The Rising," his 9/11-inspired song. He was accompanied by the Joyce Garrett Singers, a Washington, DC-based gospel choir.

back into the community. In 1980, I started to play "This Land Is Your Land." That, and then "Born in the U.S.A.," was when we knew what we were going to do, both as a band, a bit as a social unit, and as an entertainment unit, and how we were going to blend all these things together. And that was where I found my full satisfaction.

PRESIDENT OBAMA: I like how you're talking about blending it all together, because you know that's been the essence of all great American musicians. And that's one of the reasons why Michelle and I thought it was so important during the course of our presidency—at a moment when the country felt so divided—to really put an emphasis on these music series that we did.

We would have a Motown night. But also a country music night. Or a fiesta Latina. Or a Broadway tunes night. Or a gospel night. Part of what we would do is draw musicians from various traditions to be a part of something that wasn't traditionally in their space. We'd have the country music singer in the gospel concert. Or we'd have an R & B singer singing rock to emphasize and underscore how all these traditions do, in fact, blend together once you start breaking down some of these silos and categories that we carry around in our heads.

BRUCE SPRINGSTEEN: Right.

PRESIDENT OBAMA: I was always struck by the generosity of musicians toward each other. Usually the musicians would come in and rehearse the night before or the day before. They'd usually rehearse at night. I might be in the Treaty Room, which was right upstairs. I could hear suddenly the bass come in and sometimes I would sneak down and watch. I'd sit in the back and try not to be noticed as the rehearsals were going on. I remember one time I was watching Mick Jagger and Gary Clark Jr. trying to work out a blues number they were doing. And Jagger is Gary's grandpa's age, right? By that time he's already seventy. Although he was moving onstage like he was twenty-five. And Gary Clark Jr. is basically a carrier of the traditions the Stones drew from. So the old, grizzled icon and the new up-and-comer, they are just musicians, and there is a respect there and they are listening to each other.

BRUCE SPRINGSTEEN: Life among musicians is good.

> SEEING THAT SPIRIT MADE ME THINK, "IT'D BE GOOD IF POLITICS WAS LIKE THIS, WHERE FOLKS WERE JUST TRYING TO MAKE A GOOD SONG."
>
> —PRESIDENT OBAMA

PRESIDENT OBAMA: Seeing that spirit made me think, "It'd be good if politics was like this, where folks were just trying to make a good song."

BRUCE SPRINGSTEEN: That is a huge part of rock 'n' roll. And why most bands don't stay together.

PRESIDENT OBAMA: Because it's hard to sustain that spirit.

Now, Bruce, as you and Patti can testify, some of the best music that happened in the White House happened off camera during some of our parties.

BRUCE SPRINGSTEEN: Well, we were at a few, and all I can say is they were historic. And they're not gonna see another one like that at the White House for a loooong time.

PRESIDENT OBAMA: They will not. We had some amazing moments. The performances that took place late into the evening . . . that was fun. I remember one in particular.

Let's set the stage here: I am in my last month of my presidency. I want to do something for the staff that has been with me for the entire journey, and has gone through a really remarkable but grueling process. So we get this idea. Maybe we can just do something small and quiet and private—a hundred people. And maybe Bruce will be willing to come in and just do a quick concert.

And you show up and we've got about ten guitars sitting over there on a rack, and we've got the piano. Patti says to me, "Yeah, I don't really know what he's going to do. . . ." Because you hadn't really done the whole thing for her either.

BRUCE SPRINGSTEEN: I'd never done it for anybody. I only did it for a few hours in this room we're sitting in before I came down. I got the invitation and I thought, "Well, I am not gonna put the band together and make a big noise. I'll go down and play some acoustic songs." Then I thought, "What could I do to make that a little different? Well, I'll read from my book and I'll play a few songs."

So I came in here and I started to read from the book and play a few songs. And I realized reading from the book was a

OPPOSITE, TOP: The Queen of Soul, Aretha Franklin, prepares to perform at the "Women of Soul" concert, March 6, 2014. OPPOSITE, BOTTOM: President Obama showcases his dance moves onstage with Prince and his daughter Sasha during a performance at the White House, 2015.

"IN PERFORMANCE AT THE WHITE HOUSE" SERIES, 2009-2015

FEBRUARY 26, 2009
THE LIBRARY OF CONGRESS
GERSHWIN PRIZE FOR
POPULAR SONG

ANITA JOHNSON performs "I Never
Dreamed You'd Leave in Summer"

DIANA KRALL performs
"Blame It on the Sun"

ESPERANZA SPALDING performs
"Overjoyed"

TONY BENNETT

MARTINA MCBRIDE performs
"You and I"

MARY MARY performs
"Higher Ground"

STEVIE WONDER performs
"Signed, Sealed, Delivered"
and "Sir Duke"

INDIA ARIE performs
"Summer Soft"

MAY 12, 2009
AN EVENING OF POETRY,
MUSIC, AND SPOKEN WORD

ESPERANZA SPALDING performs
"Tell Him" on the double bass

LIN-MANUEL MIRANDA performs
"The Hamilton Mixtape"

OCTOBER 13, 2009
FIESTA LATINA

GLORIA ESTEFAN performs
"Mi Tierra"

GLORIA ESTEFAN, SHEILA E.,
AND JOSE FELICIANO perform
"No Llores"

SHEILA E. AND PETE ESCOVEDO

TITO EL BAMBINO

THALIA

MARC ANTHONY

LOS LOBOS

JOSE FELICIANO

OPPOSITE: B.B. King. ABOVE: Paul McCartney.

NOVEMBER 4, 2009
AN EVENING OF
CLASSICAL MUSIC

JOSHUA BELL, AWADAGIN PRATT, AND ALISA WEILERSTEIN perform Felix Mendelssohn's Piano Trio No. 1 in D minor, Op. 49, 4th movement: Finale, Allegro assai appassionato

JOSHUA BELL AND SHARON ISBIN perform Niccolò Paganini's Cantabile

JOSHUA BELL AND AWADAGIN PRATT perform Maurice Ravel's Tzigane

CELLIST ALISA WEILERSTEIN AND SIXTEEN-YEAR-OLD PERCUSSIONIST JASON YODER perform Camille Saint-Saëns's The Swan

CELLISTS ALISA WEILERSTEIN AND EIGHT-YEAR-OLD SUJARI BRITT perform Luigi Boccherini's Sonata for Two Cellos in C major, 1st movement: Allegro moderato

CELLIST ALISA WEILERSTEIN performs Zoltán Kodály's Sonata for Solo Cello, Op. 8, 3rd movement: Allegro molto vivace

CONCERT PIANIST AWADAGIN PRATT performs J. S. Bach's Passacaglia and Fugue in C minor, BWV 582

CLASSICAL GUITARIST AARON ISBIN performs Isaac Albeniz's Asturias and Agustin Barrios Mangoré's Waltz, Op. 8, No. 4

FEBRUARY 10, 2010
MUSIC OF THE CIVIL RIGHTS
MOVEMENT

THE BLIND BOYS OF ALABAMA perform "Free at Last"

SMOKEY ROBINSON performs "Abraham, Martin and John"

THE FREEDOM SINGERS perform "(Ain't Gonna Let Nobody) Turn Me Around"

GOSPEL MUSIC STAR YOLANDA ADAMS performs "How Great Thou Art" and "A Change Is Gonna Come"

JENNIFER HUDSON performs "Someday We'll All Be Free"

JOAN BAEZ performs "We Shall Overcome"

NATALIE COLE performs "What's Going On"

JOHN MELLENCAMP performs "Keep Your Eyes on the Prize"

SMOKEY ROBINSON AND JENNIFER HUDSON perform "People Get Ready"

BOB DYLAN performs "The Times They Are a-Changin'"

PRESIDENT BARACK OBAMA AND THE FIRST FAMILY join the performers onstage in the East Room of the White House as they sing "Lift Every Voice and Sing"

JULY 19, 2010
A BROADWAY CELEBRATION

DANIELLE ARCI, CONSTANTINE ROUSOULI, AND DANCERS FROM THE DUKE ELLINGTON SCHOOL perform "You Can't Stop the Beat"

TONYA PINKINS performs "Gonna Pass Me a Law"

NATHAN LANE AND BRIAN D'ARCY JAMES perform "Free"

KAREN OLIVO AND DANCERS perform "America"

IDINA MENZEL performs "Defying Gravity"

IDINA MENZEL AND MARVIN HAMLISCH perform "What I Did for Love"

ELAINE STRITCH performs "Broadway Baby"

CHAD KIMBALL performs "Memphis Lives in Me"

BRIAN D'ARCY JAMES performs "Blue Skies"

AUDRA MCDONALD performs "Can't Stop Talking About Him" and "Happiness Is a Thing Called Joe"

ASSATA ALSTON performs "Gimme Gimme"

FEBRUARY 24, 2011
THE MOTOWN SOUND

LEDISI

NATASHA BEDINGFIELD,
JORDIN SPARKS, AND LEDISI

STEVIE WONDER

SMOKEY ROBINSON
AND SHERYL CROW

SHERYL CROW

SEAL

NICK JONAS

JOHN LEGEND, NICK JONAS,
JAMIE FOXX, AND SEAL

JORDIN SPARKS

JOHN LEGEND

NATASHA BEDINGFIELD

AMBER RILEY

NOVEMBER 21, 2011
COUNTRY MUSIC

THE BAND PERRY performs
"If I Die Young" and
"I Will Always Love You"

DARIUS RUCKER AND KRIS KRISTOFFERSON
perform "Pancho and Lefty"

MICKEY performs "Crazy"

ARNOLD MCCULLER AND LYLE LOVETT
perform "Funny How Time
Slips Away"

LYLE LOVETT performs
"Cowboy Man"

LAUREN ALAINA performs
"Coal Miner's Daughter"

KRIS KRISTOFFERSON performs
"Me and Bobby McGee"

JAMES TAYLOR performs
"Wichita Lineman" and
"Riding on a Railroad"

DIERKS BENTLEY performs "Home"

DARIUS RUCKER performs
"I Got Nothing"

DIERKS BENTLEY AND LAUREN ALAINA
perform "Always on My Mind"

ALISON KRAUSS performs
"When You Say Nothing at All"

FEBRUARY 21, 2012
RED, WHITE, AND BLUES

BUDDY GUY AND ENSEMBLE perform
"Sweet Home Chicago"

TROMBONE SHORTY performs
"St. James Infirmary"

SUSAN TEDESCHI, DEREK TRUCKS, AND
WARREN HAYNES perform "I'd
Rather Go Blind"

MICK JAGGER performs
"I Can't Turn You Loose"
and "Miss You"

KEB' MO' performs "Henry"

MICK JAGGER AND JEFF BECK perform
"Commit a Crime"

BUDDY GUY, GARY CLARK JR.,
JEFF BECK, AND MICK JAGGER perform
"I'd Rather Go Blind"

BUDDY GUY AND JEFF BECK perform
"Let Me Love You"

SHEMEKIA COPELAND AND GARY CLARK JR.
perform "Beat Up Old Guitar"

GARY CLARK JR. performs
"Catfish Blues"

B.B. KING AND ENSEMBLE perform
"Let the Good Times Roll"

**MAY 9, 2012
THE LIBRARY OF CONGRESS
GERSHWIN PRIZE FOR
POPULAR SONG**

SHERYL CROW performs
"Walk on By"

STEVIE WONDER performs "Alfie"

SHERYL CROW AND LYLE LOVETT
perform "I'll Never Fall
in Love Again"

SHELÉA AND ARTURO SANDOVAL perform
"Anyone Who Had a Heart"

RUMER performs "A House Is
Not a Home"

MIKE MYERS performs
"What's New Pussy Cat"

MICHAEL FEINSTEIN performs
"Close to You"

LYLE LOVETT performs "Always
Something There to Remind Me"

DIANA KRALL performs
"The Look of Love"

BURT BACHARACH performs
"What the World Needs Now
Is Love"

ARTURO SANDOVAL AND STEVIE WONDER
perform "Make It Easy on
Yourself"

**APRIL 9, 2013
MEMPHIS SOUL**

SAM MOORE AND JOSHUA LEDET
perform "Soul Man"

BOOKER T. JONES AND ENSEMBLE
perform "In the Midnight Hour"

WILLIAM BELL performs "You Don't
Miss Your Water"

JUSTIN TIMBERLAKE AND STEVE CROPPER
perform "(Sittin' On) The
Dock of the Bay"

SAM MOORE performs "When
Something Is Wrong
with My Baby"

QUEEN LATIFAH performs
"I Can't Stand the Rain"

OPPOSITE: Carole King. **ABOVE:** Joan Baez.

MAVIS STAPLES performs
"I'll Take You There"

JOSHUA LEDET performs
"When a Man Loves a Woman"

CYNDI LAUPER AND CHARLIE MUSSELWHITE
perform "Try a Little
Tenderness"

EDDIE FLOYD performs
"Knock on Wood"

**ALABAMA SHAKES, STEVE CROPPER,
AND BOOKER T. JONES** perform
"Born Under a Bad Sign"

MAY 22, 2013
**THE LIBRARY OF CONGRESS
GERSHWIN PRIZE FOR
POPULAR SONG**

CAROLE KING

NOVEMBER 6, 2014
A SALUTE TO THE TROOPS

WILLIE NELSON AND JOHN FOGERTY

MARCH 6, 2014
WOMEN OF SOUL

JANELLE MONAE

PATTI LABELLE performs
"Over the Rainbow"

MELISSA ETHERIDGE performs
"Neither One of Us"

ARIANA GRANDE performs
"Tattooed Heart" and
"I Have Nothing"

ARETHA FRANKLIN performs
"Amazing Grace"

APRIL 14, 2015
THE GOSPEL TRADITION

ARETHA FRANKLIN performs
"Plant My Feet on Higher
Ground"

SHIRLEY CAESAR performs
"Sweeping Through the City"

MICHELLE WILLIAMS performs
"Say Yes"

RHIANNON GIDDENS performs
"Up Above My Head"

TAMELA MANN performs
"Take Me to the King"

Ben Harper, William Bell, Cyndi Lauper, Justin Timberlake,
Queen Latifah, Sam Moore, Charlie Musselwhite, and
Steve Cropper. **FOLLOWING:** Bruce Springsteen brought
his sound to the East Room on January 12, 2017, as a
send-off for the Obamas and 250 of their staffers.

little stilted, because the way you write for your book is not the way you speak. So I started to paraphrase the writings in the book as if I was just telling a story, and I spent a couple hours for two days in this studio and then we came down.

PRESIDENT OBAMA: And you essentially ended up doing—what would you say, maybe ninety minutes of—

BOTH: What became the Broadway show.

BRUCE SPRINGSTEEN: I have to give you credit, because the two of you were sitting right in front of me and I was thrilled to be there, honored to be playing for you. I can honestly say that I felt, after that performance, like I had never felt after any performance I'd done, because it was something different.

Afterwards, you were the first one onstage, and you leaned down into my ear and you said, "Hey, look, I know you did this just for us, but this ought to be a show somewhere or something, you know." When we went home that night, we were talking all the way back. And Patti and Jon [Landau] were saying, "We think we ought to do something with this." And then one thing led to another. I thought, "Well, I need a really small space because I need complete quiet for this to work out, as we had in the East Room." And we went out and we found that tiny theater on Broadway and—

PRESIDENT OBAMA: You end up having to work a real job.

BRUCE SPRINGSTEEN: I ended up being there for five nights a week at two hours and twenty minutes a show. One of the best times in my life.

Are you a shower singer?

PRESIDENT OBAMA: Absolutely.

BRUCE SPRINGSTEEN: Ha!

PRESIDENT OBAMA: I sing in the shower. I sing outside of the shower. I am unembarrassed about singing. My daughters and my wife sometimes roll their eyes. I have been known to have been scolded by my staff for doing some air-guitar stuff on Air Force One.

BRUCE SPRINGSTEEN: I'm sorry I missed that. The reason I ask is because you did a pretty damn nice version of Al Green— "Let's Stay Together." Am I right there? Is that the one?

PRESIDENT OBAMA: Here's the story: We're in the legendary Apollo Theater in Harlem for a fundraiser. Al Green has performed. But, as is always true, I don't get to see the act because they've got me somewhere else. I'm getting there late after the performance. So I'm sitting backstage with Valerie Jarrett. And I say, "Man. I missed Al Green!" And then I start singing backstage. *I'm . . . so in love with you.* A couple of the sound guys, smart alecks, say, "Mr. President, why don't you sing that onstage?"

And I say, "Well, you don't think I will do that?"

Valerie says, "Uh, don't do that."

BRUCE SPRINGSTEEN: Funny.

PRESIDENT OBAMA: Because she . . . she's the surrogate for Michelle in these circumstances. And I probably wouldn't have done it were it not for the fact that I think I was on my fifth event that day and I was a little loopy.

BRUCE SPRINGSTEEN: Good for you.

PRESIDENT OBAMA: I was a little tired. And Al Green was still there. He was sitting up in the lower seats. So I got up onstage and I said, "Ah, Al was here. I'm sorry I missed him."

And then I looked to see if the stage guys were watching. And I burst out into song.

BRUCE SPRINGSTEEN: What I really want to ask you about, of course, is "Amazing Grace," because that really shook the whole country. How on that day did you come to decide to sing that song?

PREVIOUS: President Obama and Michelle Obama greet Bruce Springsteen in the Blue Room prior to the Presidential Medal of Freedom ceremony on November 22, 2016. Bruce received the prestigious award alongside twenty other honorees. **ABOVE:** Bruce and Patti Scialfa sharing a moment, and the mic, onstage. **OPPOSITE:** *Springsteen on Broadway* opened for previews on October 3, 2017, and celebrated its official opening on October 12, 2017. Its first run, which won Bruce a Special Tony Award, was extended twice and ended on December 15, 2018, after 236 performances. A new limited run at the St. James Theatre was announced for late 2021. **FOLLOWING (PAGES 106-107):** Bruce in his dressing room at the Walter Kerr Theatre in New York City. **FOLLOWING (PAGES 108-109):** A Broadway standing ovation.

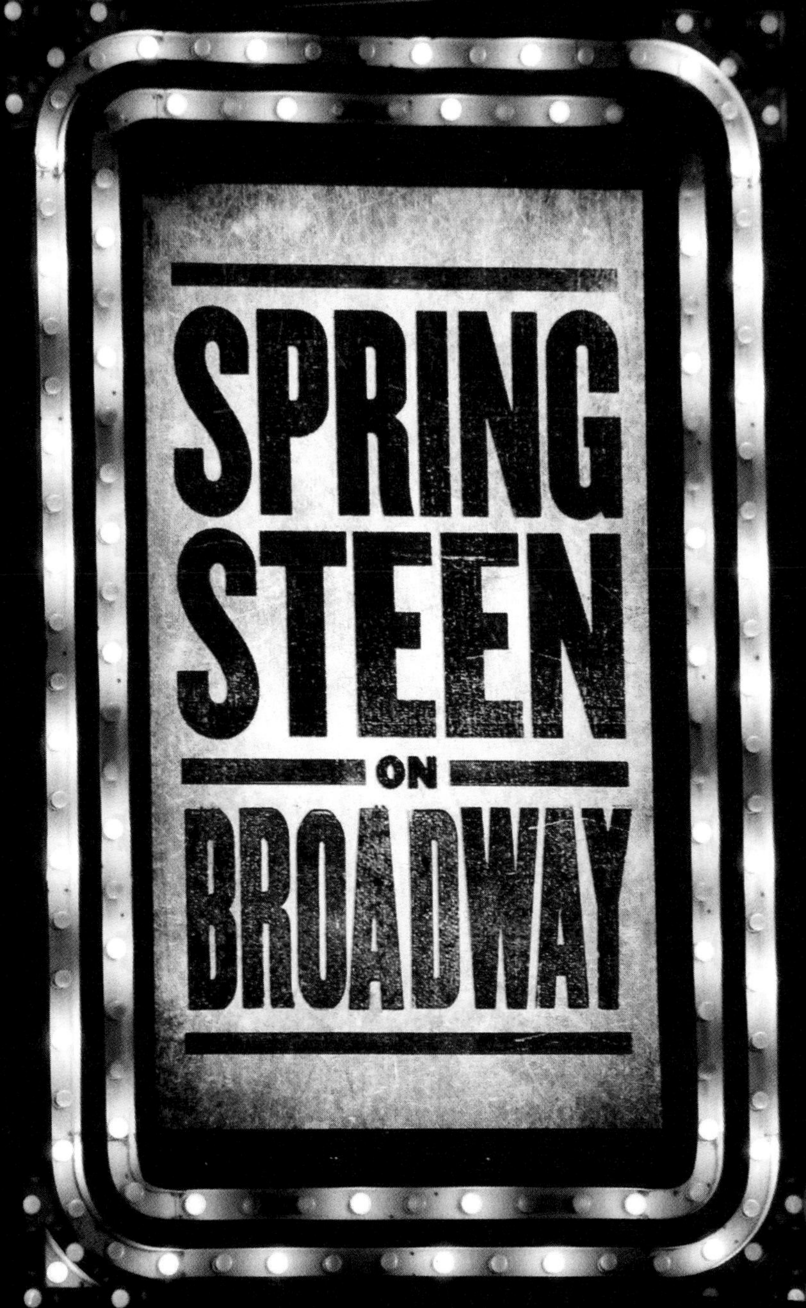
SPRING
STEEN
ON
BROADWAY

PRESIDENT OBAMA: That's an interesting story. That was a magical day that began in grief—or we had anticipated would begin in grief, but it turns out that's also the day in which the Supreme Court hands down the ruling saying that it is unconstitutional to not let LGBTQ partners get married. So that's a joyful moment. But we are traveling down to Charleston after this young white man who's been filled with hatred guns down a Bible study class that had welcomed him in. I actually had met the pastor, Reverend Pinckney, in previous visits to South Carolina. He had two little girls that were a little younger than Malia and Sasha.

And this was coming on the heels of what seemed like a mass shooting every three months. After each of these mass shootings—sometimes Michelle would go with me, although at a certain point it became difficult for her—I would spend a couple hours with a family who just had their child or their father or their brother or their son gunned down senselessly. After Newtown, when twenty six- and seven-year-olds had been gunned down in this fashion by a deranged young man—who had basically an arsenal in his house—I thought, "All right, Congress is gonna do something about this." And the closest I ever came to just losing hope about this country was probably after efforts for modest gun safety laws were defeated. They never even really got called up in the Senate. After twenty children had been slaughtered like that. The only time I saw a Secret Service person cry while I was speaking was at Newtown. So it happens again, and I say, "You know, I'll want to go to the funeral, but I don't want to speak. I don't have anything left to say. I feel like I've used up all my words. I made practical, rational arguments, emotional arguments, I've shown anger in speaking about this topic, I've shown sorrow, and nothing seems to have any impact. I'm out of words."

Of course, they ask that I speak, and I conclude, "All right, it's part of the job." But I'm stuck, I have nothing to say.

It just so happened at the time I'm corresponding with a friend, Marilynne Robinson, who's a wonderful author who wrote *Gilead*, and one theme that she writes about is grace. We've been writing each other and talking about the notion of grace as a recognition that we are fundamentally flawed and weak and confused. We don't deserve grace, but we get it sometimes.

Just as we've been writing to each other about this, the families of those slain in Charleston, during the shooter's

On June 26, 2015, the US Supreme Court legalized same-sex marriage when it issued a 5-4 ruling in the highly anticipated *Obergefell v. Hodges* case. Soon after the historic decision, the White House was lit up in rainbow colors to honor the LGBTQ community. Thousands of people gathered outside in celebration—including First Lady Michelle Obama and her daughter Malia, who snuck out of their residence and watched the jubilant crowd from the White House lawn.

110

arraignment, say, "We forgive you." It didn't click right away. I'm still thinking, "I don't know what to say." I tell my head speechwriter, Cody Keenan, "I don't know what's going to work here." He gives me something that just doesn't meet the moment. Not because it's his fault, but because he's gone through the same thing I have. We've done this too many times.

So I'm sitting there about ten o'clock at night. And I'm just stuck and I don't know what it is that I'm going to say tomorrow. Marilynne's letter is sitting on a desk and I see the word *grace* and, somehow, I start singing to myself. *Amazing grace . . .*

And I think about the families who said, "We forgive you." Suddenly, I write the eulogy in ten minutes, maybe twenty. It just pours out of me.

We get on Air Force One, and I say to Valerie and Michelle—again, they're the two who are most likely to express skepticism toward some of my shenanigans—"Listen, I just want you guys to know—I don't know for certain, but it's possible—I may sing." Then they said, "Hold it, what do you mean?" "I don't know," I said, "we'll just see if the spirit moves."

And so we get down there. It's obviously a big auditorium. Reverend Pinckney was an AME pastor, so you've got all the clergy behind me. And I get up and I deliver the eulogy. I come to the point in which I'm speaking about amazing grace and it just felt as if it was important for me to do. And it felt important for me to do precisely because I wasn't certain that I could pull it off. I need to show people that I will put myself out, I will try this. I need to just lay out what it is that I'm feeling. Which is why there is a long pause before I start singing. There's a part of me that's gathering myself to go ahead and say, "I don't know how this is going to come out." At this point I'm already pretty emotional and I'm worried that it's conceivable that I might start crying as I start singing.

So I had to kind of settle myself down. The thing that allowed me to do it was that it was church. It was a stadium, but it was church. It's the Black church and that's our home. And I knew that all I had to do was hit the first bar. And the organ is going to come in, and I knew that all my clergy behind me are gonna stand up. And no matter how bad I sound, they'll lift us up.

> YOU ARE AT YOUR BEST WHEN YOU UNDERSTAND THAT YOU ARE SIMPLY AN INSTRUMENT FOR EVERYONE ELSE, FOR THE PEOPLE WHO ARE COUNTING ON YOU, AND THAT THIS IS NOT ABOUT YOU OR EGO AND AMBITION AND TALENT AND SKILL. . . . I WAS AT MY BEST WHEN ALL THAT STUFF BURNED AWAY.
>
> —PRESIDENT OBAMA

BRUCE SPRINGSTEEN: It was an amazing moment of your presidency.

PRESIDENT OBAMA: Well, it's an example of the idea that you are at your best when you understand that you are simply an instrument for everyone else, for the people who are counting on you, and that this is not about you or ego and ambition and talent and skill. But, for me at least, I was at my best when all that stuff burned away and I was just trying to figure out how I could provide a platform or give voice to or serve. The larger purpose requires you to get out of the way sometimes or to do things that are out of your comfort zone. To walk the tightrope a little bit. To take the leap of faith.

And I'm assuming that, you know, when you're at your best as a performer, you probably feel that same way. You practice, you practice, you practice. You get your skills. You do all that, but you gotta let go.

BRUCE SPRINGSTEEN: Yeah, I think the emotional stakes are so high. I always felt that, as a band, we always played our best on the nights when the stakes were high.

PRESIDENT OBAMA: For me this was also a moment when I thought, "Will words be enough?" And they would have been. But I thought the music, the song, the leap of faith involved—particularly because I knew that I wouldn't sound like a professional singer, I would sound like just one other guy in the choir—that would be the grace note, the thing that drew people out.

And part of the reason I think that it somehow met the moment was because not only is it a beautiful song, but it also captures this unifying element in America represented in its music. You've got an old-world English hymn that has been used by everybody, in every church, all across this country. White churches, Black churches, the Black gospel tradition has transformed it. And it spoke then to the fact that underneath even a tragedy like this, there's something that is there for all of us. Something that we share.

OPPOSITE: President Obama and Michelle Obama arriving in Charleston, SC, June 26, 2015.

COLLEGE
OF CHARLESTON

———————

CHARLESTON,
SOUTH CAROLINA

———————

2:49 P.M. EDT

DRAFT 6/26/15 900am
Keenan
6-4698 desk | 503-5633 mobile

Remarks of President Barack Obama
Eulogy for Reverend Clementa C. Pinckney
Charleston, South Carolina
June 26, 2015

The Bible calls us to hope. To persevere, and have faith in things not seen.

"They were still living by faith when they died," the Book of Hebrews says of the prophets.
*"They did not receive the things promised; they only saw them and welcomed them from a
distance, admitting that they were foreigners and strangers on Earth."*

We are here today to remember a man of God who lived by faith. A man who believed in things
not seen. A man of service who persevered, knowing full well that he would not receive all
those things he was promised, because he believed his efforts would deliver a better life for those
who followed. ~~but saw and wel~~

To Jennifer, his beloved wife; to Eliana and Malana, his beautiful daughters; to this Mother
Emanuel family and the people of Charleston:

I did not *have the good fortune to* know Reverend Pinckney very well. ~~I was not that fortunate~~ *graciousness at*. But I did have the
pleasure of meeting him, here in South Carolina, back when we were both a little bit younger.
~~And~~ the first thing I noticed was his ~~grace~~, his ~~easy~~ smile, his reassuring baritone, his deceptive
sense of humor -- all qualities that helped him wear a heavy burden of expectation so effortlessly.

Friends of his remarked this week that when Clementa entered a room, it was like the future
arrived; that even from a young age, folks knew he was special. Anointed. He was the progeny
of a long line of the faithful -- a family of preachers who spread God's word, and protesters who
sowed change to expand voting rights and desegregate the South.

Clem heard their instruction, and did not forsake their teaching. He was in the pulpit by 13,
pastor by 18, public servant by 23. He did not exhibit any of the cockiness of youth, nor did he
possess youth's insecurities; instead, he set an example worthy of his position, wise beyond his
years, in his speech, his conduct, his love, faith, and purity.

As a senator, he represented a sprawling swath of the Lowcountry, a place that has long been one
of the most neglected *were too* in America. A place still wracked by poverty and inadequate schools; a
place where children can still go hungry and the sick too often go without treatment. A place
that needed someone like Clem. His position in the minority party meant the odds of winning
more resources for his constituents were often long, his calls for greater equity in the allocation
of resources often unheeded, the votes he cast sometimes lonely. But he never gave up; stayed
true to his convictions; would not grow discouraged. After a full day at the capitol, he'd climb
into his car and head to the church to draw sustenance from his ministry, and from the
community that loved and needed him; to fortify his faith, and imagine what might be.

1

Reverend Pinckney embodied a politics that was neither mean nor small, conducting himself [*, seen the world through their eyes*] quietly, and kindly, and diligently. He encouraged progress not by pushing his ideas alone, but by seeking out yours, and partnering with you to make it happen. He exemplified empathy, ~~the~~ [*was full of*] ~~idea of walking~~ [*able to*] in someone else's shoes. No wonder one of his senate colleagues remembered Senator Pinckney this week as "the most gentle of the 46 of us – the best of the 46 of us."

Clem was often asked why he'd choose to be a pastor and a public servant. [*about*] But as our brothers and sisters in the AME church know well, they're one and the same. "Our calling," Clem once said, "is not just within the walls of the congregation, but…the life and community in which our congregation resides." It's the idea that our Christian faith demands deeds and not just words; that the "sweet hour of prayer" actually last the whole week long; that to put our faith in action is about more than our individual salvation, but our collective salvation; that to feed the hungry and clothe the naked and house the homeless is not merely a call for isolated charity but the imperative of a just society.

Preacher by 13. Pastor by 18. Public servant by 23.

What a life Clementa Pinckney lived. What an example he set. What a model for his faith, and for us all.

And to lose him at 41 – slain in his sanctuary with eight wonderful members of his flock, each at different stages in life, but bound together by a common commitment to their God.

Cynthia Hurd. Susie Jackson. Ethel Lance. DePayne Middleton-Doctor. Tywanza Sanders. Daniel L. Simmons, Sr. Sharonda Coleman-Singleton. Myra Thompson.

Good and decent people, so full of life, and kindness, and perseverance, and faith. [*a too often hostile world*]

To the families of these fallen, the nation shares in your grief. Our pain cuts that much deeper because it happened in church. The ~~black~~ church is ~~the spiritual heart~~ of ~~the black community~~ – [*and has always been the beating center*] [*African American life*] a place to call our own in ~~American life~~, a sanctuary from so many ~~of our~~ hardships. Over the course of centuries, black churches ~~have been a rock to stand on:~~ [*have been, and served as*] "hush harbors" where slaves could worship in safety; praise houses where their free descendants could gather on the coast; rest stops for the weary along the Underground Railroad, and bunkers for the foot soldiers of the Civil Rights Movement. They are community centers where we organize for jobs and justice; ~~for quality schools and health care~~; where children are loved and kept out of harm's way and told that they matter. [*places*] [*places of worship and economic networking;*] [*celebrating*]

That's what the black church means. Our beating heart; the ~~special~~ place where our dignity as a people is inviolate. ~~And~~ There is no better example of this centrality than Mother Emanuel – a church built by blacks seeking their liberty, burned to the ground because its worshipers sought to end slavery, only to ~~be built anew~~. When there were laws banning all-black church gatherings, services happened here, in defiance of unjust laws. When there was a righteous movement to ~~change such laws~~, Dr. King preached from its pulpit, and marches began from its steps. A sacred place, this church, not just for blacks or Christians, but for every American who cares about ~~the steady~~ liberty and justice for all. [*dismantle Jim Crow*] [*expansion of human rights in this country; as a foundation stone*] [*rise up again, a Phoenix from the ashes*]

2

It is doubtful that the killer of Reverend Pinckney and eight others knew this history. But he surely sensed the meaning of his ~~actions~~ -- ~~actions~~ that drew on a long history of bombs and ~~fires~~ and shots at churches as a means to terrorize and control. ~~He may have seen this~~ as an opportunity to incite fear and recrimination; violence and suspicion; to deepen divisions that trace back to our nation's original sin.

[handwritten annotations: fried · violent · an act · It reported that · all · saw this terrible violation · arson · and oppress]

Oh, but God works in mysterious ways, doesn't he?

Blinded by hatred, ~~their assassin~~ could not see the grace of Reverend Pinckney and that Bible Study group – their light ~~shining~~ as they opened the church doors and invited a stranger to join their ~~circle of fellowship~~. He could ~~not~~ have anticipated the way ~~their~~ families would respond – even in the midst of unspeakable grief – with words of forgiveness. ~~He~~ could not imagine how the city of Charleston, and the state of South Carolina, and the United States of America would respond – with not merely revulsion at this evil act, but with a big-hearted generosity and, more importantly, a thoughtful introspection and self-examination so rarely seen in our public life.

[handwritten annotations: the alleged killer · never · surrounding · of the fall · when they saw him in court · of love that shone · when the rise leadership of Mayor Riley · The killer alleged killer · The alleged killer]

Blinded by hatred, he failed to comprehend what Reverend Pinckney so well understood – the power of God's grace.

This whole week, I've been reflecting on this idea of grace – the grace of the families who lost loved ones, the grace Reverend Pinckney would ~~talk~~ about in his sermons; the grace in my favorite hymnal.

[handwritten annotations: preach · described · the one we all know:]

Amazing grace, how sweet the sound, that saved a wretch like me;
I once was lost, but now I'm found; was blind but now I see.

According to Christian tradition, grace is not ~~merited~~, it's not something we deserve, ~~but rather, it~~ is the free and benevolent favor of God, as manifested in the salvation of sinners and the bestowal of blessings.

[handwritten annotations: earned. Not something · grace]

As a nation, out of terrible tragedy, God has visited grace upon us. For he has allowed us to see where we've been blind. He has given us the chance to find our best selves, where we've been lost. We may not have earned it, this grace, but it is up to us now to make the most of it, to receive it with gratitude, and make ourselves worthy of the gift.

[handwritten annotations: we may ... with our rancor and complacency · and rightly short ... fear of each other, but we got it all the same. He's once more given us grace ... and]

For too long, we were blind to the pain that the Confederate flag stirred in too many of our citizens. It's true – a flag didn't cause these murders. But as people from all walks of life, Republicans and Democrats, including Governor Haley, ~~have so~~ eloquently ~~stated~~, the flag has always represented more than just ancestral pride. To many, black and white alike, it has been a reminder of systematic oppression and racial subjugation. We see that now. Removing the flag from the state capitol isn't an act of political correctness or an insult to the valor of Confederate soldiers. It is an acknowledgment that the cause for which they fought – the cause of slavery – was wrong. It is one step in an honest accounting of ~~our~~ history, and a balm for so many unhealed wounds. It is an expression of the amazing changes that have transformed this country for the better because of the work of so many people of good will, people of all races striving to form a more perfect union. By taking down that flag, we express God's grace.

[handwritten annotations: whose record · on the ... subject is worthy of praise · America's]

It's possible that we now bias realize the way racial pre-prejudice can infect us even when we don't realize it so that we must guard against racial slurs, but also guard against not only using the impulse to call Johnny back for a job interview but not Jamal; so that we search our hearts when considering laws that makes it harder for some of our fellow citizens to vote.

For too long, we've been blind to the way past injustices continue to shape the present. Perhaps we see that now. Perhaps this tragedy causes us to ask some tough questions about how we can permit so many of our children to languish in poverty, or attend dilapidated schools, or grow up without prospects for a job or career. Perhaps it softens hearts towards those lost young men, thousands, millions, caught up in the criminal justice system, and leads us to make sure it is not infected with bias; that we embrace changes in how we train and equip our police so that the bonds of trust between law enforcement and the communities they serve make us all safer and more secure. By recognizing our common humanity, by treating every child as important, regardless of the color of their skin or the station into which they were born, and do what is necessary to make opportunity real for all, we express God's grace.

For too long, we've been blind to the unique mayhem that gun violence inflicts upon this nation. Yes, our eyes open when eight of our brothers and sisters are cut down in a church basement, and twelve in a movie theater, and twenty-six in an elementary school. But do we see the thirty precious lives that guns cut short in this country every single day? Can we see the countless more whose lives are forever changed – the survivors crippled with permanent pain; the husband who will never again feel his wife's warm touch; the entire communities whose grief ~~rises again~~ overflows every time they have to watch this happen somewhere else?

the children traumatized and fearful every day on their walk to school

Can we see, now, that we are unique among nations in the number of firearms we stockpile, the frequency with which we turn them on each other, the wretched anguish we inflict upon ourselves, and realize that it does not make us more free? The vast majority of Americans, the majority of gun owners even, want to do something about this. We see that now. By acknowledging the pain and loss of others, by respecting the traditions and values of others, to make the moral choice to change if it will save even one precious life, we express God's grace.

We don't earn God's grace, but we choose how to receive it. We decide how to honor it. None of us can expect a transformation in race relations overnight; none of us should believe that a handful of gun safety measures will prevent any tragedy. People of goodwill will continue to debate the merits of various policies, as our democracy requires, and whatever solutions we find will necessarily be incomplete.

But it would be a betrayal of everything Reverend Pinckney stood for, I believe, if we allowed ourselves to slip into a comfortable silence again, once the eulogies have been delivered and the media has moved on. To avoid uncomfortable truths about the prejudice that still infects our society; to settle for symbolic gestures without following up with the hard work of change – that's no way to receive grace. Likewise, it would be a refutation of the forgiveness expressed by those families if we merely slipped into the old habits, whereby those who disagree with us are not merely wrong but bad; and we shout instead of listen, and barricade ourselves behind our preconceived notions, *or a well-practiced cynicism.*

Reverend Pinckney once said, "Across the South, we have a deep appreciation of history – we haven't always had a deep appreciation of each other's histories." What is true in the South applies to America. Clem recognized that justice grows out of recognition, of ourselves in others; that my liberty depends on my respect for yours; that history cannot be a weapon to justify injustice, but must be a manual for how to avoid the mistakes of the past, and set us on a better course. He knew that the path to grace involves an open mind, but more importantly an open heart.

That's what I've felt this week — an open heart. That's, on That, more than any policy or analysis, in what's called upon right now, what a friend of mine calls "that reservoir of goodness, beyond, and of another kind, that we are able to do each other in the ordinary course of things." If we can find that grace, anything is possible. If we can tap that grace, everything will change.

Amazing grace, how sweet the sound, that saved a wretch like me;
I once was lost, but now I'm found; was blind but now I see.

Clementa Pinckney found that grace.

Cynthia Hurd found that grace.

Susie Jackson found that grace.

Ethel Lance found that grace.

DePayne Middleton-Doctor found that grace.

Tywanza Sanders found that grace.

Daniel L. Simmons, Sr. found that grace.

Sharonda Coleman-Singleton found that grace.

Myra Thompson found that grace.

Through the example of their lives ~~their tragic deaths,~~ they have now passed it on to us. May we find ourselves worthy of this precious and extraordinary gift, as long as our lives endure. ~~And~~ May grace lead them home, and ~~may~~ may God continue to shed his grace on the United States of America.
Amen.

AMERICAN
SKIN

Talking about race isn't always easy. Bridging America's racial divide is going to require concrete policies to address the ongoing legacy of slavery and Jim Crow, but it also requires each of us–in our workplaces, our politics, and our places of worship, and in a million daily interactions–to make more of an effort to understand one another's reality.

Not to mention our own unspoken attitudes.

As a lot of us have learned—whether from a childhood, like mine, of growing up different, or from a lifetime partnership like Bruce had with "the Big Man," Clarence Clemons; whether from the great old protest songs or the new kinds of protest movements across the country—that kind of reckoning can be uncomfortable. Even—or maybe especially—when it's with the people we love.

PRESIDENT OBAMA: We talked about racial tension in Freehold, but when you started what became the E Street Band, it was integrated. How intentional was that? Or was it a matter of just, "Man, I'm trying to get the best musicians I can. This is the sound I want"?

BRUCE SPRINGSTEEN: It started when I saw Clarence. He had a sound that raised the roof. He was just one of the greatest-sounding sax players I'd ever heard.

PRESIDENT OBAMA: Was he older than you?

BRUCE SPRINGSTEEN: Yeah, Clarence was about eight years older than I was.

PRESIDENT OBAMA: Okay, so he's already well into his twenties. He's been around. He's seen some things.

BRUCE SPRINGSTEEN: He'd been to college and he'd had some experiences already. He almost went into pro football but ended up somehow an itinerant sax player on the edges of Asbury Park playing in the Black clubs at the time.

He walked into the club one night, walked up onstage, stood to my right, started playing. I said, "There's something about him and I together." We struck up a friendship, started to play with the band, and people started to come and respond. And eventually the band developed. For a year or two it was three white guys and three Black guys. And that was around '74.

It was just something that happened. Davey Sancious walked into the mostly white Upstage Club—I would say almost completely white—and had the balls to get onstage and blow everybody's ass away. He's a sixteen-year-old, skinny kid from Belmar, from E Street. That's why it's called the E Street Band.

I know I need that guy, because he's incredible.

Then we had a gig at a place called the Satellite Lounge in Fort Dix, New Jersey. But we'd just fired our drummer, a fabulous guy called Vincent "Mad Dog" Lopez who had some anger-management issues. I love Vini, he's one of my great friends today. But we were just doing something slightly different at the time. So I called and said, "We can't make the gig."

The club happened to be owned by the local mob, who said if we didn't make the gig, my fingers were going to be broken.

So, this being New Jersey, I said, "Maybe we'll play."

PRESIDENT OBAMA: Oh, man!

OPPOSITE: Clarence Clemons with his iconic saxophone, circa 1972. **FOLLOWING:** The early days of the E Street Band, circa 1975.

BRUCE SPRINGSTEEN: But we don't have a drummer and the show is the next night. So Davey Sancious says, "I know a guy named Boom Carter." Young Black guy from Asbury Park. He spends twenty-four hours without sleep learning the entire show. We play the Satellite Lounge. That's how we end up with three Black guys and three white guys in the E Street Band. There was no self-consciousness about it, and you forget this . . . this is the early seventies. You're kids . . . you're a different generation than your parents. And I don't remember people being . . .

PRESIDENT OBAMA: Shocked by it or . . .

BRUCE SPRINGSTEEN: No. And we played a lot of music that was rooted in Black culture. It was powerful and a lovely band and it would have been interesting to see where it went. Except Dave and Boom were so good they quit my band to have their own band where they played jazz. And then I just put an ad in the newspaper. I auditioned thirty drummers, thirty piano players; I picked the two best guys, who were two white guys. It was as simple as that.

PRESIDENT OBAMA: Nobody would know you had that integrated band today, by the way.

BRUCE SPRINGSTEEN: Nope. And—

PRESIDENT OBAMA: I didn't know that because, look, I hate to date ya, brother, but when *Born to Run* came out I was still—

BRUCE SPRINGSTEEN: You were a child.

PRESIDENT OBAMA: I was in high school, so I didn't know that you had a half-Black, half-white band. Like, I knew the Average White Band was all white—those are some Scottish guys. And those guys can jam, by the way.

BRUCE SPRINGSTEEN: Yes, they could.

PRESIDENT OBAMA: Loved them. You knew Earth, Wind & Fire were all Black guys. But part of the reason that I wouldn't have necessarily known that about your original lineup is, not only did you not have the internet and video, but music was still pretty categorized.

> I'VE NEVER WRITTEN A SONG THAT TOLD A BIGGER STORY THAN CLARENCE AND I STANDING NEXT TO EACH OTHER ON ANY OF THE 1,001 NIGHTS THAT WE PLAYED. HE LENT HIS POWER TO MY STORY, TO THE STORY THAT WE TOLD TOGETHER, WHICH WAS ABOUT THE DISTANCE BETWEEN THE AMERICAN DREAM AND THE AMERICAN REALITY.
>
> —BRUCE SPRINGSTEEN

BRUCE SPRINGSTEEN: Very much! And we had a primarily white audience.

PRESIDENT OBAMA: And Clarence isn't on the cover of *Time* magazine, right?

BRUCE SPRINGSTEEN: No.

PRESIDENT OBAMA: It's Bruce Springsteen with his curly hair looking cute with his cap and all that. . . .

And how was the power balance inside the band? Because I'm assuming every team, any group, has some dynamics, and Clarence on the one hand is an iconic figure in the E Street Band, but he is also still a sideman and you are still the front man.

BRUCE SPRINGSTEEN: It's a funny thing because it was a dynamic that both happened naturally and that we contrived together. There was a moment when I said, "Hey, C, ya know, tomorrow night when I go to the front of the stage and I play this, come on up with me and play it next to me."

And we took those steps the next night.

PRESIDENT OBAMA: It's like a buddy movie onstage.

BRUCE SPRINGSTEEN: And the crowd went crazy. There was an idealism in our partnership; I always felt our audience looked at us and saw the America that they wanted to see and wanted to believe in.

And so this became the biggest story I ever told. I've never written a song that told a bigger story than Clarence and I standing next to each other on any of the 1,001 nights that we played. He lent his power to my story, to the story that we told together, which was about the distance between the American Dream and the American reality.

PRESIDENT OBAMA: And maybe what you were trying to recapture with Clarence on the stage was a time that was a little more innocent? Sort of a better version of what might have been?

OPPOSITE: Bruce Springsteen, 1975. During the final week of October that year, Bruce appeared on the cover of both *Time* and *Newsweek*, marking his arrival as a rock star.

BRUCE SPRINGSTEEN: Like I said, we tried to take a piece out of that no-man's-land between the American Dream and the American reality. I think one of the reasons why people were moved by my partnership with Clarence was the idea "Oh, this is the world as it could possibly be." But we also told a lot of stories about the world as it was.

PRESIDENT OBAMA: There's a story behind the *Born to Run* album cover.

BRUCE SPRINGSTEEN: Before that cover, Clarence was, as I say in my book, a very large Black saxophonist in my band. There were five of us, and he was one of the five.

But after the cover of *Born to Run*, Clarence became the Big Man. The Big Man was invented, and we were invented as a group and as a duo on that cover. When you bought the album, if you looked at the front of it, what do you see? You see a very charming photo of a young, white punk rock 'n' roller, but when it opens, a band is born.

I brought Clarence to the session because I wanted to be photographed with him. Instinctively, I knew there was something we wanted to say about the two of us standing side by side. It was dramatic and it was exciting and it was a little bit more. We were trying to create and present to our audience our own musical version of John Lewis's beloved community. That's what I wanted our audience to see when they came in to see our band at night.

I wanted the band to mirror back to the audience a sense of themselves. The cover captured what I felt the first night that Clarence and I jammed onstage at the Student Prince, that little club where he came down and we met each other for the first time. I said, "That night a real story was born." It's a story that can be nurtured and evolve, but first it has to be there in the dirt, the beer, the bands, and the bars that give it birth. When you saw that cover, it was filled with the resonance and the mythology of rock's past, and freshness calling toward its future.

What are these two guys doing together? What story are they sharing? If you look at the front of that album, it looks like I'm whispering something in Clarence's ear. *What's that story? I want to hear that.* The story began before you dropped the needle on the first cut of that record. It was the story of our pursuit of the musical version of the beloved community.

PRESIDENT OBAMA: But part of what you're describing is that Clarence provided something to you, personally, and to the band that helped capture what would end up being your sound, your spirit. Also at some level, here's an older Black man who's been hustling out there for a long time and he's gotta hook up with a young white guy—

BRUCE SPRINGSTEEN: A little skinny white kid, you know?

PRESIDENT OBAMA: Who is less experienced than him. Now, it works out beautifully for the both of you. But there are also complications, right? To that whole relationship. And I don't know if you guys ever talked about it.

BRUCE SPRINGSTEEN: He had to give more than I had to give in the sense that once our keyboardist and drummer left, Clarence was the only Black man in the room a lot of the time. He had to swim in white culture for most of his work life, you know?

PRESIDENT OBAMA: I wrote about this in my first book. My friends in high school, they're white, Hawaiian, Filipino. I'm making friends with these older Black kids who are taking me to parties on the base, and I invite my school friends along to one of those parties. When we get to the party, I look over at those guys, and they are cool, but they are also experiencing for the first time in their lives what I have to go through a bunch. They're the only white guys in the room. Or, non-Black guys in the room. Right?

BRUCE SPRINGSTEEN: This happened to us on the Ivory Coast. It was during the Amnesty International tour and we came out to a stadium of entirely Black faces. We stand there for a moment, and Clarence comes over and he says, "Well . . . now you know how it feels."

PRESIDENT OBAMA: Did he say that?

BRUCE SPRINGSTEEN: Yeah!

ABOVE: Bruce Springsteen's third studio album, *Born to Run*, was released on August 25, 1975. Critically acclaimed and commercially successful, it engaged a broader audience and showcased more mature lyrics. **OPPOSITE:** Bruce with Clarence Clemons during the *Born to Run* cover shoot, June 20, 1975. **FOLLOWING (PAGE 134):** Barack Obama and his friend Greg Orme, dressed up for the prom, circa 1979. **FOLLOWING (PAGE 135):** President Obama's high school friends Greg Orme (left) and Robert "Bobby" Titcomb (middle) meet baby Malia, with Michelle Obama, on Malia's first trip to Hawaii, 1998.

PRESIDENT OBAMA: How'd the concert go?

BRUCE SPRINGSTEEN: We started to play, and it was about sixty seconds of everybody just kind of staring at each other's eyes . . . and then the place exploded! It was simply the most generous audience we've ever played in front of to this day.

But it was difficult for Clarence, and it was painful for him at different times. And we did talk about it, usually on evenings when, for some reason or another, we were reminded of it.

PRESIDENT OBAMA: Such as . . .

BRUCE SPRINGSTEEN: One evening, Clarence and I went out to a local club. And I was watching the band, and the next thing I see, Clarence is at the front door and there's a scuffle going on. I go up and see that Clarence has got a couple of guys pinned down and the owner has got a guy pinned down and everybody breaks apart and the owner throws them out.

On the way out, one of the guys says the N-word. Clarence had been around. He was a pretty worldly guy, but he disappeared. I go out in the parking lot looking for him because I don't know where these other guys have gone. I don't know where he might have gone. And he was just standing near the hood of a car, and he looked at me and said, "Brucie, why'd they say that? I play football with those guys every Sunday. Same people." He says, "Why'd they say that?"

And rather than saying, "Well, they're assholes," I just said, "I don't know. I don't know what that's about."

PRESIDENT OBAMA: Where it comes from?

BRUCE SPRINGSTEEN: Yeah.

PRESIDENT OBAMA: And why would you pull that out? Because the same thing happened to me. When I was in school, I had a friend. We played basketball together. One time we got into a fight and he called me a coon.

Now, first of all, ain't no coons in Hawaii, right? He might not even have known what a coon was—what he knew was, "I can hurt you by saying this."

BRUCE SPRINGSTEEN: Yeah.

PRESIDENT OBAMA: And I remember I popped him in the face and broke his nose! We were in the locker room.

BRUCE SPRINGSTEEN: Well done.

PRESIDENT OBAMA: It was just reactive. And suddenly blood is pouring down. He said, "Why'd you do that?" I explained to him—I said, "Don't you ever call me something like that."

What it comes down to is an assertion of status over the other. The claim is made that "No matter what I am—I may be poor. I may be ignorant. I may be mean. I may be ugly. I may not like myself. I may be unhappy. But you know what I'm not? I'm not *you*."

And that basic psychology that then gets institutionalized is used to justify dehumanizing somebody.

At the end of the day it really comes down to that. And in some cases it's as simple as, you know, "I'm scared I'm insignificant and not important. And this thing is the thing that's going to give me some importance."

BRUCE SPRINGSTEEN: When I first saw you, you spoke to a broad sense of American hopefulness. And there was something in Clarence's presence that reflected that quality, and it's what made our band so powerful when we came to your town at night. And that partnership . . . it was just real, you know? I was at his bedside when he took his last breath.

PRESIDENT OBAMA: You miss him.

BRUCE SPRINGSTEEN: Yeah, of course.

PRESIDENT OBAMA: You loved him.

BRUCE SPRINGSTEEN: It was forty years of your life. It's not something that comes again. Forty years. And the only thing we never kidded ourselves about was that race didn't matter. We lived together. We traveled throughout the United States, and we were probably as close as two people could be. Yet at the same time, I always had to recognize there was a part of

OPPOSITE: The now-iconic "Hope poster" was created in 2008 by renowned street artist Shepard Fairey, who based his art on a photograph taken by Associated Press photographer Mannie Garcia. Designed by Fairey in one day and initially printed as a street poster, it quickly went viral and became one of the most recognizable symbols of Barack Obama's presidential campaign and its optimistic messages of hope and change. **ABOVE:** First published by the Dial Press in 1963, James Baldwin's *The Fire Next Time* contains two landmark essays on race: "My Dungeon Shook: Letter to My Nephew on the One Hundredth Anniversary of the Emancipation" and "Down at the Cross: Letter from a Region of My Mind."

Clarence that I wasn't ever really going to exactly know. It was a relationship unlike any other that I've ever had in my life.

After George Floyd's murder, I started reading James Baldwin, and this passage always stuck with me: *"White people in this country will have quite enough to do in learning how to accept and love themselves and each other, and when they have achieved this—which will not be tomorrow and may very well be never—the Negro problem will no longer exist, for it will no longer be needed."*

PRESIDENT OBAMA: Necessary.

BRUCE SPRINGSTEEN: Yeah.

PRESIDENT OBAMA: Yeah. The legacy of race is buried . . . but it's always there, right?

Depending on the community you're in, how far near the surface it is, is not always clear. And I think a lot of Black folks always talk about how what's hardest is not dealing with a Klansman. That, you know. That, you can figure out. You are prepared. What cuts is people who you know aren't bad people, and the fact that that card is still in their pocket and that at some unexpected moment it might be played is heartbreaking. Because that's when you realize, "Oh, this is a deep, big piece of business," and it's not a matter of not using racial epithets, and it's not just a matter of voting for Barack Obama. Did you see the movie *Get Out*?

BRUCE SPRINGSTEEN: I did.

PRESIDENT OBAMA: So when the father who turns out to be crazy starts saying, "Man, I'd vote for Obama a third time!," that's part of the point that this line is making.

BRUCE SPRINGSTEEN: This is a moment when it feels that as a country we've got to have that conversation, you know? If we want to create a more honest and adult and noble America, and one that's worthy of its ideals. And days like the day when John Lewis was buried are certainly not days you can be cynical about the possibilities of America.

PRESIDENT OBAMA: John embodied this very particular brand of courage. It was a courage and trust in the redemptive power.

The ability to say, "Here I stand. Do your worst. I believe that at some point there is a consciousness that will be awakened. That there is a force in you that will see me." He never gave up that hope. I told John, and I said something similar in the eulogy, "John, these are your children. They might not have known it, but you helped give birth to that sense of right and wrong in them. You helped infuse them with that expectation that we're better than we are." My mother used to say sometimes, if I wasn't acting right, she said, "Listen, I don't necessarily care if you believe in what I've told you to do, but if you do it often enough, that's who you're going to be." And I think there's a little bit of an element of young people saying, "You've told us this is who we're supposed to be, you've told us that all people are equal and we treat everybody with respect, and you've told it to us often enough that maybe *you* didn't even believe it, but we do. And we're going to force you to adapt your behavior, your policies and your institutions and your laws, to what you told us was true. Because you may have been painting a fantasy to make yourself feel better, but we believed it. And now we're going to try to make it true."

And that's why, as long as protests and activism don't veer into violence, I want and expect young people to push those boundaries and to test and try the patience of their parents and their grandparents. I remind young activists that I meet with, "Look, if you want my advice about how you can get a law passed or get enough votes to put people in power, I can give you some practical advice. But that doesn't necessarily mean that should be your goal. Sometimes your goal may just be to—"

> IF YOU WANT MY ADVICE ABOUT HOW YOU CAN GET A LAW PASSED OR GET ENOUGH VOTES TO PUT PEOPLE IN POWER, I CAN GIVE YOU SOME PRACTICAL ADVICE. BUT THAT DOESN'T NECESSARILY MEAN THAT SHOULD BE YOUR GOAL. SOMETIMES YOUR GOAL MAY JUST BE TO . . . STIR. SHIT. UP. AND OPEN UP NEW POSSIBILITIES.
>
> —PRESIDENT OBAMA

BRUCE SPRINGSTEEN: Stir shit up.

PRESIDENT OBAMA: Stir. Shit. Up. And open up new possibilities. What have you been thinking about as you watch all these young kids out protesting?

BRUCE SPRINGSTEEN: It's an exciting moment, you know? My son is out there. He's going to be thirty this week. And he's in New York City, he's out there in that crowd.

OPPOSITE, TOP: Freedom Riders, July 1961. **OPPOSITE, BOTTOM:** Black Lives Matter protesters, summer 2020.

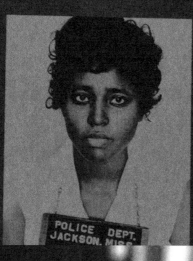

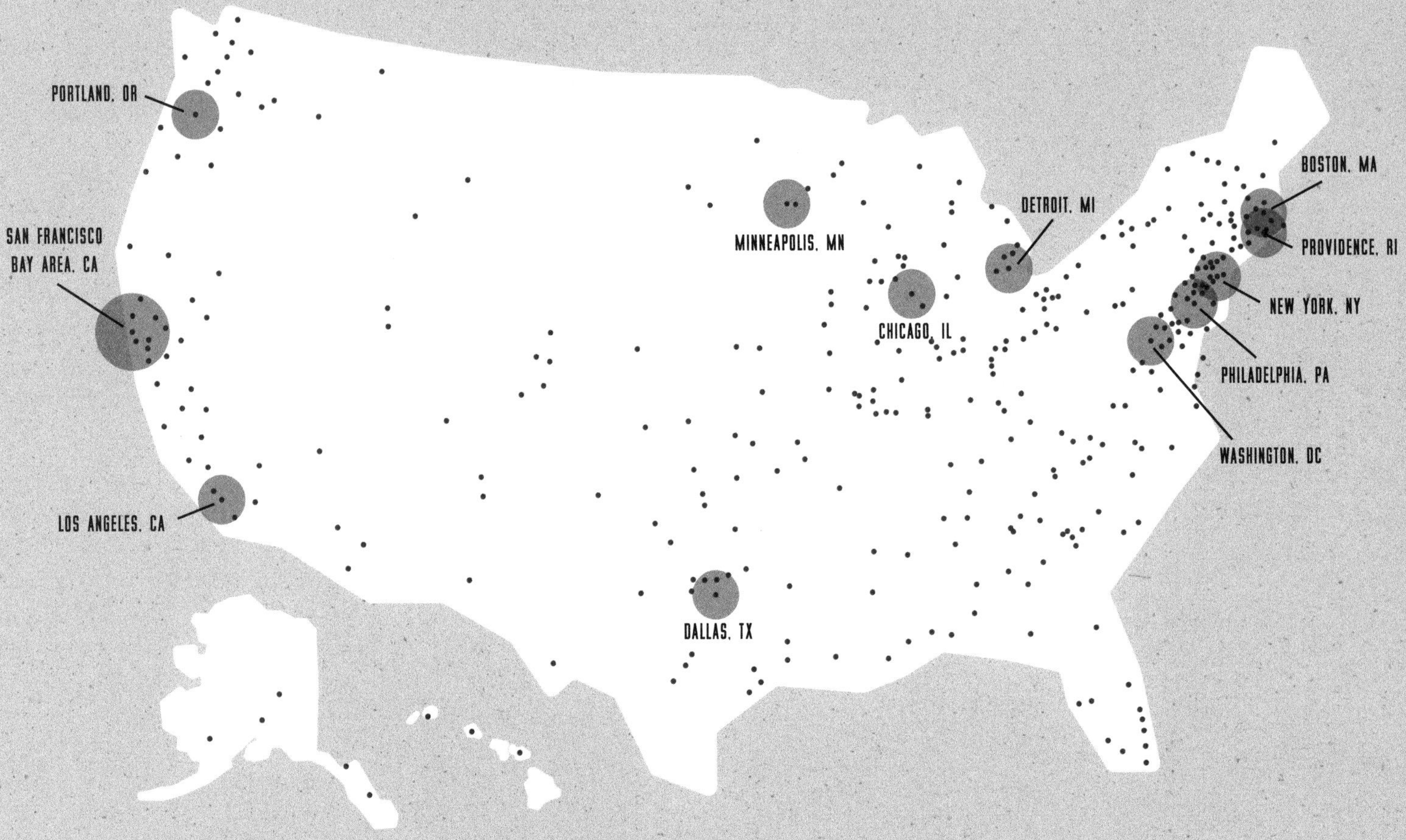

PORTLAND, OR

SAN FRANCISCO
BAY AREA, CA

MINNEAPOLIS, MN

DETROIT, MI

BOSTON, MA

PROVIDENCE, RI

NEW YORK, NY

CHICAGO, IL

PHILADELPHIA, PA

WASHINGTON, DC

LOS ANGELES, CA

DALLAS, TX

PRESIDENT OBAMA: Let me just say that having a thirty-year-old son . . . Weren't we just thirty?

BRUCE SPRINGSTEEN: I was. . . .

PRESIDENT OBAMA: Man, I don't know what happened. Well, watching these young people has been energizing and it has been hopeful. In the sixties protests, it was a more limited band of young people who were getting involved. You had these heroic white students go down for the Freedom Rides, but it was a fraction of the population. There were young activists on college campuses who were focused on racial injustice. But what you're seeing—and it's sustaining itself—seems to be a change in attitude that is generational or generation-wide. And it's not uniform, but it's still a plurality of the country. I am encouraged by the willingness of young people to not only put themselves out there but to ask themselves hard questions and to ask their parents hard questions. To look inward and not just look outward.

BRUCE SPRINGSTEEN: How do you hold the idea that the same country that sent a man to the moon is the country of Jim Crow? You don't make peace with that, obviously, but how do you hold that being the same America?

PRESIDENT OBAMA: I think that it is partly because we never went through a true reckoning, and so we just buried one huge part of our experience and our citizenry in our minds.

BRUCE SPRINGSTEEN: Now, you mentioned a reckoning hadn't taken place, so here we sit today where it feels like a reckoning is being called for. Is the country ready to deconstruct its founding myths, its mythic stories, its mythic history? Or is it prepared to consider reparations? Do you think we're at that place right now?

PRESIDENT OBAMA: If you ask me theoretically, "Are reparations justified?," the answer is yes. There's not much of a question that the wealth of this country, the power of this country, was built in significant part—not exclusively, maybe not even the majority of it, but a large portion of it—was built on the backs

BRUCE SPRINGSTEEN: The White House

PRESIDENT OBAMA: They built the house that I stayed in for a while.

What is also true is that, even after the end of formal slavery, and the continuation of Jim Crow, the systematic oppression and discrimination of Black Americans resulted in Black families' not being able to build up wealth, not being able to compete, and that has generational effects. So if you're thinking of what's just, you would look back and say, "The descendants of those who suffered those kinds of terrible, cruel, often arbitrary injustices deserve some sort of redress, some sort of compensation—a recognition."

BRUCE SPRINGSTEEN: How do you as president, knowing all of the above, push or prepare the nation for something that feels, as you say, so justified—or not?

PRESIDENT OBAMA: Well, that then brings us to the question "Can you actually get that kind of justice? Can you get a country to agree and own that history?" And my judgment was that as a practical matter, that was unattainable. We can't even get this country to provide decent schooling for inner-city kids!

What I saw during my presidency was that the politics of white resistance and resentment, the talk of welfare queens and the talk of the undeserving poor and the backlash against affirmative action—all that meant the prospect of actually proposing any kind of coherent, meaningful reparations program strikes me as, politically, not only a nonstarter but potentially counterproductive.

Presidents' House Carpenter's Roll

We acknowledge severally to have re[ceived] ... Signatures being in full for Wages due ... in the City of Washington in the Month ...

	Days	Rate		
Pierce Purcell	23	15/	17.5.–	Seventeen Poun[ds] ...
Rich.d Dowling	22	8/4	9.3.4	Nine Pounds three ...
Peter Lenox should be 22	23	"	9.3.4	Nine Pounds three ...
James Duncan	7½	"	3.2.6	Three pounds two ...
Redmond Purcell	13	"	5.8.4	Five Pounds Eig[ht] ...
Samuel Curtis	11	"	4.11.8	Four Pounds E[leven] ...
Timothy Sheedy	18½	"	7.14.2	Seven Pounds fo[urteen] ...
Robert Aul	17½	"	7.5.10	Seven Pounds f[ive] ...
Simon Toole	18½	"	7.14.2	Seven Pounds fo[urteen] ...
John McCaskill	10	7/6	3.15.–	Three Pounds f[ifteen] ...
Tom.s McCaskill	23	7/	8.1.–	Eight Pounds O[ne] ...
Peter Smith	22½	6/6	7.6.3	Seven Pounds s[ix] ...
Negros Peter	15½	"	5.–.9	Five Pounds ...
Tom	15½	"	5.–.9	Five Pounds ...
Ben	23	5/	5.15.–	Five Pounds f[ifteen] ...
Harry	23	4/	4.12.–	Four Pounds ...
Daniel	23	4/	4.12.–	Four Pounds ...

£115.11.1 Eq.l to 308 Dollars ...

9 2/4
115-10
1-1

...es of Chas. Richmond the Sums, pursuant to our respective
... as Carpenters & Joiners employed at their Presidents Ho...
...ary 1795 Witness our Hands this 7th March 1795

...five Shillings — " "	by	Pedr. Purcell
...llings and fourpence " "		Michael Dowling
...llings and fourpence " "		Peter Lenox
...llings and sixpence " "		Jas. Duncan
...Shillings and fourpence " —		Pedr. Purcell
...Shillings and Eightpence —		Samuel Curtis
...Shillings and twopence "		Timothy Sheedy
...Shillings and tenpence " "		Robt Aull
...Shillings and twopence " — "		Simon Tool
...ee Shillings " " "		James Hoban
...Shilling " " "		Pedr. Purcell
...Shillings & three pence "		Pedr. Purcell
...pence " " " "		James Hoban
...pence " " " "		Pedr. Purcell
...Shillings " " "	}	
...e Shillings " " "	}	James Hoban
...ve Shillings " " "	}	

24

It's perfectly understandable why working-class white folks, middle-class white folks, folks who are having trouble paying the bills or dealing with student loans or don't have health care, who feel like government has let them down, wouldn't be thrilled with the idea of a massive program that is designed to deal with the past but isn't speaking to their future.

BRUCE SPRINGSTEEN: You're saying we live in a country where we could do that for bankers on Wall Street, but we can't do it for a part of the population that's been struggling for so long.

PRESIDENT OBAMA: I am saying that the resentments, the fears, the stereotypes, the tribal lines that are drawn in our country remain very deep. And so my assessment has been that the best way to actually provide programs and pathways to opportunity and success and equality for African Americans is to frame it as "Let's make sure *all* kids get a good education. Let's make sure all people get health care. We're a wealthy enough country; everybody should be able to get a job that pays a living wage."

And by framing it in universal terms, as opposed to specifically benefiting a racial group that has been done wrong in the past, we're more likely to get a majority. Now, the challenge—and look, it's a question I've asked myself, and that I think any progressive politician who cares about this country and cares about justice has to ask him- or herself—is: Does in fact the truth of our history demand reparations? If our criminal justice system and the way we police are broken and we have to start it from scratch, are we obliged to just say that, even if the country is not ready for it? Even if you lose votes, even if you forgo the possibility of making more incremental progress, is it worth it just to articulate that truth?

That is the kind of question that I constantly struggled with, and part of my conclusion was and has been that it's less of an "either-or" question. It's a "both-and" question, but there's a recognition that, at any given time, each of us has different roles to play.

The activist has a different role to play than the politician. The writer and the poet have different roles to play than the journalist. And so there is a role for the prophetic Jeremiah, who comes in and says, "This is wrong, and this is unjust, and you need to all look at yourselves and your sins." And then there is the person who is occupying the here and now and not looking down from an eternal perch, who inhabits a more profane day-to-day. "How do I get this guy a job? How do I get this person health care? How do I get this person an education?"

There have been times when I have been criticized from the left—despite being a politician of the left—for not more roundly criticizing the structural imbalances and injustices. There have been times African Americans, academics, and public intellectuals have said that I have told too hopeful a story about progress in race relations in this country. And I have to acknowledge that I have made a bet that I can—without papering over the past—better inspire and move the country closer to the ideal if I hold it up as being possible and lift up moments where it was possible. And not simply indicting the country for all its sins but also saying we can overcome those sins.

But even though I was convinced that reparations was a nonstarter during my presidency, I understand the argument of people I respect, like Ta-Nehisi Coates. I believe that we should talk about it anyway, if for no other reason than to educate the country about a past that too often isn't taught. And, let's face it, we'd rather forget. It goes back full circle to everything we've been talking about. The bridge between America as it is and as we mythologize it to be. The only way that you can bring those two things together is to do an honest accounting and then do the work. I'm not willing, and I know you're not either, to abandon the ideal, because the ideal is worthy. But the ideal, this more perfect union of ours, is far from where the reality has been. There's some who argue, "Let's just get rid of the ideal." I think you need a North Star, you need some place to point to—

BRUCE SPRINGSTEEN: I'm completely with you on that.

PRESIDENT OBAMA: But what I also think is you can't get to where you want to go if you don't know where you are.

BRUCE SPRINGSTEEN: Absolutely.

ABOVE: President Obama participates in a literacy lesson with students while visiting a pre-kindergarten classroom at Moravia Park Elementary School in Baltimore, MD, May 17, 2013. OPPOSITE: In 2014, after researching systemic racism in America, writer Ta-Nehisi Coates published a 16,000-word essay titled "The Case for Reparations" in the *Atlantic* magazine. Coates's essay reinvigorated the national conversation about what the US government owes the descendants of enslaved people and, in 2019, the House of Representatives passed HR 40, a bill that established a commission to research and propose reparations.

THE ARC OF HISTORY BENDS TOWARD JUSTICE, BUT NOT IN A STRAIGHT LINE.

The sociopolitical arc of the second half of the twentieth century, and the first few decades of the twenty-first, has bent toward forms of justice that demand inclusivity, diversity, and equity. Black Americans, young people, Latinx farmworkers, the working poor, the LGBTQIA and disabled communities, and many more people whose identities have been marginalized and whose rights have been denied continue to form coalitions and organize for change.

CIVIL RIGHTS

1954–1968

VOTING RIGHTS

1965

WE DEMAND VOTING RIGHTS NOW!

WE DEMAND VOTING RIGHTS NOW!

WE MARCH FOR JOBS FOR A DECENT PAY

DISABILITY RIGHTS

LATE 1960s–1990

OCCUPY MOVEMENT

2011–PRESENT

BLACK LIVES MATTER MOVEMENT

2013–PRESENT

FARMWORKERS' RIGHTS

1962–1983

ENVIRONMENTALISM MOVEMENT (THROUGH LATEST YOUTH MOVEMENT)

PEOPLES CLIMATE MARCH

1962–1970s

ANTIWAR MOVEMENT

What for? Stop the War!

1964–1973

WOMEN'S RIGHTS

LATE 1960s–1970s

LGBTQIA RIGHTS

LATE 1960s–1985

lives, not guns!

NO GU

GUN CONTROL MOVEMENT

1968–PRESENT

HEALTH-CARE REFORM MOVEMENT

HEALTH INSURANCE REFORM NOW
HEALTHCARE.BARACKOBAMA.COM

1992–2010

#METOO MOVEMENT

Me Too

PRESIDENT OBAMA: First thing is to get your current coordinates.

BRUCE SPRINGSTEEN: What I've been shocked about recently is finding our current coordinates were not quite as firm as I thought they were, you know?

PRESIDENT OBAMA: You thought we'd already passed some of those landmarks?

BRUCE SPRINGSTEEN: The marching with the polo shirts with your tiki torches. I thought that that was kind of over, you know?

PRESIDENT OBAMA: Yeah, you thought—you thought we weren't debating Nazism anymore? You thought that was settled back in '45?

BRUCE SPRINGSTEEN: Those little things, you know?

PRESIDENT OBAMA: Yeah.

BRUCE SPRINGSTEEN: To find out that these are not just meandering veins in our extremities but that they continue to be running through the heart of the country . . . that's a call to arms and lets us know obviously how much work we have left.

PRESIDENT OBAMA: I always say to people, I believe in the upward, forward trajectory of humankind. But I do not believe that it is a straight and steady line.

BRUCE SPRINGSTEEN: It's very crooked.

PRESIDENT OBAMA: You are zigging and zagging and you go backward and you do some loops—

BRUCE SPRINGSTEEN: The arc of history, was that it?

PRESIDENT OBAMA: The arc of the moral universe, it bends toward justice but not in a straight line. You can bend down. And that's been true throughout our history.

We talked about civil rights. We talked about rock 'n' roll, music, and social change.

BRUCE SPRINGSTEEN: Right.

THE ACTIVIST HAS A DIFFERENT ROLE TO PLAY THAN THE POLITICIAN. THE WRITER AND THE POET HAVE DIFFERENT ROLES TO PLAY THAN THE JOURNALIST. AND SO THERE IS A ROLE FOR THE PROPHETIC JEREMIAH, WHO COMES IN AND SAYS, "THIS IS WRONG, AND THIS IS UNJUST, AND YOU NEED TO ALL LOOK AT YOURSELVES AND YOUR SINS."

—PRESIDENT OBAMA

PRESIDENT OBAMA: So okay, lightning round: best protest songs. Top three, or four or five, however many you can think of—

BRUCE SPRINGSTEEN: "Fight the Power," Public Enemy.

PRESIDENT OBAMA: That is a great song.

BRUCE SPRINGSTEEN: I would say "Anarchy in the UK," the Sex Pistols. Or "God Save the Queen." Those are great protest songs.

PRESIDENT OBAMA: "Maggie's Farm" is a great protest song—

BRUCE SPRINGSTEEN: Fabulous!

PRESIDENT OBAMA: *I ain't gonna work on Maggie's farm no more.*

BRUCE SPRINGSTEEN: You sound good.

PRESIDENT OBAMA: "A Change Is Gonna Come"—Sam Cooke.

BRUCE SPRINGSTEEN: Beautiful.

PRESIDENT OBAMA: There's something about when he starts singing.

BRUCE SPRINGSTEEN: The historical pain that's in it. And yet the elegance and generousness of his voice.

PRESIDENT OBAMA: And Billie Holiday singing "Strange Fruit."

BRUCE SPRINGSTEEN: Boom, to the top of the list.

PRESIDENT OBAMA: You know what's a great protest song? Although people don't think of it as a protest song.

BRUCE SPRINGSTEEN: Go ahead—

OPPOSITE: Sam Cooke wrote his now-classic song "A Change Is Gonna Come" at the end of 1963, after he and his wife were turned away from a whites-only motel in Louisiana. Inspired by Dr. Martin Luther King Jr.'s speech at the March on Washington for Jobs and Freedom, as well as Bob Dylan's song "Blowin' in the Wind," Cooke took the risk of writing and recording a song distinctly more personal and political than his previous R & B hit singles. The song reflected on a change that was "a long, a long time coming," and it became a civil rights anthem after his untimely death in 1964.

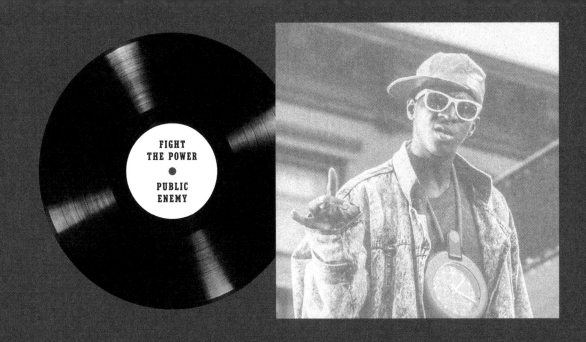

FIGHT
THE POWER
•
PUBLIC
ENEMY

STRANGE
FRUIT
•
BILLIE
HOLIDAY

ANARCHY
IN THE UK
•
THE SEX
PISTOLS

GOD SAVE
THE QUEEN
•
THE SEX
PISTOLS

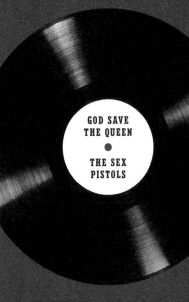

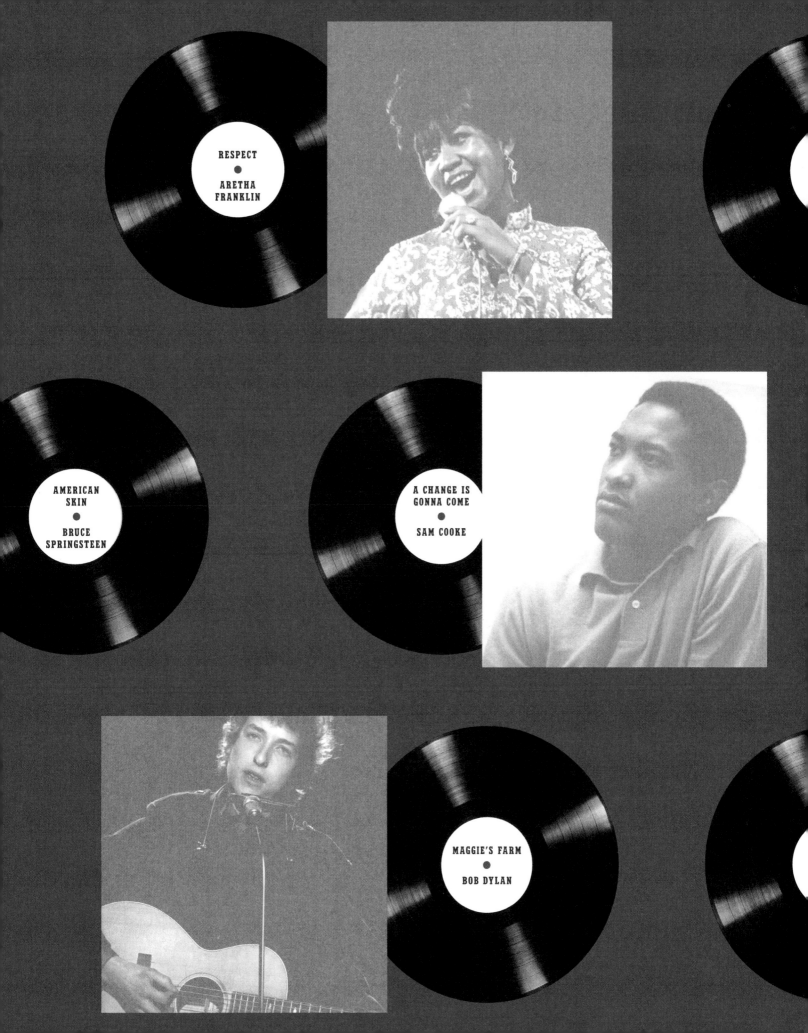

PRESIDENT OBAMA: "Respect," Aretha Franklin. *R-E-S-P-E-C-T*, right? That's a protest song.

BRUCE SPRINGSTEEN: That is one of the best.

PRESIDENT OBAMA: She was saying to every man out there, "Get your act together." But it's not a lecture.

BRUCE SPRINGSTEEN: No. I think my favorite protest songs are the ones that capture a spirit more than any particular diatribe or a dogma.

PRESIDENT OBAMA: Well, here's a good example. "American Skin" is about a very specific event. It's a sign of our age that although the story sadly has been repeated many times since then, a lot of folks might not remember exactly what happened.

BRUCE SPRINGSTEEN: Well, Amadou Diallo was an African immigrant who, in a case of mistaken identity, was stopped by the police. He was in the vestibule of his apartment building. He went to reach for his wallet and was shot nineteen times—forty-one total shots were fired by the officers, who were acquitted.

PRESIDENT OBAMA: And, important for context, these officers were in plainclothes. So Diallo doesn't even necessarily know why these four guys are telling him to stop and suggesting that they somehow got business with him.

BRUCE SPRINGSTEEN: This incident occurs and I start to think, "Okay, skin. Skin is destiny," and what a privilege it is to forget that you live in a particular body. White people can do that. Black people can't do that. So that was what was at the center of that piece of music. And the rest was addressing our mutual fear of one another. It all starts with fear. A mother's fear for her child, when he just walks to school every day. The police officers' own fear that they carry.

Hatred comes later. Everything that we've got going in the systemic racism we have here in America today, where does it come from? People are scared. What are they scared of? Demographic change. They're scared of the country

becoming someplace where Black and brown voices become louder, more influential, more powerful, more equal.

PRESIDENT OBAMA: Losing status.

BRUCE SPRINGSTEEN: Yeah, losing status.

PRESIDENT OBAMA: Did you get any kind of reaction after you wrote that?

BRUCE SPRINGSTEEN: I played it first in Atlanta, which is a great place to debut. People mildly applauded. But by the time I got back to the city before we played Madison Square Garden, we were on the front page of the *New York Post* . . . there was a lot of name-calling going on. Our upcoming concert became a minor cause célèbre in the city.

Amadou Diallo's parents came to Madison Square Garden and they were really lovely. I got the band together backstage and said, "We're just gonna go out and play it. This is what we're built for. This is what we're about. Just go out and play the music."

And we went out and played six or seven songs and went into the beginning of this song. How they even knew this was it I don't know, but the stage got rushed—there were some police officers giving us the New Jersey state bird. There was some booing. We took a lot of heat from the police for several years after that, which I always felt was a result of not really listening to the song.

If you listen to it, you'll understand that it wasn't fundamentally controversial. It wasn't a diatribe. It wasn't a finger-pointing song. It just tried to tally up the human cost of those kinds of killings and murders that go on day after day. The human cost. This song is twenty years old. This is what we're paying in blood for not having sorted through these issues. For not having come to terms with one another. It just goes on.

ABOVE, TOP: A ticket from Bruce Springsteen's 2000 performance at Madison Square Garden, which landed him on the front of the *New York Post*. **ABOVE, BOTTOM:** Patti Scialfa's guitar pick. **OPPOSITE:** Patti Scialfa and her guitar take center stage during the Reunion tour, circa 2000. A member of the E Street Band since 1984, Patti was inducted to the Rock and Roll Hall of Fame with the band in 2014.

(A)

41 shots

41 shots — well, take that ride
cross this muddy, bloody river
to the other side
41 shots — my boots caked in mud
baptized in these waters + in each others
blood
is it a wallet   is it a knife
is it a gun   this is your life
And no secret   no secret my friend
round here you can get killed just for
livin in   your American skin

41 shots — how many it take to die
your life wrestles in the vestibule
prayin for his life
dam dunes eyes
is it in your heart   is it in your eyes   / soul

(16) 41 shots   clip empty   cur... negro
kneel over him (y— vestibule prayin...
41 shots   fol the ride   lancer
bloody river side
was it a gun

41 shots   Mary   Mary dresses her little boy   10 yr old son
for school
says listen to me son   now love you got
heaven above softly
as know the rules   understand

41 shots   if a police officer stops you, always be
polite   don't reach for anything   don't run
swallow don't reach for anything in your pockets
promise mom   keep your hands in sight

AMERICAN SKIN (41 SHOTS)

41 shots . . . and we'll take that ride / 'Cross this bloody river to the other side / 41 shots . . . cut through the night / You're kneeling over his body in the vestibule / Praying for his life / Is it a gun, is it a knife / Is it a wallet, this is your life / It ain't no secret / It ain't no secret / No secret my friend / You can get killed just for living / In your American skin / 41 shots . . . Laina gets her son ready for school / She says "on these streets Charles / You've got to understand the rules / If an officer stops you / Promise me you'll always be polite, that you'll never ever run away / Promise Mama you'll keep your hands in sight" / Is it a gun, is it a knife / Is it a wallet, this is your life / It ain't no secret / It ain't no secret / No secret my friend / You can get killed just for living / In your American skin / Is it a gun, is it a knife / Is it in your heart, is it in your eyes / It ain't no secret . . . / 41 shots . . . and we'll take that ride / 'Cross this bloody river / To the other side / 41 shots . . . got my boots caked in this mud / We're baptized in these waters and in each other's blood / Is it a gun, is it a knife / Is it a wallet, this is your life / It ain't no secret / It ain't no secret / No secret my friend / You can get killed just for living / In your American skin

THE
ALMIGHTY
DOLLAR

Benjamin Franklin—who did pretty well for himself in his day—is quoted as saying that "money never made a man happy yet, nor will it. . . . The more a man has, the more he wants. Instead of its filling a vacuum, it makes one."

Wise man, Mr. Franklin. When we were growing up in the sixties and early seventies, my family and Bruce's didn't have a lot. And didn't expect a lot when it came to money. But we had enough. American society wasn't so stratified then. Life was still a struggle for a lot of people, and the doors of opportunity were too often closed for women and people of color.

But thanks to strong unions and government investment, upward mobility wasn't a myth. Hard work didn't just deliver financial stability and the promise of a better life for your kids, it also provided people with a sense of dignity and self-worth. It's something that Bruce and I have both spent a lot of time thinking about: how the American economy changed, how America became more unequal, and how, in the chase for the almighty dollar, we lost some of the values of community, solidarity, and shared sacrifice that we are going to need to make us whole once again.

PRESIDENT OBAMA: Part of your story about the draft is that you suddenly realize there's a class basis to this entire thing. How is it that the kids who are going to college don't have to go? Part of what separates World War II, that Greatest Generation, from the Vietnam generation is suddenly the sense that "We are gonna hook it up so that the privileged don't have to make sacrifices for bad decisions being made in Washington." And I think there's a consciousness of that injustice that ends up disillusioning people as well.

BRUCE SPRINGSTEEN: We just took that for granted. That we're not up there, we're down here. And we're playing by the rules of down here. And if we don't want to go, there are street pre-scriptions that you're going to have to follow to get out, and it's going to involve some crazy-ass shit, you know? Nobody could afford the doctors' notes or getting back into college. I barely got in the first time. I don't even remember feeling aggrieved by it.

PRESIDENT OBAMA: You don't feel some class resentment?

BRUCE SPRINGSTEEN: No, I didn't.

PRESIDENT OBAMA: You'd just think, "Yeah, of course the rich kids are going to have a different deal." But you don't think that raises questions about the whole myth of the American Dream and upward mobility and "anybody can make it"?

BRUCE SPRINGSTEEN: I think you lost your faith in life, liberty, and the pursuit of meaning for all. You lost your faith in that. I didn't have the idea that I was going to have any great success because I had simply never known anyone who ever had. There were no great success stories in my neighborhood; everybody was pure blue-collar working-class. I knew no one who had ever signed a record contract—no one at all. I knew no one who had ever been on an airplane. Kids in the neighborhood, we were like the lost tribes. We saw them fly over, we knew people were in them. So all this was outside of the bounds of your experience. And you just took it in stride.

And there was a little bit of "Ooooh, it's every man for himself."

The economic picture in Freehold in my childhood, the 1950s, was a very different picture than the economic picture in the country today. If you were middle-class in Freehold or if you were the wealthiest people in Freehold, there was a street you lived on. I remember it was called Brinckerhoff Avenue. It was the widest, most tree-lined street in town. And to find poverty, you had to really look for it.

OPPOSITE, TOP: "The Greatest Generation" refers to Americans born in the early decades of the twentieth century. Their childhoods were marked by technological advances like the telephone, but also the economic hardship of the Great Depression. When America entered World War II, millions of men enlisted and went overseas, while millions of women joined the workforce to support their families and the war effort. The struggles and sacrifices that the economic turmoil and devastating war required of Americans still defines the generation. Here, World War II veteran Kenneth "Rock" Merritt shares stories of D-Day with President Obama aboard Marine One at the seventieth French-American D-Day commemoration ceremony, June 6, 2014. OPPOSITE, BOTTOM: With its uniform houses and carefully planned community, the hamlet of Levittown, NY, was a model for the postwar suburban dream in America, circa 1955.

It was there, usually in the communities of color, but the income inequality felt so much less pronounced. My parents lived hand-to-mouth. They spent all the money they had this week until they had money next week and then spent all of that—we all lived that way. But we never thought of ourselves as struggling. We were clothed, we had food, we had a roof over our heads. Our home was pretty funky, but it sat there in the midst of other homes and it wasn't that dramatically different.

PRESIDENT OBAMA: It wasn't like you were ashamed of the house or you thought, "Man, we need to get fancier curtains."

BRUCE SPRINGSTEEN: In our house I did have a little bit of that going. I lived in one of the oldest houses in town and it got pretty dilapidated. But, even then, I never thought of myself as a poor kid, until my father said, "We are going to the movies tonight, we gotta sell the spare tire."

PRESIDENT OBAMA: Did that really happen?

BRUCE SPRINGSTEEN: Yeah.

PRESIDENT OBAMA: But look, it was not rubbed in your face that you did not have as much as other people.

BRUCE SPRINGSTEEN: No. I lived in the middle of a middle-class neighborhood.

PRESIDENT OBAMA: Part of what you're saying, though, is if you're growing up as a kid there and you're looking around, you think, "All right, I'm pretty much on par with everybody else."

BRUCE SPRINGSTEEN: With Bobby Duncan down the street or with Richie Blackwell over here . . .

PRESIDENT OBAMA: Yes, and maybe his dad runs the bank. Whereas my dad works at the bank or works in the factory. But you don't feel as if you somehow are on the outside looking in.

BRUCE SPRINGSTEEN: No, you don't feel like you're victimized or a victim. You're aware of some class differences, of course. But that awareness is much less dramatic than it is today.

PRESIDENT OBAMA: But did you have folks in the neighborhood, kids who said, "Man, you know, I'm getting out of here because

I'm going to make a lot of money. I'm going to get that new Chevy and that's a sign, a marker that I've made it." Was there any kind of notion that you needed to make a certain amount of money, or have a certain amount of stuff, because if not, you were a failure or you were going backward or you hadn't been ambitious enough?

BRUCE SPRINGSTEEN: In my experience, it's a much more modern phenomenon. I don't remember that being the huge topic of conversation in high school. Everybody wanted to make a living and if you were going to do really well, you were going to go to college.

PRESIDENT OBAMA: Right, that was a marker.

BRUCE SPRINGSTEEN: Big marker. Huge marker.

PRESIDENT OBAMA: If you went to college, that indicated something a little bit different.

BRUCE SPRINGSTEEN: You were special. But that changed dramatically in the United States in the seventies, certainly the eighties. The Gilded Age of the eighties.

PRESIDENT OBAMA: I'm in middle school and then high school in the seventies. And I see all this through the lens of my grandparents, who I lived with most of the time. And they are Depression-era, World War II–era folks.

BRUCE SPRINGSTEEN: Right, as my grandparents were.

PRESIDENT OBAMA: And we lived in an apartment in Honolulu. Maybe twelve hundred square feet? I remember as an adult going back to the apartment and thinking, "Yeah, you know, this is really modest." But at the time I never, ever thought, "Wow, I don't have much." We weren't blue-collar, in the sense that my grandparents had office jobs. My grandmother was pink-collar. She had started as a clerk in a bank. She didn't have a college degree even though she was smart as a whip, because the GI Bill did not apply to Rosie the Riveter. She had worked in a factory while my grandfather was off at war. He comes back; he gets the GI benefit, goes to college for almost a year and a half, and then decides to drop out.

> I DIDN'T HAVE THE IDEA THAT I WAS GOING TO HAVE ANY GREAT SUCCESS BECAUSE I HAD SIMPLY NEVER KNOWN ANYONE WHO EVER HAD. THERE WERE NO GREAT SUCCESS STORIES IN MY NEIGHBORHOOD; EVERYBODY WAS PURE BLUE-COLLAR WORKING CLASS.
>
> —BRUCE SPRINGSTEEN

OPPOSITE: Barack Obama in his Punahou blazer, with his mother, Ann, circa 1978.
FOLLOWING: The Freehold 175th anniversary parade, 1953.

She doesn't get to go to college. But she ends up becoming a vice president in the bank—the Bank of Hawaii. And my grandfather was a salesman. They were on the low end income-wise, but middle-class in Hawaii. I went to a prep school. So let's call it 80 percent of the kids at the school are more well-off than I am. But the interesting thing is, we did not feel poor.

I didn't consider the world foreclosed to me because I was not wealthy. My grandparents wanted me to go to college and sacrificed for me to go to prep school, which more or less assured, unless I got kicked out for drinking, that I'd get to college.

I'm saying all this, and you know . . . we sound like these old guys—

BRUCE SPRINGSTEEN: It's terrible. It's so bad.

PRESIDENT OBAMA: "Man, I used to walk to school barefoot."

When I move to Chicago, I'm working with folks who've lost their jobs, because the steel plant moved. And that's where I also see most clearly the intersection between race and class, because the story you describe in Freehold was never fully available to African Americans, or it was always a poorer, more hazardous version, a more tenuous version.

BRUCE SPRINGSTEEN: Right.

PRESIDENT OBAMA: Michelle's parents are examples of folks who were able to aspire to the working-class life. A working middle-class life that you describe in Freehold.

But it's always a little more tenuous. And the rungs they get on the ladder are always a little more slippery. I remember talking to folks when I got to the South Side of Chicago who described how it was a really big deal, for example, to get a post office job. Because that meant you had a regular salary, and you had a pension.

BRUCE SPRINGSTEEN: Yeah. When my dad worked on the line, it was a huge deal.

PRESIDENT OBAMA: But I think you and I had the same sense that this shift took place right around the early eighties. A

few months after Reagan gets elected, he breaks the air traffic controllers' union, and we've got stagflation.

BRUCE SPRINGSTEEN: Right. And then you have the beginning of the kind of media that *Lifestyles of the Rich and Famous* introduces, which brings the culture of materialism into everyone's home, twenty-four hours a day, and suddenly we're being told, "You are not good enough unless you have this stuff."

PRESIDENT OBAMA: This is right around the time I move to New York. And New York is coming out of near bankruptcy. But Wall Street is surging, right? Soon the movie *Wall Street* comes out. "Greed is good." Michael Douglas in the high collars.

BOTH: And the huge cell phones.

BRUCE SPRINGSTEEN: The size of a backpack!

PRESIDENT OBAMA: Manhattan in '81, '82, '83 is a good perch to watch this shift in culture. It was the epicenter. And as you said, it is suddenly in your face. It's like that David Mamet play, *Glengarry Glen Ross,* where you got a boss talking to a bunch of salesmen. The guy says, "First place, you get a Cadillac. Second place, steak knives. Third place, you're fired."

There's suddenly the sense that, "Hey, you are either going to win or you are going to lose in this capitalist game, and you don't want to be on the back side of that thing." What I saw then in my peers was the shift in thinking to the notion that "If I don't get to Wall Street or a white-shoe law firm to punch my ticket, then I could start slipping down the scales."

> THERE'S SUDDENLY THE SENSE THAT, "HEY, YOU ARE EITHER GOING TO WIN OR YOU ARE GOING TO LOSE IN THIS CAPITALIST GAME, AND YOU DON'T WANT TO BE ON THE BACK SIDE OF THAT THING."
>
> **—PRESIDENT OBAMA**

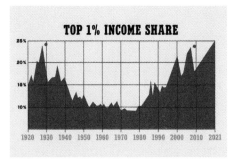

TOP 1% INCOME SHARE

1920 1930 1940 1950 1960 1970 1980 1990 2000 2010 2021

ABOVE: Income inequality in America has worsened dramatically since the 1970s. In 1970, the top 1 percent of American earners made 9 percent of America's income. Today, they make almost 25 percent, and the 400 richest Americans have more wealth than the bottom 150 million Americans combined. While this extreme consolidation has happened, middle-class incomes have stayed the same or even dropped since the 1970s. At the same time, the cost of living—including housing, childcare, and education—continues to increase. **OPPOSITE:** The cutthroat spirit of corporate America in the 1980s was best exemplified by the movers and shakers working in New York City's financial district, who were dramatized in the 1987 film *Wall Street.* In it, Michael Douglas plays Gordon Gekko, an unscrupulous corporate raider who delivers an infamous speech to the shareholders of a failing paper company, declaring "Greed is good."

GREED. YOU MARK MY WORDS. WILL NOT ONLY SAVE TELDAR PAPER.
BUT THAT OTHER MALFUNCTIONING CORPORATION CALLED THE USA.

1. Bye Bye Johnny
2. Starkweather (Nebraska)
3. Atlanta City
4. Mansion on the Hill
5. Born in the U.S.A.
6. Johnny 99
7. Downbound Train
8. Losin kind
9. State Trooper
10. Used Cars
11. Wanda (open All Night)
12. Child Bride
13. Pink Cadillac
14. Highway Patrolman
15. Reason to Believe

Meanwhile, I am swimming backward to a different idea of America. And my idea of America was defined by the Freedom Riders. My idea of America was defined by the coal miners, and folks who were working the settlement houses in Chicago with Jane Addams. And my idea of America was the grunts in World War II who were fighting fascism and making sacrifices. So I guess in my head there were always these two contrasting ideas. There was an America that's all about me getting mine. And then there was this other America that's about "We're all raising the barn together. And we're all pitching in."

I'm basically coming of age in the Reagan era. And so when I am thinking about America, and I am thinking about my place in it, rather than seeing a culture around me of service, sacrifice, and community, I am seeing a country where we are being defined by greed.

BRUCE SPRINGSTEEN: Let me give you a "for instance." My kids are going to a nice little school across the street from my house. I go for "first day" parents' introduction. The first thing that happens is the headmaster gets up and he says, "Now, I don't want you parents worrying that when your child has its first day at Bear Stearns . . ."

PRESIDENT OBAMA: Oh, man!

BRUCE SPRINGSTEEN: This is the *opening salvo.* My kid is only four! But that was what was in the air at that point of time.

PRESIDENT OBAMA: Yeah, you could feel it: that anxiety. When I told people that I was going to work as a community organizer, nobody could really even understand. This is all happening against the backdrop of manufacturing moving offshore; unions getting busted; CEOs, who were making maybe thirty times what the average guy or gal on the assembly line was making in the fifties and sixties, now making three hundred times.

Suddenly in the 1980s Ronald Reagan is describing government being the problem. "Let's cut taxes, let's cut public services." It also means cutting public jobs, cutting union jobs, and that combination of manufacturing going away and public-sector jobs going away decimates the opportunity for Black men and Black women to get work. And just as, post–civil rights movement, the door is finally cracking open to get some of these jobs that previously had been banned to them, the rug gets pulled out from under them. So there's a real shift

in how capitalism operates, and people's wages really are stagnating and the inequalities really are getting greater.

BRUCE SPRINGSTEEN: And the middle class is now getting squashed.

PRESIDENT OBAMA: They're getting squeezed.

BRUCE SPRINGSTEEN: And so one question is, were the forties and fifties, and somewhat the sixties, just a break in between two Gilded Ages?

PRESIDENT OBAMA: And the answer is . . . mostly yes.

BRUCE SPRINGSTEEN: All right, so in '81 I wrote "Atlantic City."

In the early eighties, there's a dread in the air. Maybe you can trace it back to the end of the Vietnam War. And I wrote a very strange album called *Nebraska*, this very quiet record that dealt with all of these issues at that moment. Now, I'm writing about these things when I'm not that conscious about them. I'm following what I'm feeling in the air.

That and the combination of my father's life, my experiences in Freehold, where I saw what happens when there's some union problems and suddenly the factory is moving down south and everybody is unemployed, and the cost that was paid by the families in town and my own—all that moved me to write in this direction. And like I said, I didn't write the album with the idea of being socially conscious. I was just telling stories that I was feeling at the time.

PRESIDENT OBAMA: Here's a topic for both of us: we start off not thinking a lot about money, but thinking, in your case, about music and your art, and I'm deliberately saying I'm not taking that path—

> IN THE EARLY EIGHTIES, THERE'S A DREAD IN THE AIR. MAYBE YOU CAN TRACE IT BACK TO THE END OF THE VIETNAM WAR. AND I WROTE A VERY STRANGE ALBUM CALLED *NEBRASKA*, THIS VERY QUIET RECORD THAT DEALT WITH ALL OF THESE ISSUES AT THAT MOMENT.
>
> —BRUCE SPRINGSTEEN

OPPOSITE (inset): A draft track list for *Nebraska*, sent by Bruce Springsteen to manager Jon Landau. When the album was completed, the songs included were "Nebraska," "Mansion on the Hill," "Highway Patrolman," "Used Cars," "My Father's House," "Atlantic City," "Johnny 99," "State Trooper," "Open All Night," and "Reason to Believe." **FOLLOWING:** Community ties that Barack Obama developed in his years as an organizer were a driving factor in his decision to embark on a political career by running for an Illinois state senate seat representing Chicago's South Side, circa 1996.

Well they blew up the chicken man in Philly last night / now they blew up his house too / Down on the boardwalk they're gettin' ready for a fight gonna see what them racket boys can do / Now there's trouble busin' in from outta state and the D.A. can't get no relief / Gonna be a rumble out on the promenade and the gamblin' commission's hangin' on by the skin of its teeth / Well now everything dies baby that's a fact / But maybe everything that dies someday comes back / Put your makeup on fix your hair up pretty / And meet me tonight in Atlantic City / Well I got a job and tried to put my money away / But I got debts that no honest man can pay / So I drew what I had from the Central Trust / And I bought us two tickets on that Coast City bus / Well now everything dies baby that's a fact / But maybe everything that dies someday comes back / Put your makeup on fix your hair up pretty / And meet me tonight in Atlantic City / Now our luck may have died and our love may be cold but with you forever I'll stay / We're goin' out where the sand's turnin' to gold so put on your stockin's baby cause the nights gettin' cold / And everything dies, baby, that's a fact / But maybe everything that dies someday comes back / Now I been lookin' for a job but it's hard to find / Down here it's just winners and losers and don't get caught on the wrong side of that line / Well I'm tired of comin' out on the losin' end / So honey last night I met this guy and I'm gonna do a little favor for him / Well I guess everything dies baby that's a fact / But maybe everything that dies someday comes back / Put your hair up nice and set up pretty / and meet me tonight in Atlantic City / Meet me tonight in Atlantic City / Meet me tonight in Atlantic City

—FROM NEBRASKA (1982)

BRUCE SPRINGSTEEN: Now, that's a big choice to make coming out of the kinds of schools you came out of and given the opportunities that you would've had. How did you come to make that choice?

PRESIDENT OBAMA: Part of it was because my mom was a little bit of a freethinker. And she wandered around, became an anthropologist, went into development work. She was not all that practical to begin with, and kind of a romantic. And I'm sure she put a little bit of that into me. But part of it was a recognition that the American Dream had never been fully available to Black folks. When I thought about what I should aspire to, it wasn't "Man, let me be Jay Rockefeller." It was "Look at John Lewis. Look at Dr. King. Look at these folks who went out there trying to make the world better and open up opportunities for people." So partly because of my own need to figure out who I was as a Black American, that path looked like it was necessary for me to take. My salvation was there.

BRUCE SPRINGSTEEN: That's an interesting word, *salvation*. Because it turns what you're doing into a redemptive exercise.

PRESIDENT OBAMA: Right. And that's what it was for me. I find myself in Chicago working with folks who are going through these struggles and trying to figure out, how am I going to get work and how am I going to get my kid work and how am I going to get my kid into college, or at least into a trade? What's happening to the value of my house? They're going through this stuff and I'm seeing it in concrete terms. And that does become redemptive for me, because now my story merges with theirs and the larger American story. And if I can figure out how to help that community that I've now become a part of—and, as it turned out, that my wife grew up in—maybe I can redeem a piece of America, too, and make it my own. That becomes my mind-set.

BRUCE SPRINGSTEEN: Those are fundamentally my own motivations. And there's a deeper question of where that comes from, because it's a response to something.

PRESIDENT OBAMA: We're trying to figure out, how do we feel whole and make the world around us feel whole?

BRUCE SPRINGSTEEN: Well put.

PRESIDENT OBAMA: But the interesting thing is that Michelle, partly because she was very clear about who she was—with loving parents, a sense of family, community—she doesn't feel like she needs to get redeemed. She feels like, "I just need some money."

BRUCE SPRINGSTEEN: Funny.

PRESIDENT OBAMA: So when I meet her, she is driving a Saab, and she's joined a wine club. From her perspective, initially, she punched her ticket.

I remember the first time she invites me to a party with a bunch of her friends, and they're all these young professionals. I am very much the misfit. Because one of my responses to this era was I went in the opposite direction. I had like three shirts. I had one plate. And I lived in these scruffy-looking apartments and all of my furniture was scavenged from out on the street. I knew that there lay temptation. Like if I went down the path of starting to want stuff, that was a hamster wheel you never got off of.

So I'm with all these young professionals. They're looking all like Richard Gere in *American Gigolo*.

BRUCE SPRINGSTEEN: That was the look!

PRESIDENT OBAMA: I walk in, and I had one sports jacket that didn't quite fit me right, which I'd gotten at some discount store. Ironically, I do think it was part of my power as a politician. People could sense that Michelle and I had lived through and understood what it was like to have a whole bunch of student loans to pay, what it was like to have some credit card debt, and what it was like to have to say no to things. And it wasn't an act.

BRUCE SPRINGSTEEN: Right.

PRESIDENT OBAMA: I'm interested in how you dealt with money. You started off chasing music, but what's the point when you suddenly say, "Shit, I'm rich"?

BRUCE SPRINGSTEEN: Thirty, I would say, thirty-two, thirty-three. What happened was that I signed so many bad deals

---

ABOVE: The community organizer days, circa 1988. OPPOSITE: Barack and Michelle Obama as young parents, with daughter Malia, circa 1998. FOLLOWING: Obama, early in his political career, encouraging Chicago voters to hit the polls, 1992.

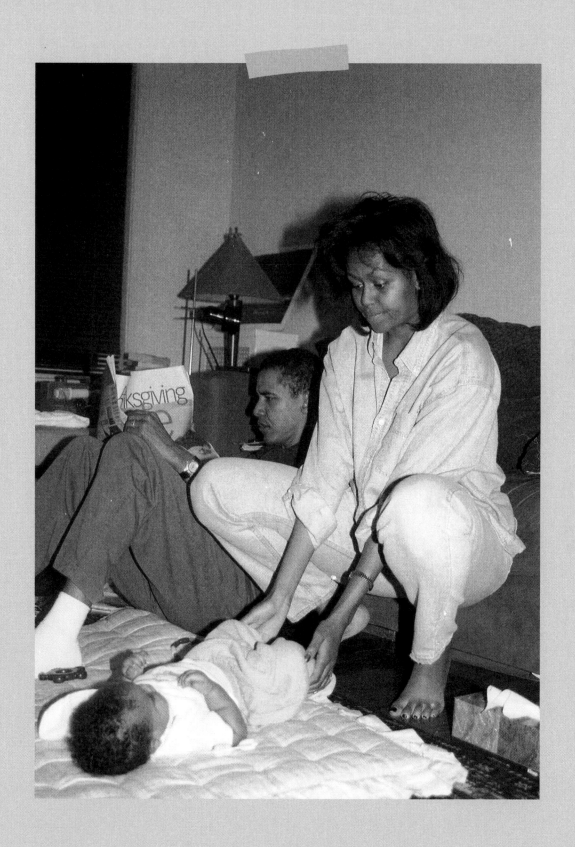

that for ten years I was pretty broke. Here's an example of how little money I had. It was 1972 and I was flat broke. My manager told me if I got to New York, he could give me thirty-five dollars. So I said, "I'm going to the city." I went in my drawer, dug up all my pennies, and I figured out exactly what it would take me to get to New York . . . just enough. My girlfriend lent me her car, but it had a push-button transmission.

I got to the Lincoln Tunnel and it was a buck to get through. I had a hundred pennies, right? I gave the woman the pennies and she said, "I can't take these pennies."

There was a sign that said "No Pennies." I said, "Ma'am, this is all the money I have. I don't have enough gas to get back to where I came from. I need to get into the city, so we're going to sit here while I count every penny."

She busted open the rolls, scraped each one, one, two, and after a minute she looks at me and says, "You can't go through." "Why not?" She sticks her hand in the window. There was one Canadian penny.

I said, "There ain't a self-respecting car in the whole fucking world that don't have a penny somewhere under the seats." And I got out of that freaking car with everybody beeping their asses behind me and I searched that car and, believe it or not, I found a penny and I got through to New York. But that taught me . . . In America, ninety-nine cents ain't gonna get you where you want to go. You need the full dollar, my friend.

PRESIDENT OBAMA: I'm impressed. And you didn't cuss the woman out.

BRUCE SPRINGSTEEN: No, no. I was just gonna find that penny or I don't know what.

But in my early thirties, several things happened. One, the live concert industry began to become very lucrative. We went out and played a lot of shows. And I had finally paid off most of my debts from all my stupid mistakes. I had twenty grand in the bank when I started—almost ten years after I signed my record deal, that's what I had to my name—and I came home at the end of that tour with a lot more than that, and my first thought was, "Oh my god. As far as I'm concerned, I'm rich." Second thought, "I hate myself!" Because now I'm in a trap!

So my first luxury was the luxury of ignoring my money. But I remember I bought one new thing. I bought a ten-thousand-dollar Chevrolet Camaro. Every time I got in it, I felt like I was driving in a solid-gold Rolls-Royce, and I was embarrassed.

> IN AMERICA, NINETY-NINE CENTS AIN'T GONNA GET YOU WHERE YOU WANT TO GO. YOU NEED THE FULL DOLLAR, MY FRIEND.
>
> —BRUCE SPRINGSTEEN

PRESIDENT OBAMA: You didn't feel good about it. You felt self-conscious about it.

BRUCE SPRINGSTEEN: Very self-conscious.

PRESIDENT OBAMA: Well, the other thing is, it runs contrary to your brand. In terms of who you are thinking about as both your audience and your subject.

BRUCE SPRINGSTEEN: And who I feel like . . . so I don't want to settle for that. I want that wholeness that you were talking about. That's what I'm after.

PRESIDENT OBAMA: Redemption.

BRUCE SPRINGSTEEN: That's correct.

PRESIDENT OBAMA: Salvation.

BRUCE SPRINGSTEEN: So I consider myself healthily skeptical when I started to change station.

PRESIDENT OBAMA: Even as this whole atmosphere just accelerates, right? I mean, all through the eighties into the nineties, not only are you making more and more money, but the temptations of how to spend your money become more and more lavish. And your peers, folks in your musical stratosphere, are not quite as restrained in terms of how their money is being spent.

BRUCE SPRINGSTEEN: Everybody has a different attitude about it. And I don't really judge anybody.

PRESIDENT OBAMA: I'm not saying you judge them—what I am saying though is, during this period, are you thinking to yourself, "Why am I not buying a huge mansion?"

BRUCE SPRINGSTEEN: I am thinking that, and I don't have the answer, which is a big problem because I got to a place where I said, "I want a home. A home is a part of that wholeness."

I can't find one. I can't get one. I can't buy one. And I realize, "Oh, I get it. I can't buy one because I don't deserve one."

OPPOSITE: Bruce Springsteen, circa 1973. **FOLLOWING:** Bruce performing at the Stone Pony in Asbury Park, NJ, circa 1970 and 2011.

Why don't I have a partner and a home life and children and satisfactions of my own? "Well, I don't deserve any of those." When I finally made some money, it forced me to interrogate myself about who I was.

I remember feeling rootless and dissociated, afraid of losing who I was, where I belonged, where I was connected to. My basic values. And I said, "Well, I could go off and take my individual freedoms, my personal license, and turn that into a way of life, but I don't think that's where the action is."

I think the action is within the community. I'm interested in:

A. Being a part of that community, which is very difficult for me to do.

B. Understanding the social structure that has impacts on all those folks' lives.

C. Writing about that existence and giving some voice to it. Just because, at the bottom, that's who I think I still am.

So I got to wondering, "What do we owe each other?" At the end of the day, if you see America as this beloved community, then the bottom line is you owe something to your neighbors and they owe something to you. Recognize each other for who we are. See each other for who we are. Continue collectively building a country whose gifts and blessings fall upon all.

I've enjoyed my success as much as the next guy. But I didn't think that it meant you had to abandon these ideas, these values.

I was very conscious about remaining physically, emotionally, mentally, spiritually a part of the community that I came from. That was really important to me. I stayed in New Jersey. I hung out in the same bars. I played in the same bars on the weekends when I could. I had the same group of friends, and I probably took it to an extreme. But, looking back on it, I would rather have taken those things to an extreme than gone the other way. I'm interested in the story I want to tell, and I know that that story and my very self are inextricably connected to the people and the place that I came from. And if I sever that connection, I've lost something, and I've lost something essential. So I'm skeptical, moving forward very carefully, tiny step by tiny step, until I buy a house in the most exclusive community in this little part of New Jersey.

And I feel terrible about it. First night I'm in that house I'm like, "What the fuck!? Have I lost my fucking mind?! Have I gone crazy!? What am I doing in this place!?" But what I realized was, looking back on it now, if you drove by the house, it's got a nice lawn and it's a sort of upscale house. It was a big house, but what did I hope to do? Fill it. That was why I got it. I got it to fill. To fill that wholeness that I was searching for. We raised our kids in it for thirty years.

PRESIDENT OBAMA: I know it's true for you, Bruce, and certainly true for me, that we're always questioning in this culture: "Am I losing touch? Am I falling prey to this huge consumer engine that's being fed to us every single day? Am I forgetting what's important?" And that requires you sometimes to step back and reflect and get that perspective.

Last year, as my Christmas present to Michelle, I arranged for us to have a dinner on the top deck of this hotel overlooking Waikiki. Left the girls behind. Some friends arranged this Hawaiian trio that played some songs. The torch was lit.

BRUCE SPRINGSTEEN: It sounds good!

PRESIDENT OBAMA: It was a good setup. We watched the sun go down. I was quite pleased with myself. The best part of the evening was right at the beginning, when we started tracking all the places that we had stayed over the twenty years that we had been coming to Hawaii, starting with the first, when we slept on my grandparents' couch. Then the second we got actually a motel room, which was like five miles from the beach. And then we moved to a legit hotel that had a pool in the general vicinity of the beach. Then we went to, like, a Sheraton. This is over the course of ten years.

BRUCE SPRINGSTEEN: You're getting there!

PRESIDENT OBAMA: And then there was a place, when we had the girls, and there was a separate room that's sort of like a junior suite—I think that's what they called it.

So that you can close the door, so that it's possible to have a little bit of privacy.

BRUCE SPRINGSTEEN: Very nice.

ABOVE: Michelle and Malia Obama in Hawaii at Christmastime, 1998. OPPOSITE: The Obamas exploring Hawaii before their children were born, midnineties.

PRESIDENT OBAMA: You can track your economic status over the years through your vacations with your spouse. Michelle and I could almost see every place that we had stayed, but the pleasure of it was reminding ourselves that we were just as happy in each of those places. The constant was our time together, and the setting really had not made any difference.

Initially, there had been a little burst of excitement—oh, you see they got the little shampoos in the bathroom. Then you go to a place that actually has, like, a robe, and you are like, "Man, try on the robe."

After that initial moment, though, it was still the sunset that mattered and you holding hands. It was still the sound of the girls laughing as they were running after each other in the sand. It was the free stuff that had nothing to do with the places you were staying at.

BRUCE SPRINGSTEEN: Those are the elements of joy.

PRESIDENT OBAMA: That was what made you whole. And I think communicating that as part of our politics, our stories, our songs, and reminding ourselves of that feeling of connection to what matters, is how you then get to the point where you can build a coalition to actually change the policies.

You can't do that unless the folks at the top recognize, "Hey, what's going to make me happy is living in a healthy, fair society. It's not how much stuff I have and that I'm living behind a gate. I can give up some of this and I'll feel better. If every kid's getting a good education, that's a better future for my kids."

BRUCE SPRINGSTEEN: "Used Cars" is a song that probably captures the feeling of my family life, my childhood, and my neighborhood—the threadbareness of a lot of our lives—as well as anything that I've ever written. All I remember was when my dad drove in that driveway with that new used car, we got so excited it may as well have been a freaking brandnew Lincoln Continental.

Looking back at it now, I guess there's a happiness and a sadness to it.

PRESIDENT OBAMA: There are the very real economic inequalities that have arisen that have to be fixed.

BRUCE SPRINGSTEEN: If we don't fix those, the country is going to fall apart.

The Obama family arrives in Hawaii, circa 2010.

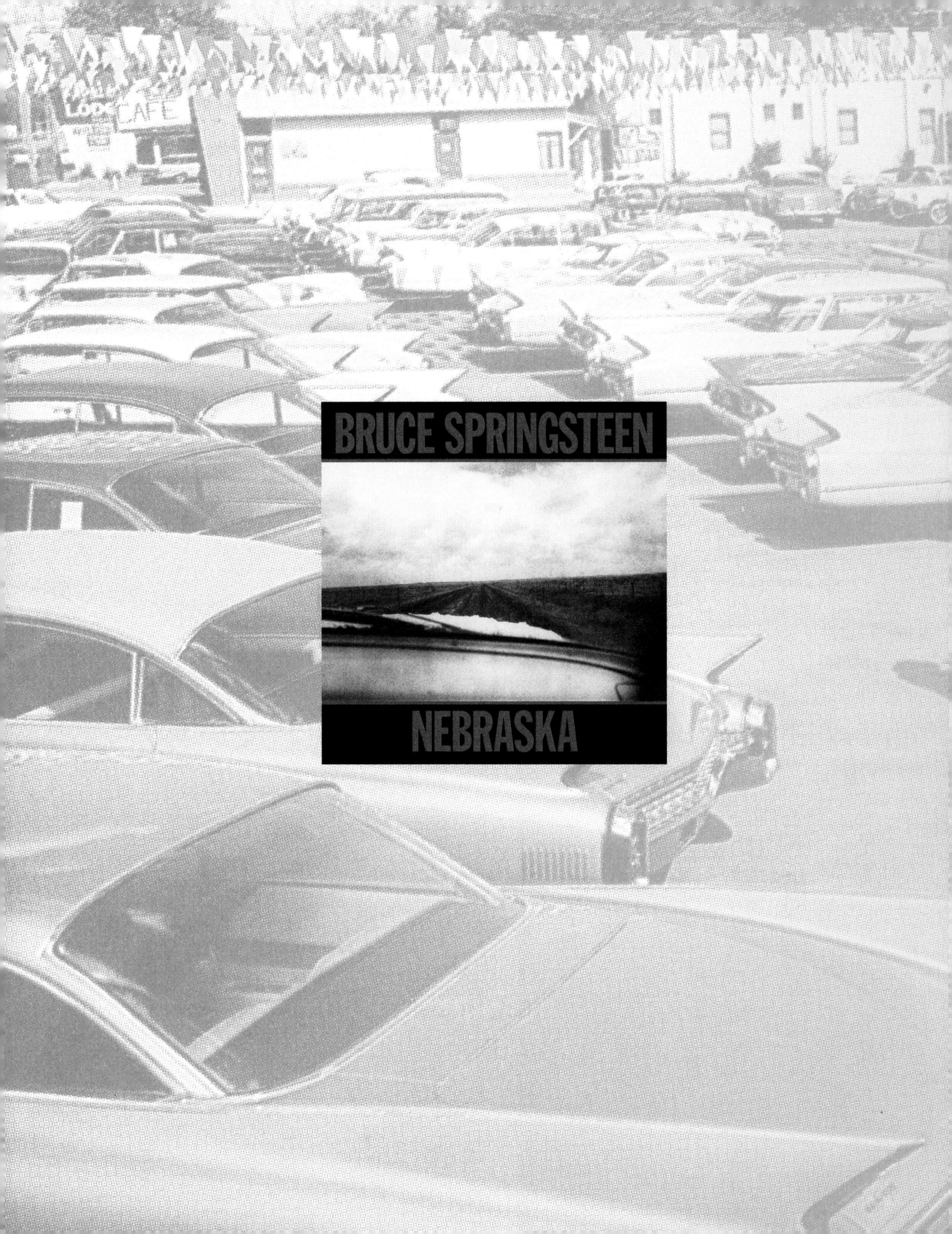
CAFE
BRUCE SPRINGSTEEN
NEBRASKA

USED CARS

My little sister's in the front seat with an ice cream cone / My ma's in the back seat sittin' all alone / As my pa steers her slow out of the lot for a test drive down Michigan Avenue / Now, my ma, she fingers her wedding band / And watches the salesman stare at my old man's hands / He's tellin' us all 'bout the break he'd give us if he could, but he just can't / Well if I could, I swear I know just what I'd do / Now, mister, the day the lottery I win I ain't ever gonna ride in no used car again / Now, the neighbors come from near and far / As we pull up in our brand new used car / I wish he'd just hit the gas and let out a cry and tell 'em all they can kiss our asses goodbye / My dad, he sweats the same job from mornin' to morn / Me, I walk home on the same dirty streets where I was born / Up the block I can hear my little sister in the front seat blowin' that horn / The sounds echoin' all down Michigan Avenue / Now, mister, the day my number comes in I ain't ever gonna ride in no used car again

—FROM NEBRASKA (1982)

PRESIDENT OBAMA: Because when folks lose that sense of place and status, when suddenly steady work alone isn't enough for you to support your family or to be respected, and when you have chronic insecurity, there's a bunch of policy stuff that has to be fixed.

But the policy fixes are necessary in part because the country starts telling a different story about what's important: a shift away from what we were talking about in the eighties, that "greed is good" attitude that never really went away. It accelerated. And the argument between conservatives and liberals, right and left, a lot of times has to do with how much redistribution of wealth there should be, how much taxation, but it never really gets to some of the core issues about why it is that we're measuring ourselves just with how much stuff we got.

And if there is a way for us to think about that differently, it becomes easier for those who have a lot to maybe give some up in order to make sure that those who have a little have enough.

BRUCE SPRINGSTEEN: That's right. There's been this rush of a certain kind of life-distorting information and it's not going away. Ever. People need interpretive abilities that generations before us possibly did not need to have. They're going to have to make decisions about what's valuable. What's truly, deeply valuable.

PRESIDENT OBAMA: That's the point: there's a collective story we tell about what we value. How can we create a new story in which the shared values that you sing about and that I've tried to express in my politics, the values of family—having a code in terms of how you live an honest life and a generous life and a full life, and what kind of friend you are and what kind of neighbor you are to people—are what confer status? One way or another, somehow, I think we're going to muddle through. But you know what helps? When you got bards and poets like yourself, who help steer us back onto the path of righteousness and love. And so I'm grateful that you're out there, and I know a lot of people are, too. And you just gotta keep on making some music, man.

BRUCE SPRINGSTEEN: I kind of like having you there, too.

PRESIDENT OBAMA: If we get too self-congratulatory, you know our wives will come in and talk to us!

> HOW CAN WE CREATE A NEW STORY IN WHICH THE SHARED VALUES THAT YOU SING ABOUT AND THAT I'VE TRIED TO EXPRESS IN MY POLITICS, THE VALUES OF FAMILY . . . ARE WHAT CONFER STATUS?
>
> —PRESIDENT OBAMA

BRUCE SPRINGSTEEN: You can say we have a great story: the story I've told my whole life, the story you've dedicated your life to. But you need waiting ears to hear that story. What are the conditions that allow people to hear and believe that that's true?

PRESIDENT OBAMA: A part of what I tried to do in my political career, part of what I'm trying to do post-politics, is to tell a story that is counter to the story that says the American Dream is defined by you ending up on top of that pyramid that's getting steeper and steeper, and the more people below you, the better off you are.

Our expectations and taste in terms of what it means to have made it have shifted, and then obviously that's reflected in our politics, which is how you get somebody like a Donald Trump elected, because he represents success in the minds of a lot of folks. Everything is gold plated. You've got the big plane. And you got the buildings with your name on them, and you're going around firing people. Particularly for men, that is a sign that you have succeeded, right?

One of the things that I never understood is why people would want individual success at the exclusion of other people. There are entire communities that are premised on living behind a gate, cut off from the larger community. Isolated. That just always felt lonely to me. It's like Citizen Kane sort of rattling around in his big mansion, muttering about Rosebud. But that is the attitude of so many in power. That's the model of success. That is the end point of the culture we so often promote.

The good news is, I think you can see a potential convergence among the religious impulses that are in the church and the spiritual impulses of a lot of young progressives who say, "Look, you know, I want to preserve the planet. I believe in sustainability. I believe in equality." There is a spiritual dimension to our politics and how we define success, and to our connection to each other and status in our society, that is out there waiting to be tapped, and that's a big part of the work we've got to do to make America feel whole again.

OPPOSITE: The crowd awaits President Obama's arrival at the memorial service for the former South African president Nelson Mandela, in Johannesburg, South Africa, December 10, 2013.

WRESTLING WITH GHOSTS

6

A topic that comes up between Bruce and me all the time is the message American culture sends to boys about what it means to be a man. It's a message that, for all the changes that have taken place in our society, hasn't really changed all that much since we were kids: the emphasis on physical toughness and suppressing your feelings, having success defined mainly by what you own and your ability to dominate rather than by your ability to love and care for others. The tendency to treat women as objects to possess rather than full-fledged partners and fellow citizens.

The more we talked, the more obvious it became how these narrow, distorted ideas of masculinity contributed to so many of the damaging trends we continue to see in the country, whether it is the growing inequality in our economy or our complete unwillingness to compromise on anything in our politics. And maybe, Bruce and I realized, we're more attuned to these issues because of the complicated relationships we both have had with our fathers—flawed role models that we spent much of our lives coming to terms with.

BRUCE SPRINGSTEEN: You know, my dad was the kind of guy who—I can remember one day I brought him a video camera and I said, "Dad, I want you to tell me the story of your life." It lasted for five minutes. . . .

And he said basically nothing. . . . What I know about my father, I know from secondhand information. He came from the Irish side of our family, who were very old-school, very provincial, very religiously active in the Catholic Church. Many generations lived in one home. I've been told he grew up on a farm that was so far outside of Freehold that it was claimed he rode a pony to the school bus—and then the pony knew to go back to the barn.

He quit school at sixteen, went to work in a rug mill as a floor boy, and then went to war shortly after. He was the kind of guy who was sent off to war, and, when he came home, he never budged again. He never had that desire.

He met my mother through our relatives. They were married shortly thereafter, with his only promise being that he'd get an actual job. He worked on the Ford line, took a variety of factory jobs, and was a truck driver and a guard at the Freehold jail for a while. He went through a variety of jobs for the rest of his life, really.

Whatever I ended up knowing about my father was what I observed and a little bit of what my mother told me about him, which was not a lot but contradicted the man that I knew. I got absolutely no information from my grandmother and my grandfather, who were as quiet as he was. I had to make my peace with the fact that I was never going to get to know my father and that was just the way it is.

He was simply an unknowable man with a great penchant for secrecy. And I believe he got this from his father; the only thing I knew about my grandfather was he disappeared for periods of time and returned home.

PRESIDENT OBAMA: And nobody knew where he went?

BRUCE SPRINGSTEEN: No, no, no . . .

PRESIDENT OBAMA: Or what he was doing?

BRUCE SPRINGSTEEN: My father carried on that tradition of secrecy about his own life. Really, when I think about it, my father disappeared for a day a week and he was always on his own, and my mother was at home with us, and I couldn't tell you where he went or what he did during that particular period of time. And it was something that was handed down, and something I had to work hard not to emulate.

OPPOSITE: Bruce Springsteen's father, Douglas, circa 1960. Douglas's presence haunts many of Bruce's songs, including *Darkness on the Edge of Town's* "Adam Raised a Cain": "Daddy worked his whole life for nothing but the pain / Now he walks these empty rooms looking for something to blame / You inherit the sins, you inherit the flames."

PRESIDENT OBAMA: You know, the interesting thing for me was not having my own father in the house. I had a stepfather for a while.

BRUCE SPRINGSTEEN: How long did you have the stepfather?

PRESIDENT OBAMA: I lived with him probably for four years, from the ages of six to ten. And he was a kind man, treated me well, taught me how to box, and then . . .

BRUCE SPRINGSTEEN: What happened to him?

PRESIDENT OBAMA: Well, he's Indonesian. We moved to Indonesia. We lived there for four years. When I'm ten, my mom, who's worried about my education, decides, "Okay, I need to send Barry"—that was my nickname back then—"I need to send him back to Hawaii so he can get an American education." And so I come back to live with my grandparents in the States, and by that time my mother's marriage to my stepfather is already fraying a little bit. They separate amicably. And then he has a liver ailment and dies very young. I remember sobbing when he died.

BRUCE SPRINGSTEEN: Yeah . . .

PRESIDENT OBAMA: Even though . . .

BRUCE SPRINGSTEEN: Well, if you cried when he died—

PRESIDENT OBAMA: Yeah, he had an impact. One of the things about not having a father in the house was also not seeing someone who had a craft or a trade or a profession that looked like something that I should emulate or do.

BRUCE SPRINGSTEEN: How old is your grandfather?

PRESIDENT OBAMA: He's relatively young. I mean, he was probably—because my mom was only eighteen when she had me—he's probably forty-five when I'm born, which means that by the time I'm a teenager he's probably not much older than I am now. Although he looked a whole lot older. And he *lived* a whole lot older, right? Some of that is generational.

BRUCE SPRINGSTEEN: And you're having to look toward a fifty-five-year-old white man—

> ONE OF THE THINGS ABOUT NOT HAVING A FATHER IN THE HOUSE WAS ALSO NOT SEEING SOMEONE WHO HAD A CRAFT OR A TRADE OR A PROFESSION THAT LOOKED LIKE SOMETHING THAT I SHOULD EMULATE OR DO.
>
> —PRESIDENT OBAMA

PRESIDENT OBAMA: I loved him deeply and I still see parts of him in me, but there was nothing in him that made me say, "Oh, that's what I should be." And he was somebody who at the end of the day wasn't satisfied with his life, because he had big dreams that were never really fulfilled. He was the kind of guy that would, when I was ten, sit down on the weekends and draw out the kind of house he would love to build.

And he'd make sort of architectural drawings that he had looked up in some magazine on how to do it, with great detail. But the house never got built.

And my grandmother was a practical one. She had worked her way up from being a clerk to becoming a vice president of the local bank, and ended up being our primary breadwinner in the family, which was, for that generation, a source of resentment.

BRUCE SPRINGSTEEN: Yeah, that was like my mom—

PRESIDENT OBAMA: But it was unspoken. I say all this just because, to get back to what we were talking about earlier, there weren't really any obvious role models out there for me to follow. And the fact that I was in Hawaii, where there were almost no African American men, meant that you really had to piece this thing together on your own.

So now, as a teenager, I'm trying to figure out, "All right, what does this mean, to be a man?" It means you gotta be an athlete. Right? And so basketball becomes my obsession. It means you got to chase girls, successfully or not.

BRUCE SPRINGSTEEN: I'm not doing good so far, but go ahead, keep going.

PRESIDENT OBAMA: Right? You got to do that. How much beer could you consume?

BRUCE SPRINGSTEEN: Oh, man.

OPPOSITE, TOP LEFT: Barack Hussein Obama Sr., during his Harvard years, circa 1963. **OPPOSITE, TOP RIGHT:** Barack Obama with his stepfather, Lolo Soetoro; his mother, Ann; and his sister Maya in Indonesia, circa 1970. **OPPOSITE, BOTTOM:** Bruce Springsteen's mother, Adele, on the job, circa 1958. **FOLLOWING (PAGE 198):** Obama channeling Dr. J, circa 1979. **FOLLOWING (PAGE 199):** Obama as a young man in Indonesia, circa 1980.

PRESIDENT OBAMA: How high could you get? How were you in a scrap?

BRUCE SPRINGSTEEN: Yeah.

PRESIDENT OBAMA: That was what the culture told you was manly. And if you didn't have a father in the house, then a lot of it you're picking up just from popular culture. So you're watching James Bond movies or you're watching, in my case, you're watching *Shaft* and *Super Fly* and, especially, athletes—everyone loves Dr. J. That becomes the model of cool and strength—

BRUCE SPRINGSTEEN: All of those things . . . I mean, if I could've done any of those things you listed, I would never have become a rock star! Never! People in my line of work were people who couldn't do any of those things, so they had to find an alternate route.

PRESIDENT OBAMA: To getting girls—

BRUCE SPRINGSTEEN: To get the girls. To get loaded. To dominate. I mean, the arc of my work life was a little funny because I was at my most popular, I feel, when I had an image that was least like myself.

PRESIDENT OBAMA: I like to think of myself as somebody who has worked through a lot of those issues and now I'm sensitive and in touch with my feelings and, you know, the enlightened male and all that stuff.

BRUCE SPRINGSTEEN: From a distance and from us knowing each other in general, let me say I believe that you are.

PRESIDENT OBAMA: That is what I would like to think, and yet, every so often there will be times when we'll be at the dinner table, or we're playing a board game, and then, you know, alpha behavior comes out, and Michelle will look at me and say, "You are such an . . ."

BRUCE SPRINGSTEEN: "Asshole," you know . . .

PRESIDENT OBAMA: The girls will roll their eyes and say, "You know, you're just such a boy."

BRUCE SPRINGSTEEN: I had a very alpha-male image right in the middle of the Reagan-era eighties.

PRESIDENT OBAMA: The Boss.

BRUCE SPRINGSTEEN: Right. And that view of the United States as something powerful and domineering was resurgent. It's funny how I look and see, in my own way, I pursued that archetype myself. I mean, what's more domineering than coming out in front of a stadium of fifty thousand people—

PRESIDENT OBAMA: With some drums and some smoke.

BRUCE SPRINGSTEEN: It's gladiatorial, all right? It's a gladiatorial experience on some level. So I can't deny that played upon me and that I took satisfaction in it.

PRESIDENT OBAMA: The interesting thing is the degree to which that hasn't changed that much. As women entered the workforce, as they gained a voice and they got more empowered, a lot of what's been driving our politics has been rooted also in this fear: "Am I being emasculated?" You see it in popular culture, and you see it in sort of some of the cultural politics that go around. You saw it, obviously, in Donald Trump. In this caricature of . . .

BRUCE SPRINGSTEEN: Manhood.

PRESIDENT OBAMA: Never apologizing, no weakness, no emotions . . .

ABOVE: Bruce as "alpha-male," 1980. **OPPOSITE:** Like many young men—particularly those without a father in the house—President Obama largely shaped his teenage conception of masculinity around the popular culture of the time. Key influences included the following: *Diamonds Are Forever* (top left) was the last James Bond film to star Sean Connery as the hypermasculine international secret agent also known as 007. Connery played Bond as smooth-talking, arrogant, and promiscuous—and always seeking to outsmart and/or seduce the scantily clad femme fatale counterparts who came to be known as Bond Girls. Ronald Reagan (top right) was the president from 1981 to 1989; his conservative political style and approach to domestic and global affairs defined the decade in numerous ways. An actor before turning to politics as the governor of California, he was seen by many as a symbol of masculinity and manliness. *Shaft* (center) is a 1971 action film directed by Gordon Parks Jr. and starring Richard Roundtree as the suave, sexy Harlem-based private detective John Shaft. It's one of the definitive "Blaxploitation" movies, and is also known for the Grammy-winning soundtrack by Isaac Hayes. *Super Fly* (bottom left), directed by Parks's son, Gordon Parks Jr., came out in 1972 and is considered a Blaxploitation classic. It stars Ron O'Neal as Youngblood Priest, a rich cocaine dealer who lives large in New York City but who wants to get out of the drug business. It featured another iconic soundtrack, this one by Curtis Mayfield. "Dr. J" (bottom right) is the nickname for basketball great Julius Erving, who is widely considered to be one of the greatest players in National Basketball Association and American Basketball Association history. He's especially known for popularizing the "slam dunk."

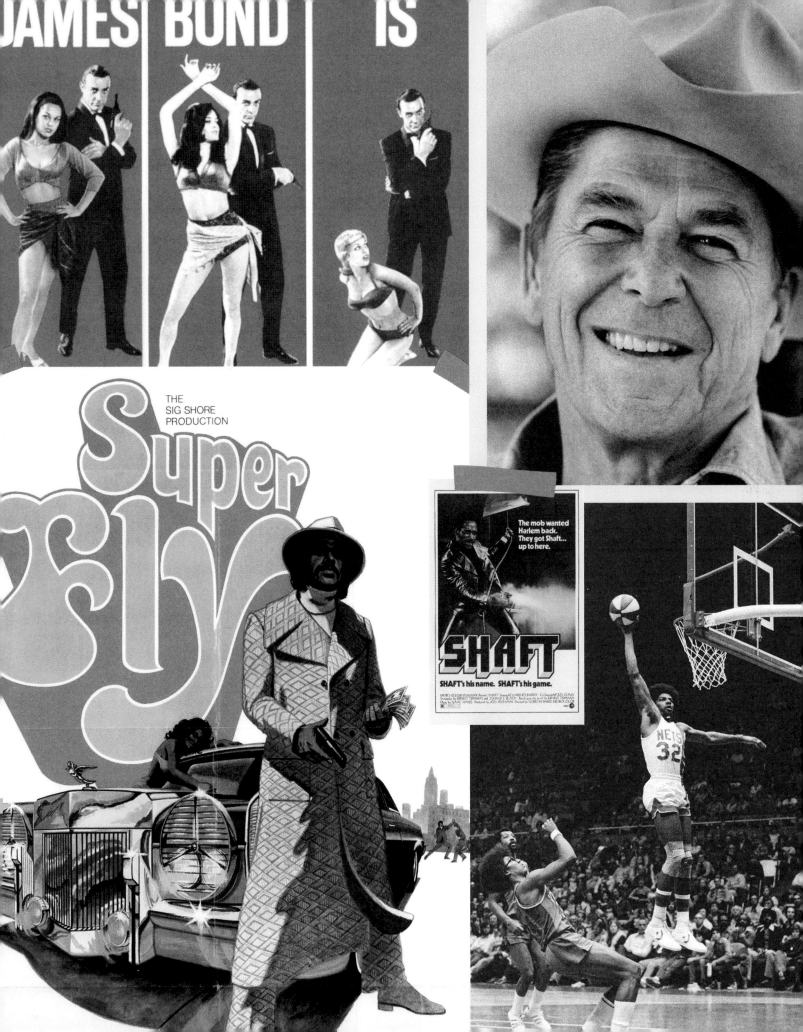

BRUCE SPRINGSTEEN: No transparency. And so you remain isolated and alone, particularly if you're going through painful times.

PRESIDENT OBAMA: You also see it in the statistics around suicide and opioid abuse. And what happened in the African American community as men lost jobs and status with deindustrialization and factories closing. And now you're seeing it happening in working-class white communities, where for the first time you're actually seeing life expectancy decline among a lot of working-class white men. And, you know, there's the loneliness, particularly as we get older. Michelle always points this out, that she can talk for ten hours with her friends; you know, they'll sit there, and they will talk about everything.

And I talk a lot with my male friends, but, after about an hour, I kind of run out of stuff and then we'll turn on a ball game or we'll play a ball game, so there is some activity. But the sort of sustained ability to share and connect—we don't teach our boys to do that.

BRUCE SPRINGSTEEN: From when I was a young man, I lived with a man who suffered that loss of status and I saw it every single day. It was all tied to lack of work, inconsistency working, and I just watched the low self-esteem. That was a part of my daily life living with my father. It taught me one thing: work is essential. That's why if we can't get people working in this country, we're going to have an awful hard time.

PRESIDENT OBAMA: It is. It is central to how people define themselves in the sense of self-worth.

And I think about young men coming up behind me. For all the changes that have happened in America, when it comes to "What does it mean to be a man?" I still see that same confusion, and the same limited measures of manliness today, as I had back then. And that's true, whether you're talking about African American boys or white boys. They don't have rituals, road maps, and initiation rites into a clear sense of a male strength and energy that is positive as opposed to just dominating.

I talk to my daughters' friends about boys growing up, and so much of popular culture tells them that the only clear, defining thing about being a man, about being masculine, is excelling in sports and sexual conquest—

BRUCE SPRINGSTEEN: And violence.

PRESIDENT OBAMA: And violence. Those are the three things. Violence, if it's healthy at least, is subsumed into sports. Later, you add to that definition: making money. How much money can you make?

And there are some qualities of the traditional American male that are absolutely worthy of praise and worthy of emulating. That sense of responsibility, meaning you're willing to do hard things and make some sacrifices for your family or for future generations. The Greatest Generation showed that again and again. And that sense of handling your business, of being an adult.

But there is a bunch of stuff in there that we did not reckon with, which now you're seeing with Me Too, with women still seeking equal pay, with what we're still dealing with in terms of domestic abuse and violence. There was never a full reckoning of who our dads were, what they had in them, how we have to understand that and talk about that. What lessons we should learn from it. All that kind of got buried.

BRUCE SPRINGSTEEN: Yeah, but we sort of ended up being just sixties versions of our dads, carrying all the same sexism.

PRESIDENT OBAMA: Yeah—carrying all the same baggage. All the same anger, all the same pent-up frustrations, all the same messages. And there was one other thing that I know you can relate to: it was, you don't show weakness.

BRUCE SPRINGSTEEN: That's right.

PRESIDENT OBAMA: You don't show emotion, you don't talk too much about how you're feeling—your fears, your doubts, your disappointments. You project a general "I've got this." Everything is under control. I'm fine. I'm not worried.

BRUCE SPRINGSTEEN: Now, I had that tempered by having a father who was pretty seriously mentally ill, and so in high school I began to become very aware of his weaknesses even though, outwardly, he presented as kind of a bullish guy who totally conformed to that standard archetype.

Things went pretty wrong in the last years of high school and in the last years that I lived with him at our house. There was something in his illness or in who he was that involved a tremendous denying of his family ties. And this created

OPPOSITE: On January 21, 2017, the day after the inauguration of Donald Trump, an estimated 7 million people around the world took part in the Women's March. The massive show of resistance was intended to send a message to the new administration that Trump's racist, misogynistic comments and proposed policies were unacceptable. Nearly half a million protesters attended the Women's March on Washington, making it the largest demonstration in the nation's capital since the antiwar marches of the 1960s and '70s.

enormous problems for me as I got older because I couldn't make a family connection.

I always remember him complaining that if he hadn't had a family he would've been able to take a certain job and go on the road. It was a missed opportunity. And he sat there over that six-pack of beers night after night after night after night and that was his answer to it all, you know? So we felt guilt. And that was my entire picture of masculinity until I was way into my thirties, when I began to sort it out myself because I couldn't establish and hold a relationship, I was embarrassed simply having a woman at my side.

I just couldn't find a life with the information that he'd left me, and I was trying to over and over again.

All the early years I was with Patti, if we were in public I was very, very anxious. I could never sort that through, and I realized, "Well, yeah, these are the signals I got when I was very young—that a family doesn't strengthen you, it weakens you. It takes away your opportunity. It takes away your manhood."

PRESIDENT OBAMA: It neuters you.

BRUCE SPRINGSTEEN: Exactly.

PRESIDENT OBAMA: Constrains you.

BRUCE SPRINGSTEEN: And this is what I carried with me for a long, long time. I lived in fear of that neutering, and so that meant I lived without the love, without the companionship, without a home. And you have your little bag of clothes and you get on that road and you just go from one place to the next.

PRESIDENT OBAMA: And you're free.

BRUCE SPRINGSTEEN: You think you are.

PRESIDENT OBAMA: That's the notion.

BRUCE SPRINGSTEEN: Right. You think you are. And I thought I was.

I thought that way for a long time, until I tried to have something beyond what was allowed. Beyond what I was allowing myself. And you don't notice it when you're in your twenties. But, right around thirty, something didn't feel quite right. Did you have to deal with that at all?

PRESIDENT OBAMA: So there's some stuff that's in common and then there's stuff that tracks a little differently. So my father leaves when I'm two. And I don't see him until I'm ten years old, when he comes to visit for a month in Hawaii.

BRUCE SPRINGSTEEN: What brought him to visit you eight years after he left?

PRESIDENT OBAMA: So the story is that my father grows up in a small village in the northwestern corner of Kenya. And he goes from herding goats to getting on a jet plane and flying to Hawaii and traveling to Harvard, and suddenly he's an economist—

BRUCE SPRINGSTEEN: Unbelievable.

PRESIDENT OBAMA: And in that leap from living in a really rural, agricultural society to suddenly trying to pretend he's this sophisticated man-about-town, something was lost. Something slipped. Although he was extraordinarily confident and charismatic and, by all accounts, could sort of run circles around people intellectually, emotionally, he was scarred and damaged in all kinds of ways that I can only retrace from the stories that I heard later, because I didn't really know him. Anyway, when he's a student in Hawaii, he meets my mother. I am conceived. I think the marriage comes after the conception.

But then he gets a scholarship to go to Harvard and he decides, "Well, that's where I need to go." He's willing to have my mother and me go with him, but I think there are cost issues involved and they separate. But they stay in touch. He goes back to Kenya, gets a government job, and he has another marriage and another set of kids.

BRUCE SPRINGSTEEN: When he comes back to visit you, he has another family—

PRESIDENT OBAMA: He's got another family, and I think he and his wife are in a bad spot.

What he's probably coming back for is to see my mother, who still sees him as he was at that point in his life when

everything was a possibility. And I think he was probably trying to court my mother and to convince her to grab me and move all of us to Kenya, and my mother, who still loved him, was wise enough to realize that was probably a bad idea.

But I do see him for a month. And . . . I don't know what to make of him.

Because he's very foreign, right? He's got a British accent and he's got this booming voice and he takes up a lot of space. And everybody kind of defers to him because he's just a big personality. And he's trying to sort of tell me what to do.

He's like, "Anna"—that's what he'd call my mother; her name was Ann—"Anna, I think that boy . . . he's watching too much television. He should be doing his studies." So I wasn't that happy that he had showed up. And I was kind of eager for him to go. Because I had no way to connect to the guy. He's a stranger who's suddenly in our house.

BRUCE SPRINGSTEEN: Right.

PRESIDENT OBAMA: So he leaves. I never see him again. But we write.

When I'm in college I decide, "If I'm going to understand myself better, I need to know him better." So I write to him and I say, "Listen, I'm going to come to Kenya. I'd like to spend some time with you." He says, "Ah, yes. I think that's a very wise decision, you come here." And then I get a phone call, probably about six months before I was planning to go, and he's been killed in a car accident.

But two things that I discovered, or understood, later. The first was just how much influence that one month that he was there had on me, in ways that I didn't realize.

BRUCE SPRINGSTEEN: Amazing . . .

PRESIDENT OBAMA: He actually gave me my first basketball. So I'm suddenly obsessed with basketball. . . . How'd that happen, right? But I remember that the other thing we did together was, he decided to take me to a Dave Brubeck concert.

Now, this is an example of why I didn't have much use for the guy, because, you know, you're a ten-year-old American kid and some guy wants to take you to a jazz concert.

BRUCE SPRINGSTEEN: "Take Five"—you're not going to love—

PRESIDENT OBAMA: "Take Five"! So I'm sitting there and . . . I kind of don't know what I'm doing there.

It's not until later that I look back and say, "Huh." I become one of the few kids in my school who's interested in jazz.

And when I got older my mother would look at how I crossed my legs or gestures and she'd say, "It's kind of spooky."

The second thing that I learned was, in watching his other male children—who I met and got to know later when I traveled to Kenya—I realized that, in some ways, it was probably good that I had not lived in his home. Because, much in the same way that your dad was struggling with a bunch of stuff, my dad was struggling, too. It created chaos and destruction and anger and hurt and long-standing wounds that I just did not have to deal with.

BRUCE SPRINGSTEEN: I think what's fascinating is the impact he had on you in one month. That's in one month.

PRESIDENT OBAMA: Yeah.

BRUCE SPRINGSTEEN: The thing that happens is—when we can't get the love we want from the parent we want it from, how do you create the intimacy you need? I can't get to him and I can't have him. I'll be him. That's what I'll do. I'll be him. . . . I'm way into my thirties before I even have any idea that that's my method of operation. I'm onstage. I'm in workmen's clothes. I've never worked a job in my life.

My dad was a beefy, bulky guy. I've played freaking guitar my whole life, but I've got twenty or thirty extra pounds on me from hitting the gym. Where'd that come from? Why do I spend hours lifting up and putting down heavy things for no particular reason whatsoever? My entire body of work, everything that I've cared about, everything that I've written about, draws from his life story. Not my own. Primarily from his.

I went down a lot of roads that did not lead me where I wanted to be. I don't think I got to where I wanted to be as a man until Patti was in my life and schooled me on some things I needed serious schooling on, you know?

> THE THING THAT HAPPENS IS—WHEN WE CAN'T GET THE LOVE WE WANT FROM THE PARENT WE WANT IT FROM, HOW DO YOU CREATE THE INTIMACY YOU NEED? "I CAN'T GET TO HIM AND I CAN'T HAVE HIM. I'LL BE HIM. THAT'S WHAT I'LL DO. I'LL BE HIM."
>
> —BRUCE SPRINGSTEEN

OPPOSITE: Barack Obama sharing the holiday with his father, Barack Obama Sr., on the latter's only trip to Hawaii during President Obama's childhood, circa 1971.

Here is where I was lucky. At thirty-two, I go into hard-core analysis. I don't have my children until I'm forty, so I'm eight years into looking into a lot of these things, because what I found out about that archetype was it was fucking destructive in my life.

It drove away people I cared about. It kept me from knowing my true self. And I realized, "Well, if you wanna follow this road, go ahead. But you're going to end up on your own, my friend. And if you want to invite some people into your life, you better learn how to do that."

And there's only one way you do that: You've got to open the doors. And that archetype doesn't leave a lot of room for those doors to be open because that archetype is a closed man. Your inner self is forever secretive and unknown—stoic, silent, not revealing of your feelings. Well, you've got to get rid of all of that stuff if you want a partnership. If you want a full family, and to be able to give them the kind of sustenance and nurture and room to grow they need in order to be themselves and find their own full lives, you better be ready to let a lot of that go, my friend.

My dad never really spoke to me through the day he died. He didn't know how. He truly did not. He just didn't have the skills at all. And once I understood how ill he was, it makes up for a lot of it. But when you're a six-year-old or an eight-year-old or a nine-year-old boy, you're not going to have an understanding of what your father is suffering with, and . . .

PRESIDENT OBAMA: You end up wrestling with ghosts.

BRUCE SPRINGSTEEN: I guess that's what we all do.

PRESIDENT OBAMA: And ghosts are tricky because you are measuring yourself against someone who is not there. And, in some cases, I think people whose fathers aren't there—and whose mothers are feeling really bitter about their fathers' not being there—what they absorb is how terrible that guy was and *you don't want to be like that guy.*

In my mother's case, she took a different tack, which was that she only presented his best qualities and not his worst. And in some ways that was beneficial, because I never felt as if I had some flawed inheritance—something in me that would lead me to become an alcoholic or an abusive husband or any

of that. Instead, what happened was I kept on thinking, "Man, I got to live up to this." Every man is trying to live up to his father's expectations or live up to his mistakes.

You know, Michelle wonders sometimes, "Why is it that you just feel so compelled to just do all this hard stuff? I mean, what's this hole in you that just makes you feel so driven?" And I think part of it was kind of early on feeling as if, "Man, I got to live up to this. I got to prove this. Maybe the reason he left is because he didn't think it was worth staying for me, and no, I will show him that he made a mistake not hanging around, because I was worth investing in."

BRUCE SPRINGSTEEN: You're always trying to prove your worth. You're on a lifetime journey of trying to prove your worth to . . .

PRESIDENT OBAMA: Somebody that's not there.

BRUCE SPRINGSTEEN: Somebody that's not there anymore.

PRESIDENT OBAMA: And who may not have been thinking about you, not because of anything to do with you, but because he's confused and he's lost and he's damaged in various ways, right?

BRUCE SPRINGSTEEN: But like you say, we end up wrestling with ghosts. The trick is you have to turn your ghosts into ancestors.

Ghosts haunt you. Ancestors walk alongside you and provide you with comfort and a vision of life that's going to be your own. My father walks alongside me as my ancestor now. It took a long time for that to happen.

> GHOSTS HAUNT YOU. ANCESTORS WALK ALONGSIDE YOU AND PROVIDE YOU WITH COMFORT AND A VISION OF LIFE THAT'S GOING TO BE YOUR OWN. MY FATHER WALKS ALONGSIDE ME AS MY ANCESTOR NOW. IT TOOK A LONG TIME FOR THAT TO HAPPEN.
>
> —BRUCE SPRINGSTEEN

OPPOSITE: Bruce Springsteen, evoking his "beefy and bulky" father in his workingman clothes, 1986. **FOLLOWING:** Bruce and Patti Scialfa, 1986.

My Father's House

Last night I dreamed that I was a child
(back south) out where the pines grow wild + tall
   I was trying to make it home through
      the forest
   before the darkness falls

I heard the wind rustling through the trees
      ghostly voices rose from the fields
I ran with my heart pounding down that
      broken path
   with the (devil) night snapping at my
      heels

   I broke through the trees and there in the
      night
my fathers house stood shining hard and
      bright
   the branches + brambles tore my clothes + scratched
      my arms but I ran until I fell
      shaking in his arms

   I awoke from my dream sir and I did ride
from out on the road I could see the house standing giving off light
   A woman I didn't recognize came + spoke to
      me through A chained door
she said I'm sorry son but no one by that
      name lives here any more

my fathers house shines hard + bright
   it stands like a beacon calling me in the night
calling + calling so cold and alone
      but no matter
shining cross this dark highway where our sins lie unatoned

Last night I dreamed that I was a child out where the pines grow wild and tall / I was trying to make it home through the forest before the darkness falls / I heard the wind rustling through the trees and ghostly voices rose from the fields / I ran with my heart pounding down that broken path / With the devil snappin' at my heels / I broke through the trees, and there in the night / My father's house stood shining hard and bright the branches and brambles tore my clothes and scratched my arms / But I ran till I fell, shaking in his arms / I awoke and I imagined the hard things that pulled us apart / Will never again, sir, tear us from each other's hearts / I got dressed, and to that house I did ride from out on the road, I could see its windows shining in light / I walked up the steps and stood on the porch a woman I didn't recognize came and spoke to me through a chained door / I told her my story, and who I'd come for / She said "I'm sorry, son, but no one by that name lives here anymore" / My father's house shines hard and bright it stands like a beacon calling me in the night / Calling and calling, so cold and alone / Shining 'cross this dark highway where our sins lie unatoned

—FROM NEBRASKA (1982)

A FEARLESS
LOVE

7

For all of our outward success, Bruce and I both agree that the most important anchor over the years has been our families. We were lucky enough to find remarkable, strong, independent women to push us and challenge us and ground us—and to call us out on our BS. Women who helped us become better versions of ourselves and forced us to continually reexamine our priorities.

Michelle and Patti also gave us the single greatest gift of our lives: the chance to be fathers. To experience the joys and trials and profound humility of being husbands and dads. We spent some time trading notes about what wives and kids continue to teach us, what values we want to pass on, what examples we want to set, and what kind of country we want to leave behind for them to inherit.

PRESIDENT OBAMA: We're now dads.

BRUCE SPRINGSTEEN: Oh yeah.

PRESIDENT OBAMA: And how did that change you? How much on-the-job training did you still have to do?

BRUCE SPRINGSTEEN: Oof.

PRESIDENT OBAMA: Was there still a lot of stuff you had to work out before you got to the point where you said, "All right, this is the kind of dad I want to be"?

BRUCE SPRINGSTEEN: The problem was I didn't trust myself with someone else's feelings for a long, long, long time. All you have is faith to go on, that if you take a baby step, you'll be able to take another one. Where does that faith come from? It comes out of the love in your life.

In my case, Patti was an enormous source of love in my life. She had more emotional bravery than I did, which gave me the faith to risk parts of myself that I'd never risked before and say, "Hey, I think I'm at a place where I can hold this down and let the chips fall where they may. If it all crumbles and comes apart and winds up in ruin, then that's what happens. But what if it doesn't? Then what am I going to do? What if suddenly I find myself with a family and with a long-standing love? Who am I then?"

All of these things came into question way before being a dad. Patti and I were together and we were just loving each other. That was our business of the day: to build something. I'm thirty-five, thirty-six years old. That's getting up there, you know? And deep inside I wanted to have a family, and I felt like I had to be honest with her. I said, "Patti, I don't know if I can make this." And she said, "Well, we'll see. It's okay if we take it a day at a time." And so we did.

Then I came home one night. I think I had been away for a few days. And I walked in the room, and she said, "Oh! By the way, I'm pregnant. . . ."

PRESIDENT OBAMA: Crickets.

BRUCE SPRINGSTEEN: Crickets. That's what it sounded like. And we're on the bed. I look away and she doesn't know exactly how I'm going to respond, but there's a mirror on the inside of the door and she says, "Hey, I just saw you smile." That was it! Many smiles later, here we sit. My boy about to be thirty years old.

PRESIDENT OBAMA: It moves, man.

BRUCE SPRINGSTEEN: Yeah . . . Your oldest—how old is she?

OPPOSITE: Patti Scialfa has been a member of the E Street Band since 1984. She and Bruce Springsteen married in 1991 and are seen here on their honeymoon.

PRESIDENT OBAMA: Malia is . . . Malia is twenty-two.

BRUCE SPRINGSTEEN: Twenty-two . . .

PRESIDENT OBAMA: Sasha is nineteen. So I meet Michelle while I am working at a law firm for the summer. She's already a lawyer. She's younger but had gone straight through school. I'd taken my diversion into community organizing after college so I'm an older law student. I'm twenty-eight. She's twenty-five. And she comes from a completely orderly family and they had a big extended family beyond that.

Michelle and I always talk about how part of the attraction that we had for each other, in addition to her being very attractive, and funny and smart as a whip, was that in me she saw some things that had been missing in her childhood: adventure, the open road . . .

BRUCE SPRINGSTEEN: Right.

PRESIDENT OBAMA: A bunch of risk taking, traveling the world—that appealed to her. I looked at her and her family and I thought, "Oh, you know, well, they seem to know how to set this up." I had a vision of wanting to make sure that my kids were in a place of love and I liked the idea of not necessarily a big family, but an extended family. Like there was a community of people who were all part of their lives. And Michelle's family was very much like that.

That very first summer that we were together, I thought to myself, "This is somebody I could see spending my life with." And Michelle, she wasn't shy. You know, pretty early on she just says, "Look, I really value my career but the thing I really want to be is a mom, and I really care deeply about family." And so when I graduate from law school, I come back to Chicago and live in her apartment, which is upstairs from her parents' apartment. Her father had died in the interim. He had some health issues. I had flown back and been with her during that time. And I think, from her perspective, she maybe saw that I'm not a guy who was going to be afraid to be there for her when she needed it.

And look, once you come back to a city and you've moved into *her* place, the clock has to be ticking, because—

BRUCE SPRINGSTEEN: You were there.

PRESIDENT OBAMA: Right, it's like, "What are you doing here?" And I did not have a big panic about it, even though part of me—and this goes back to our earlier conversation about being a man—remembered growing up in a culture that said, in comedies, in television, in popular culture, "Man, they're gonna get"—

BRUCE SPRINGSTEEN: Of course.

PRESIDENT OBAMA: "They got their hooks in yet?"

BRUCE SPRINGSTEEN: That's right.

PRESIDENT OBAMA: "You gotta try to wriggle free"—

BRUCE SPRINGSTEEN: I'm surprised you didn't have a bigger issue with that, given your familial history. I really am.

PRESIDENT OBAMA: Well, maybe it actually has something to do with our relationships to our mothers? Maybe we're attracted to, and want to interact with, somebody who's not going to back down and not going to put up with our stuff?

But, you tell me: What do you think led us down this challenging and ultimately fulfilling path of being with strong women?

BRUCE SPRINGSTEEN: I think we're people that needed boundaries. Previous to my relationship with Patti, I felt adrift. I had a sense of the values that would make a good family life. But I had no emotional mechanics whatsoever as to how to put those things into place. And also, as we talked about earlier, I'd been taught that family life was emasculating. That being with a woman was embarrassing. It made you look weak.

PRESIDENT OBAMA: If you needed a woman?

BRUCE SPRINGSTEEN: That's right, if you needed a woman, you were weak. Family was restrictive to your male freedoms. I

OPPOSITE, TOP: Michelle Robinson, photographed by Barack Obama in Lamu, Kenya, on their first trip to Africa together, circa 1991. OPPOSITE, BOTTOM: Patti Scialfa, circa 1970. ABOVE: Bruce and Patti, circa 1992. FOLLOWING (PAGE 222): Patti in a quiet moment at the Meadowlands, East Rutherford, NJ, September 1986. FOLLOWING (PAGE 223): Michelle in the second-floor apartment she and Obama shared in her parents' house on Euclid Avenue in Chicago, circa 1990.

believed all of these things, and I carried them with me like a tremendous fear. Terrified of the kind of connections that you need to build a family life. And so, consequently, I was destructive in every relationship that I had until I got with Patti. And there was something in Patti's intelligence, insight, power, womanliness, that drained some of that fear out of me. It gave me confidence that I suddenly had a partner I could lean on and who I could express those fears to.

PRESIDENT OBAMA: There's also something that you have to remind yourself when it comes to settling down with a strong, challenging woman—the kind of woman I was attracted to. If you're living with them all the time, and you've got to make decisions about career and family, there's a lot of negotiation that happens on a daily basis.

And what I had to get comfortable with was the fact that, yeah, you know what? I'm alpha and I'm pretty stubborn. Well, that person I'm living with? She's got some strong opinions and she's accustomed to making decisions and owning the room. And so, now, everything becomes contested.

I find that if you are not comfortable with that, it also means there are going to be some periods where you're butting heads. Your partner may have a temper and they're not going to automatically give in to smooth things over when things get tense. And I've had a bunch of friends who just at a certain point say, "You know what, I feel threatened by being challenged all the time."

And oftentimes, those friends have separated, and they've moved on to something that they have decided is easier and more comfortable and doesn't force them into too many changes. The assumption is that the woman is going to adapt to them and what they want and what they need. With Michelle, she's certainly accommodated and made changes to stick around with me, but she's also said, "Buster, there's some changes you're going to have to make, too."

And there's a mutuality there—and there always has been. I've never been under any illusions that my family life would be one in which I could sit back and just be the lord of the manor and have my wife doting on me and fixing my meals. That just was not going to be an option.

BRUCE SPRINGSTEEN: Yeah, from the top I knew that wasn't going to happen with Patti. . . . She was trying to define a broader sense of maleness and of masculinity for me—a freer sense of

it. And that scared me. I'd met someone who could change me, and who could assist me in changing myself—that's a great influence to allow into your life. But you realize that if you don't, you are not going to have a full life, you know?

PRESIDENT OBAMA: Thinking back to my mother and my grandmother again, maybe it was because they were who I relied on most and respected most that it was natural for me to see women as my equals, as my friends, as my partners in work or play. It also meant that in the kind of relationship where a woman just batted her eyes at me and told me how wonderful I was, I'd get bored.

That certainly wasn't who my grandmother was and that wasn't who my mother was. I expected to be challenged. I expected to be questioned. And the women I found most interesting, and most attractive, were women who interested me because of how they thought. I'm not saying I wasn't paying attention to how they looked, but their ability to make me laugh, their ability to make me see something I hadn't seen before, their ability to force me into asking questions about who I was and what I wanted, what I expected—all that was something I naturally gravitated toward. And I don't know . . . I liked the idea of having something kind of hard.

BRUCE SPRINGSTEEN: Hey, very similar to my redheaded gal here.

PRESIDENT OBAMA: Yeah, absolutely.

BRUCE SPRINGSTEEN: Patti went with a lot of guys . . . and she left a lot of broken hearts in her trail—

PRESIDENT OBAMA: A lot of broken hearts out there . . .

BRUCE SPRINGSTEEN: And I said, "Damn, she's living like I live." She was a musician, so she had a lot of the same characteristics that I had. She was pretty independent and used to living on her own. She didn't like to get tied down. And I found that attractive about her. I found that "You know what? I need somebody with that kind of power."

ABOVE: Patti Scialfa and Bruce Springsteen onstage on the Born in the U.S.A. tour, circa 1985. **OPPOSITE:** President and Michelle Obama enjoy a little dancing as the Harry Connick Jr. Big Band performs in the East Room of the White House at the Governors Ball, February 21, 2010. **FOLLOWING:** Sharing a backstage moment, Fort Monmouth, Oceanport, NJ, 1999.

PRESIDENT OBAMA: This is somebody who is my equal and who I am always going to think highly of. And even when I'm mad, even when we're in an argument, I'm going to say, "Yeah, but she's something."

BRUCE SPRINGSTEEN: Period.

PRESIDENT OBAMA: Period. Full stop. Because, to me at least, if you don't have that, then you won't weather the storms. If you're going to have a family, you have to choose a partner who you're confident is going to pass on strength and values and common sense and smarts to your kids.

And when I looked at Michelle I could say she was sui generis. I didn't know anybody like her. I thought, even if the marriage didn't work out, I would always admire and respect her, and I would never regret having been with her. So I asked her to marry me that summer when I had moved in. And—

BRUCE SPRINGSTEEN: And how old were you then?

PRESIDENT OBAMA: I was twenty-nine. And so then we had this nice stretch of about three years where she was doing her thing in her career, I was doing mine.

And then we started trying to have kids. Took a while. Michelle had a miscarriage, and we had to kind of work at it. And, when Malia was finally born, we were more than ready to be parents, right?

Because there had been this six-year stretch in which, probably for about half of it, we'd been trying, so there was no surprise to it. There was no "Are you sure?" I had no doubt the minute I saw that little creature. . . .

BRUCE SPRINGSTEEN: Oh, man.

PRESIDENT OBAMA: With those big eyes looking up at me, I said, "My goodness. I will do anything for you."

BRUCE SPRINGSTEEN: I know.

PRESIDENT OBAMA: And when the second one came, when Sasha showed up, I felt the exact same way, and the love of being a father was not something I had to work on—

BRUCE SPRINGSTEEN: Oh, no, that's implicit.

PRESIDENT OBAMA: It was physical, it was emotional, spiritual. The attachment to my children I felt entirely and completely. And I thought to myself, "Okay. If the baseline is unconditional love, I've got that."

BRUCE SPRINGSTEEN: We had an incident where Patti was a few months' pregnant. She had some bleeding. So we go to the doctor's office. I'm standing there and suddenly I realize, "There isn't anything I wouldn't do in the world right now." If somebody says there's a lion in the hall, or there's a bear, can you please go and get him out of the building right now . . . there was nothing I wouldn't have done to have Patti and the baby be all right. It was . . .

PRESIDENT OBAMA: Visceral.

BRUCE SPRINGSTEEN: It was *visceral*. And it was my first acquaintance with unconditional love. I felt a fearless love for the first time in my life. First time in my *life*. I never knew I'd be capable of even feeling that. And all I wanted to do was be the man that my wife and my son need.

PRESIDENT OBAMA: You just didn't want to disappoint them. The idea of disappointing your family and not being there and doing right was something you just couldn't—and I couldn't—abide.

BRUCE SPRINGSTEEN: And I think that was the question: "Am I capable of not disappointing?"

I wasn't sure. You're never completely sure, I suppose. . . .

PRESIDENT OBAMA: Right.

BRUCE SPRINGSTEEN: But after the children are born and you start to find the resources that you have inside you that you didn't know were there, that is a gift you get from your children and from your wife. Your acknowledgment of a new self, and the realization of your manhood—it was huge. I woke up. I felt like someone—not necessarily someone different, but someone so much farther down the road than I thought maybe I'd ever get.

> IT WAS PHYSICAL,
> IT WAS EMOTIONAL,
> SPIRITUAL. THE
> ATTACHMENT TO
> MY CHILDREN I
> FELT ENTIRELY AND
> COMPLETELY.
>
> —PRESIDENT OBAMA

OPPOSITE, TOP: Wedding day, enjoying the reception at the South Shore Cultural Center, Chicago, IL, October 3, 1992. **OPPOSITE, BOTTOM:** Michelle and Barack Obama, prior to his keynote address at the 2004 Democratic National Convention, Boston, MA, July 27, 2004.

PRESIDENT OBAMA: This is one place where I do think the idea of what it means to be a man changed in a real way. By the time I had Malia, it wasn't just that I was completely absorbed and fascinated and in love with this bundle of joy and this woman who had gone through everything to give me this joy. There was I think a sense that a dad should want to spend time with their kids and should want to burp them and change diapers—

BRUCE SPRINGSTEEN: Mmm-hmm. Ideally.

PRESIDENT OBAMA: And I took the night shift.

BRUCE SPRINGSTEEN: So did I.

PRESIDENT OBAMA: Because I was the night owl.

BRUCE SPRINGSTEEN: So was I.

PRESIDENT OBAMA: And there'd be some breast milk in the freezer. I had a set of instructions and at midnight, and at two o'clock in the morning, I'd be patting them on the back and feeding them and—

BRUCE SPRINGSTEEN: I loved all of that—

PRESIDENT OBAMA: And putting them on my lap, and they're staring up at me and I'm reading to them and talking to them and playing music for them.

And I think the joys of that were something that was taboo, in the same way that, for a long time, men couldn't see the delivery, right?

BRUCE SPRINGSTEEN: Yeah, they wouldn't let you in.

PRESIDENT OBAMA: I completely loved that part of life, and the timing was good because Malia was a Fourth of July baby.

BRUCE SPRINGSTEEN: Wow.

PRESIDENT OBAMA: I was in the state legislature at that time. The state legislature was out. I was also teaching law at the time. The law school was out. I could put my law practice on hold. So I just had all this time to just wallow in it.

And then Sasha was born. She was a summer baby, same kind of thing.

Now, here's the one thing I had to wrestle with and Michelle challenged me with. The challenge of fatherhood for *me* was that my work, by nature, was exhausting, all-absorbing, and often took me out of town.

The emotional investment in fatherhood was never hard for me; there's nothing I enjoyed more than just hanging out with my kids. Listening to them as they got older and started having their own little insights and the discovery of the world—the reacquaintance with wonder that they provide. Looking at a leaf, or a snail, or asking questions about why this and why that—all that stuff. Loved children's books, loved children's movies. I was all in. The only thing I didn't love, you know, was children's pizza, those little flat cheese pizzas that don't have anything on them.

But what I was going to say, though, is eventually it wasn't summer. And eventually, I've got to go down to Springfield, Illinois, a three-hour drive, for the state legislature. And, when I get back, I've got town hall meetings I've got to do. And then eventually I'm running for office and then I'm gone for five days at a time. And, from Michelle's perspective, family was not just a matter of love or just a matter of being present when you are there. It was a matter of *physically* being present because you've made choices and organized your life so that you can be with your family more.

BRUCE SPRINGSTEEN: Right. So you had your children young in your work life.

PRESIDENT OBAMA: Yeah.

BRUCE SPRINGSTEEN: All right, I had my children relatively late in my work life.

PRESIDENT OBAMA: You were sufficiently well established that you could set your own terms. You'd be like, "If I don't want to tour right now, I don't have to tour."

BRUCE SPRINGSTEEN: Absolutely. I had already gone to the top of the hill and over the other side. I'd had a certain kind of

ABOVE: Parents on the campaign trail, circa 2004. **OPPOSITE, TOP:** President Barack Obama talks on the phone with President Lee Myung-bak of South Korea in the Treaty Room Office, November 23, 2010—one of many late nights spent in the White House. **OPPOSITE, BOTTOM:** Bruce Springsteen working the bedtime bath shift. **FOLLOWING:** According to President Obama, "The emotional investment in fatherhood was never hard for me; there's nothing I enjoyed more than just hanging out with my kids." Here, Bruce Springsteen and Obama share some happy memories of their years as young dads.

success I wasn't going to have again, and didn't expect to have again, so I wasn't pursuing it again. I was happy now. I'd wanted to be a working, playing musician, and I had all that out of the way *really* before Patti and I got together.

PRESIDENT OBAMA: That's interesting. Yeah, that makes sense.

BRUCE SPRINGSTEEN: So I was at a point in my life where the relationship and the family had really become a priority and I could give myself to it because of where I was. And also, I'm a musician. Musicians create their own schedule if they've had a certain amount of success.

You get up when you want to. You go in the studio when you want to. You put your record out when you want to. You go where you want to go. You come home when you want to. You can say, "I'm going to go away for three days, I'm going to go away for three months." But you realize, "When I go away for three months, it's *bad* when I come back. When I go away for three days, it's okay when I come back. I better start going away for three days!"

PRESIDENT OBAMA: It's the better choice.

BRUCE SPRINGSTEEN: We figured out things like "Well, whenever you're away for more than three weeks, that's bad." Now, for a touring musician, that's not much. But all we knew was that when we passed a certain point it wasn't good for our relationship. We started splitting into other and separate lives.

Anything that's going to keep and add to my stability, I want as a part of my life. The things that are destabilizing my life, I don't want those now because they will poison me and they will poison my beautiful love. And so we slowly figured all this out together, which included making some mistakes. . . . Because you're king on the road. Everybody just wants to say "Yes!"

PRESIDENT OBAMA: And you're not king at home—

BRUCE SPRINGSTEEN: Right. On the road it's "How can I do this for you?" "What can I do to make you happier?" "What can I give?" It's "My house! Here, take my house!" "My girl! Take my girlfriend!" Everybody's just like, "What can I possibly give to you, the man who writes the songs that the whole world sings?" So you're out there and you're going, "Eh, this isn't so bad. . . ." I mean, it's what you know.

But when you come back, you are not king. . . . You are the chauffeur! You are the short-order cook in the morning. And the thing is, you've got to be at the place in your life where you love it.

PRESIDENT OBAMA: What you're saying about your schedule, though, and where you were in your career, that is a difference. Because essentially Michelle and I have kids and within the span of two or three years I am suddenly being catapulted. I mean, look, when I ran for the US Senate, Sasha was only three years old.

BRUCE SPRINGSTEEN: Wow.

PRESIDENT OBAMA: When I'm sworn in as a US senator, Sasha is three and Malia is six. Four years later, I'm president of the United States, and in the interim for a year and a half I've been on the road not for three-week spans but for big chunks of time.

And it was hard. The burden I put on Michelle was enormous. It wasn't as if I was working for money that would allow her to take a break. She was still working, initially full-time and then part-time, when I started running for president. Here's this smart and accomplished woman who has her own career that she now has to adjust to my crazy ambitions.

And I'm missing the girls terribly. The first six months of me running for president I was *miserable*. And we got through that only by virtue of Michelle's heroic ability to manage everything back home and the incredible gift of my daughters' loving their daddy anyway.

What I didn't anticipate was that I would get to spend much more time with my kids once I was president. Because, now, I'm living above the store.

BRUCE SPRINGSTEEN: That's right!

PRESIDENT OBAMA: I have a thirty-second commute. And so I just set up a rule: I'm having dinner with my crew at six thirty every night unless I'm traveling. And my travel schedule is very different now because people come to see me. So, unless I'm overseas, I'm going to be home at six thirty for dinner.

OPPOSITE: Winter in New Jersey, circa 1993. **ABOVE:** President Obama and Michelle Obama share a moment on the road. **FOLLOWING:** Scenes from the campaign trail, 2008.

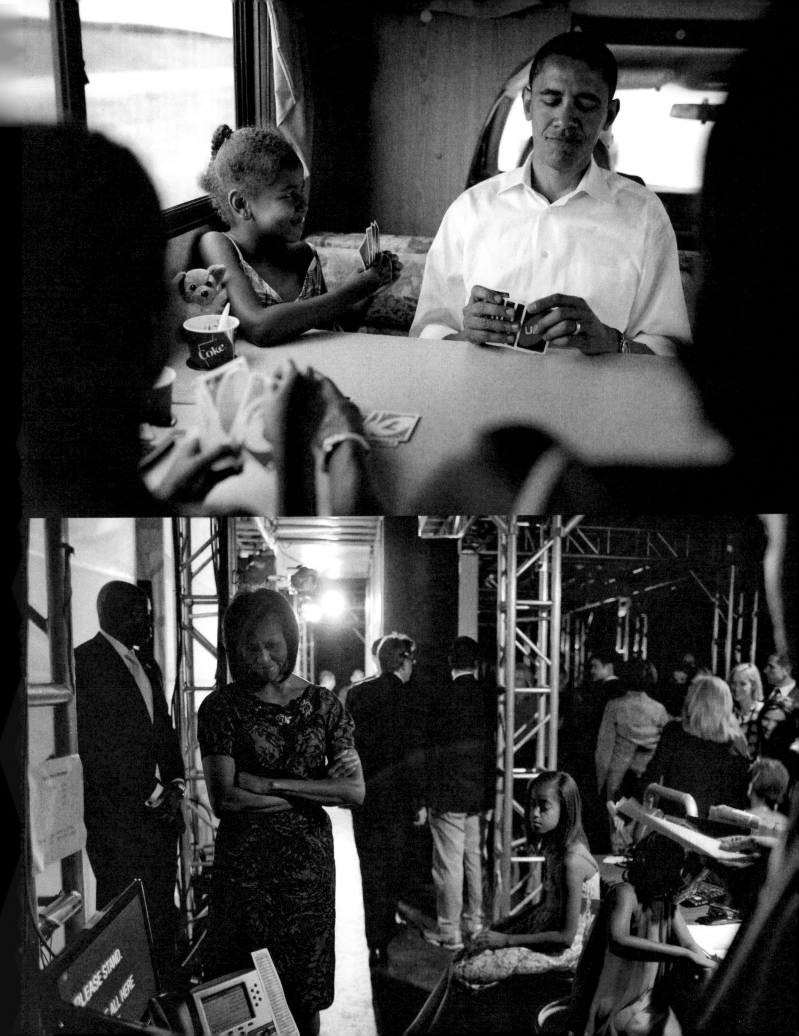

And I'm going to be sitting there and I'm going to be entirely absorbed with stories about the annoying boys and the weird teacher and the drama in the cafeteria, and then I'm going to read Harry Potter and tuck them in and listen to whatever music they're now listening to. And that actually was my lifeline in an occupation in which I'm dealing daily with mayhem, chaos, crisis, death, destruction, natural disasters. . . .

BRUCE SPRINGSTEEN: God bless . . .

PRESIDENT OBAMA: And so I always say that the degree to which Michelle and those girls sacrificed and lifted me up kept me going and prevented me from either getting cynical or despairing. It reminded me why I was doing what I was doing and spurred me on, because this job, this work, what I'd accomplished—it needed to be worth the time that I'd spent away from them, the birthday parties or the soccer games or whatever it was that I'd missed. It better count.

BRUCE SPRINGSTEEN: I know it was tough being president, but let me explain to you how hard it is making an album.

PRESIDENT OBAMA: Making an album is pretty hard.

BRUCE SPRINGSTEEN: I'm making a dumb joke.

PRESIDENT OBAMA: Listen, making an album—

BRUCE SPRINGSTEEN: I had you for a minute, though. I had you going for a minute!

PRESIDENT OBAMA: Making an album is pretty hard! But it does seem a little more fun sometimes.

BRUCE SPRINGSTEEN: I think so.

PRESIDENT OBAMA: But let me ask you this: What do you think you learned just from being a dad?

BRUCE SPRINGSTEEN: The hardest thing that I had to learn how to do was to be still. I had some habits I wouldn't give up. Old musician habits. Partly it was the schedule I liked to keep. I liked to stay up till three or four in the morning, get up at twelve in the afternoon.

And for the first several years of our children, Patti was kind of letting me do it. The kids were still babies and I was taking the night shift—

PRESIDENT OBAMA: Right.

BRUCE SPRINGSTEEN: If they cried at night or something happened at night, I was awake. And so when the late morning came around, she kind of picked up from me. But as the kids grew older, there was a lot more morning work than there was night work.

And she just came over to me and she said, "You know, you don't have to get up. But if you don't, you're going to miss it."

I said, "What do you mean?"

"Well, the kids are at their best in the morning, that's when they're their most beautiful. It's when they have reawakened from a night of dreams. They're at their most gorgeous at that moment in the morning and you're never gonna see it."

"Okay," I'm thinking, "I don't want to miss that." So I said, "What am I going to do?" She said, "You're going to make breakfast." I said, "I don't know how to do anything. I only know how to strum that freaking box. Try to put me anyplace else and I'm no good to anybody." She said, "Well, you're gonna learn." I got pretty good at it. I got pretty good at eggs. I became a pretty good short-order cook. I could get a job at any diner from, say, from six to noon, and I'd be all right.

And she was right about the children. If I saw them in the morning, it was almost like I had seen them for the entire day. And if I missed them in the morning, you could never quite make up for it for some reason. That was being present.

I learned, one, I was not my father. I didn't have to chase that ghost or worry about that anymore. That was a part of my past. And, two, be present in this world wherever you are at any given moment. Be present in their lives. Because I used to think, if somebody interrupted me while I was writing, "What the— Holy smokes! Do you know the great thoughts I'm thinking right now?"

BRUCE SPRINGSTEEN

TUNNEL OF LOVE

Well it's Saturday night / you're all dressed up in blue / I been watching you awhile / maybe you been watching me too / So somebody ran out / left somebody's heart in a mess / Well if you're looking for love / honey I'm tougher than the rest / Some girls they want a handsome Dan / or some good-lookin' Joe on their arm / Some girls like a sweet-talkin' Romeo / Well 'round here baby / I learned you get what you can get / So if you're rough enough for love / honey I'm tougher than the rest / The road is dark / and it's a thin thin line / But I want you to know I'll walk it for you any time / Maybe your other boyfriends / couldn't pass the test / Well if you're rough and ready for love / honey I'm tougher than the rest / Well it ain't no secret / I've been around a time or two / Well I don't know baby maybe you've been around too / Well there's another dance / all you gotta do is say yes / And if you're rough and ready for love / honey I'm tougher than the rest / If you're rough enough for love / baby I'm tougher than the rest

—FROM <u>TUNNEL OF LOVE</u> (1987)

PRESIDENT OBAMA: "This might've been the greatest American song ever. . . ."

BRUCE SPRINGSTEEN: It could've been!

PRESIDENT OBAMA: "Had you not walked in here."

BRUCE SPRINGSTEEN: That's where I started, all right? And where I ended up was I realized, "Oh, wait. . . . A good song is there forever. Music is there in my life forever. Children—gone."

PRESIDENT OBAMA: They grow up.

BRUCE SPRINGSTEEN: So those were the initial things I picked up from fatherhood. What about yourself? What's the biggest lesson you learned from becoming a parent?

PRESIDENT OBAMA: You know, Michelle figured out much earlier than I did that kids are like plants. They need sun, soil, water, but some of them are oaks, some of them are pines, some of them are willows, and some are bamboo, and those seeds of who they are and the pace and ways in which they're gonna unfold are just uniquely theirs. I think I had a notion with Malia and Sasha that there was sort of a way of doing things, and what Michelle understood earlier than I did, but I also ended up learning, was each one is just magical in their own ways. A branch is going to sprout when it's going to sprout. And a flower is going to pop when it's going to pop.

And you just roll with that unfolding, that unfurling of who they are, by being comfortable discovering them, as opposed to feeling as if they're a project. There's a term now—*helicopter parents* approach parenting the way I would approach some PowerPoint: "I've got to check every box, and this is when my kid has to be doing this, and this is when they . . ." They're thinking of it in terms of just throw a bunch of stuff at them, instead of be with them, play with them, teach them values.

We were good about saying to the girls things like "We're not going to sweat you on your grades, but we are going to sweat you on, did you put in some effort? We're not going to give you a hard time about making a mistake, but we will give you a hard time if you're lying about making a mistake, or if you mistreated somebody." So we put some guardrails around them in terms of values, but otherwise—and I think this was

particularly important because they were growing up in the White House—they had more than enough expectations and eyeballs on them.

BRUCE SPRINGSTEEN: Jesus.

PRESIDENT OBAMA: You know, Secret Service following them around—

BRUCE SPRINGSTEEN: Oh my god. At that age, too.

PRESIDENT OBAMA: I mean, I remember when Malia or Sasha would have a playdate, Secret Service had to go to the house of the person they were visiting and check everything out—and the poor parents, you know. So we'd have to make friends with the parents and say, "Listen, sorry about the intrusion." And when they went to the mall or to the movies, they've got somebody walking behind them—

BRUCE SPRINGSTEEN: They handled it with such grace.

PRESIDENT OBAMA: They did! And so, given all that, the last thing I wanted to do was to make them feel as if they had to be something as opposed to just being themselves. And I see that sense of certainty in Malia and Sasha—that in their relationships they're not going to make themselves small or dim their light because they are worried that the guy can't handle it. Their attitude is like, "Yeah, this is me. And if you can't handle it, then we can move on."

In our society, too often it's the woman who's expected to just make the accommodations. And one of the things that I tell younger friends of mine who are looking for relationship advice is "Look, it may be more work to be with a strong, accomplished, opinionated woman who doesn't see herself just as an appendage of you, but who has her own ambitions and dreams. But man, when I see my daughters now, knowing that they've had that role model, that they are their own women and strong and independent, that they will never allow themselves to be in a position where they are being taken advantage of, because that's just not how they view themselves as women—that makes it worth it."

> MICHELLE FIGURED OUT MUCH EARLIER THAN I DID THAT KIDS ARE LIKE PLANTS. THEY NEED SUN, SOIL, WATER, BUT SOME OF THEM ARE OAKS, SOME OF THEM ARE PINES, SOME OF THEM ARE WILLOWS, AND SOME ARE BAMBOO, AND THOSE SEEDS OF WHO THEY ARE AND THE PACE AND WAYS IN WHICH THEY'RE GONNA UNFOLD ARE JUST UNIQUELY THEIRS.
>
> **—PRESIDENT OBAMA**

And it's interesting—I learned part of what I needed to do with Michelle to make our relationship work once I started watching Malia and Sasha grow up, because they're watching you all the time. They're seeing, how are you treating Mom? How are you behaving in the house? Are you leaving it to her to do chores or are you doing chores? Are you respecting her time, or are you just kind of doing your own thing so that she has to adjust to you?

But sometimes, when I measure myself as a husband and a father, I find I still fall back on a lot of those attitudes about what does it mean to be a man. And if I'd had a son, I suspect I would have been tougher on him in some ways.

I'm wondering for you with your boys, how conscious you had to be of the difference.

BRUCE SPRINGSTEEN: You know, I'd learn the great word in my house growing up was *no*. "We don't go outside of our comfort zone. We don't talk about our feelings in this way. We don't cry over these things." And I realized, when my oldest son was very young, that I had taught him to say no to the things that he needed. And I remember going into his room one day—he might have been eight or nine, but he was still pretty young—and saying, "Evan, I think I've taught you a very bad lesson, and I would like to apologize to you for doing that. I think I've taught you to not need me because I've been afraid of what that meant as your father. I need to tell you I need you. I need you so badly in my life, so, so dearly as my son . . . that I would like to try to connect with you in a way that I haven't been doing." And I realized that was gonna take a lot of work.

And so when I was working, instead of thinking, "Oh, I'm so busy now thinking great thoughts, I don't want to be disturbed," I stopped anytime he or any of the children came into my room. I stopped working. The only way to teach them that *no* wasn't the answer was for me to start saying, "Yes. Yes. Yes. Yes. Yes." Over and over and over again.

PREVIOUS (PAGE 244): The Springsteens hit the road, circa 2003. PREVIOUS (PAGE 245, TOP): The Springsteens, circa 2005. PREVIOUS (PAGE 245, BOTTOM): The Springsteens and the Obamas share a moment onstage at a campaign rally, Cleveland, 2008. OPPOSITE, TOP: The Obama family, 2019. OPPOSITE, BOTTOM: The Springsteen family on the red carpet at the seventy-second annual Tony Awards, June 12, 2018.

THE
RISING

As Bruce and I talked, we found ourselves circling back to where we started, asking ourselves: What will it take to restore faith in America's promise? How do we tell a new, unifying story about the country that is true to our highest ideals while at the same time giving an honest accounting of where we fall short?

It's not an easy thing to do in these cynical times, especially when we've got a thousand different media outlets and internet platforms that have figured out you can make lots of money fanning people's anger and resentment.

Somehow, though, in some kind of way, we both believe that such a story is still there to be told and that folks across the country are hungry for it. We are convinced that, for all our disagreements, most of us long for a more just and compassionate America. An America where *everybody* belongs. We started exploring that spirit with the tale of an unlikely gift that a stranger gave to me on the campaign trail, and with Bruce explaining the story behind one of his most popular and misunderstood songs.

CHAPTER
— 8 —

BRUCE SPRINGSTEEN: Tell me, when did you first think you might want to run for president?

PRESIDENT OBAMA: Uh-oh.

BRUCE SPRINGSTEEN: What was your ambition? What made . . . what made you want to do that?

PRESIDENT OBAMA: Somebody must've dropped me on my head. . . . Actually, it traces back to everything we've been talking about, this idea of bringing America into alignment with its ideals. That had been my work, that had been my purpose.

The great thing about running for president is that it takes you everywhere. We started campaigning in Iowa, which is not a representative state. It is overwhelmingly white. It's got a lot of corn and a lot of hog farms. It has generally an older population. And so if you looked at a place where a young African American named Barack Hussein Obama would have the best odds of winning, Iowa would probably not be that state you choose. And yet, partly because I was in a neighboring state and I had done a lot of campaigning in downstate Illinois, I was pretty familiar with those folks. What I had discovered pretty early on—and this is during my Senate campaign—a lot of these folks were just like my grandparents. You go into their house and they are serving the same Jell-O mold. They're talking about stuff the same way. Their core values are similar. Very midwestern. Straight-talking. Friendly, not ostentatious. I was very comfortable in these settings.

You'd just go from town to town to town. And you'd talk to a hundred people. You'd talk to five hundred people. And pretty soon it was a thousand people. But you always had that

sense of being in a more intimate conversation. And what I learned in Iowa was what I had believed from the start: that, for all our differences, there were common threads among Americans, that Michelle's parents on the South Side of Chicago thought much in the same way as the farmer couple in Iowa. They both believed in hard work. They both believed in sacrificing for kids. They both believed in being true to your word. They believed in individual responsibility, but they also believed that there are some things we should do for each other, like making sure that every kid is getting a good education and making sure that seniors are not impoverished. Making sure that, if you get sick, you are not just left to fend for yourself. And pride in doing a good job. You see these common values and you say, "If I can just convince the folks in the city and the folks in the country, and the white folks and the Black folks and the Hispanic folks—if I can just get them to hear each other, they will see each other, and recognize themselves in each other, and then we've got the basis to actually move the country forward."

BRUCE SPRINGSTEEN: Did you run into anything that shocked you? Or made you question your decisions?

PRESIDENT OBAMA: Well, let me tell you, every day I question my decisions, because you're getting your ass kicked when you are on the road. Because you will make mistakes and you still say stupid things, and there will be times where the crowd is

OBAMA FOR AMERICA

dead disappointed. Most of the time, when I questioned my decision, it was not the enterprise itself, it was my seeming inability to rise to the occasion. And my disappointment in me not connecting with people, and not being able to tell their story. If you're doing it right, running for president is not actually about you. It is about finding the chorus, finding the collective.

Early in the campaign I go to this town called Greenwood in South Carolina. The reason I went there is because I was desperate for the endorsement of this state legislator and she said, "I'll give you the endorsement if you go to this town. My town."

I said, "Yeah." Turns out it's an hour and a half from the nearest large city and it's at a time I'm down in the polls. We get there and it's pouring down rain, and there's a bad article about me in the *New York Times*. Everybody is talking about how "it looks like he was all flash."

Finally we get to this little park center. I walk in and I'm damp, I'm in a bad mood, and suddenly, as I'm going around shaking hands with everybody, you hear: "Fired up!"

BRUCE SPRINGSTEEN: "Ready to go!"

PRESIDENT OBAMA: "Ready to go!" It turned out it was this wonderful woman named Edith Childs. She was a part-time private detective, and she had a great smile and she had a pretty flamboyant dress and hat on, and apparently she made a habit of saying this chant of "Fired up, ready to go." At first I thought, "This is crazy." But everybody was doing it, so I thought, "Well, I better do it. I'm here anyway," and I started feeling kind of good. And I just enjoyed the eccentricity of spirit that she was showing.

Suddenly, I'm in a better mood. We're having a good conversation with a bunch of folks. When I leave, I ask my staff, "Are you fired up? Are you ready to go?" That's what you discover when you're running for president—people would lift you up.

BRUCE SPRINGSTEEN: Sure.

PRESIDENT OBAMA: It's not . . . you. You're channeling their energy. Their hopes. Their power. Their resilience.

What you would also discover, as you'd expect, is that some of those darker strains of American life are there. So,

> THAT'S WHAT YOU DISCOVER WHEN YOU'RE RUNNING FOR PRESIDENT—PEOPLE WOULD LIFT YOU UP. . . . YOU'RE CHANNELING THEIR ENERGY. THEIR HOPES. THEIR POWER. THEIR RESILIENCE.
>
> —PRESIDENT OBAMA

you know, when I go down to South Carolina, I have that great story with Edith Childs. I also have moments where I'll go into a diner and start shaking hands with people and everybody's being very friendly, and then you'd get to a table and they won't shake your hand.

And then you'll drive out and suddenly there will be a Confederate flag being hoisted by a bunch of protesters. The message isn't that subtle.

BRUCE SPRINGSTEEN: No.

PRESIDENT OBAMA: Overall, though, for every one of those, you got ten, fifteen, twenty, thirty moments of small glory, you know? There's no such thing as one way to be an American and that's why, when you see some of the politics that have emerged—

BRUCE SPRINGSTEEN: Crazy—so ugly, man.

PRESIDENT OBAMA: During our campaign, you had Sarah Palin, who was sort of a proto-type for and a precursor of what was to come. She'd talk about "real" Americans and I, obviously, didn't qualify. And when I'd hear that, I'd say, "You haven't been around much, because Americans come in every shape and every size."

That's the joy of running for president. You visit all fifty states. You meet people of every walk of life and of every station, and there is a running thread between us. There's this link, this bond. Even among conservatives and liberals, there's a certain set of common assumptions, but they get buried very deep. Part of the intensity of our argument is precisely because what we're arguing about are the contradictions in ourselves.

And, you know, there is one question everybody wants me to ask you: tell me what was going through your mind when you were writing "Born in the U.S.A."

OPPOSITE, TOP: Campaigning is a grueling business, and sometimes you need to take a moment for yourself, as Barack Obama does here in Londonderry, NH, on October 16, 2008. **OPPOSITE, BOTTOM:** Other times, you feed on the energy of people like Edith Childs, who electrified the crowd—and Obama—in South Carolina with her rallying cry of "Fired up. Ready to go!" **FOLLOWING:** On January 6, 2021, a violent mob of pro-Trump demonstrators stormed the US Capitol, intending to disrupt a joint session of Congress and stop elected officials from counting the electoral votes to formally confirm the election of Joe Biden. Hundreds of people were involved in the unlawful breach of the Capitol; five people died as a result of the attack, and more than 140 sustained injuries.

(5)

Born in the USA.

Born down in a dead mans town
the first kick I took was when I hit the ground
end up like a dog that's been beat too much
till ya spend half your life just a coverin up
Born in the USA.....

I   got in a little hometown jam
so they put a rifle in my hands
sent me off to a foreign land
(said son)
to go and kill the yellow man

come back home to the refinery's
hirin man said "son if it was up to me"
went down to see my V.A. man
said "son don't ~~up~~ you understand"

                    brother
I had a buddy at the San
fightin of them Viet Cong
there still there   he's all gone

            A woman he loved
he had ~~a little girl~~ in Saigon
I got a picture of him in her arms

down in the shadow of the (Glendale) penetendiary
(sit + watch) by the gas fires of the refinery(s)
                out
10 yrs down the road   (down the line)
nowhere to run nowhere to go (I'm searchin but I can't find)
   I'm a long gone daddy in the USA. I'm a cool rockin daddy

Born down in a dead man's town / The first kick I took was when I hit the ground / You end up like a dog that's been beat too much / Till you spend half your life just covering up / Born in the U.S.A. / I was born in the U.S.A. / I was born in the U.S.A. / Born in the U.S.A. / Got in a little hometown jam / So they put a rifle in my hand / Sent me off to a foreign land / To go and kill the yellow man / Born in the U.S.A. / I was born in the U.S.A. / I was born in the U.S.A. / I was born in the U.S.A. / Born in the U.S.A. / Come back home to the refinery / Hiring man says "Son if it was up to me" / Went down to see my V.A. man / He said "Son, don't you understand" / I had a brother at Khe Sanh fighting off the Viet Cong / They're still there, he's all gone / He had a woman he loved in Saigon / I got a picture of him in her arms now / Down in the shadow of the penitentiary / Out by the gas fires of the refinery / I'm ten years burning down the road / Nowhere to run ain't got nowhere to go / Born in the U.S.A. / I was born in the U.S.A. / Born in the U.S.A. / I'm a long gone Daddy in the U.S.A. / Born in the U.S.A. / Born in the U.S.A. / Born in the U.S.A. / I'm a cool rocking Daddy in the U.S.A.

—FROM BORN IN THE U.S.A. (1984)

BRUCE SPRINGSTEEN: All right, so Paul Schrader, who directed *Blue Collar*, sends me a script called *Born in the U.S.A.*

It sits on my table. It's 1982. I'm writing a song about Vietnam because I have met a vet named Ron Kovic who wrote a book called *Born on the Fourth of July*. I've met a veteran named Bobby Muller. Both of these guys have been shot and confined to wheelchairs; they are veterans' activists. I met them . . . just strangely. I was driving across the desert and I stopped at a little drugstore and I picked up a copy of *Born on the Fourth of July*. Drive the rest of the way to LA. Book into a little motel, and this guy in a wheelchair is sitting by the pool. A couple of days go by and he finally wheels up to me and says, "Hi, I'm Ron Kovic." I think, "Wait, Ron . . . that sounds familiar to me." He says, "I wrote *Born on the Fourth of July*."

I said, "My god, I finished reading this book two weeks ago." So he invited me to the vet center in Venice. I spent the afternoon there, just kind of listening and learning. That set me off to write something about it. I got the script on the table. I got some verses, and then I look at the script and it says, *Born in the U.S.A.*, and I just go, "Born in the U.S.A. I was born in the U.S.A.," and I say, "Yeah! Yeah! That's it! That's it!"

This is a song about the pain, glory, shame of identity and of place. So it's a complex picture of the country. Our protagonist is someone who has been betrayed by his nation and yet still feels deeply connected to the country that he grew up in.

PRESIDENT OBAMA: Also, it ended up being appropriated as this iconic, patriotic song. Even though that was not necessarily your intention.

BRUCE SPRINGSTEEN: I think the song has been appropriated because, one, it was so powerful, and, two, its imagery was so fundamentally American. But it did demand you hold two contradictory ideas in your mind at one time, that you can both be very critical of your nation and very proud of your nation simultaneously. And that is something that you see argued about to this very day.

PRESIDENT OBAMA: When you play overseas, what's different about it? Are you conscious about saying to yourself, "Man, I need to show myself as an American rock 'n' roll balladeer"? Or do you just say, "Look, this is another audience and I'm just going to do me and hopefully they respond, but maybe they don't"?

BRUCE SPRINGSTEEN: A little bit of all that. We have a funny situation where we have two-thirds of our audience in Europe, maybe a third of our audience in the United States—so we have a much bigger audience overseas. Exactly why that is, I'm not sure, but I know that people over there have been fascinated by the American story, our films and music, for a long time.

The E Street Band, we project drama; emotional power; rush of freedom; symbolism of equality, community, comradeship; pursuit of good times. We tried to create a sound that felt as big as the country itself. We celebrate what's best about the country and we criticize the country's failings. And I think people overseas respect that.

Europe has been a very important part of my life—telling my stories over there and the reception we got over there—even at the worst of times. We played in front of fifty thousand French people soon after we invaded Iraq. There's just something about American culture, and the imagined America that you symbolize and that we tried to symbolize with my band, that still has enormous cultural power wherever you take it.

And I've been around. We've played Africa, Central America, India, and it never fails to communicate. So it's been a pretty blessed journey.

PRESIDENT OBAMA: The thing that struck me about first coming into office as president was the degree to which America's standing in the world had dropped pretty precipitously. A lot of that had to do with Iraq, but Hurricane Katrina had also hurt our reputation, and then we were responsible for triggering a global financial crisis and a great recession. So folks were not in a happy place about American policy and the American government. But what people around the world know is this: America isn't perfect. It has had chronic racial discrimination, it is violent, it has a safety net that compared to other advanced countries is lacking. Oftentimes it is ignorant of the rest of the world.

You'll hear of all these criticisms of the United States, but what everybody around the world also knows is that we are the

---

ABOVE: Bruce Springsteen's seventh studio album, *Born in the U.S.A.*, was released on June 4, 1984. In its title track, a Vietnam veteran returns home and comes to terms with a life of few options: "Nowhere to run ain't got nowhere to go." **OPPOSITE** (inset): *Born on the Fourth of July* is the autobiography of Vietnam veteran Ron Kovic. It tells the story of his upbringing, his decision to join the marines in 1964 as a pro-war patriotic teenager, and the harrowing war injury that left him paralyzed from the waist down and disillusioned with the military-industrial complex. He wrote the book in less than two months, working day and night to frantically capture his experiences and emotions. Along with director Oliver Stone, Kovic adapted the book into an Academy Award-winning film.

BORN ON THE
FOURTH
OF JULY
BY
RON KOVIC

only nation on Earth made up of people who have come from every place . . . of every faith, every race, every background, every economic station. And the world is fascinated to know: "Can this work?" Can this experiment where you throw in all of us together and you set up a democracy where everybody is supposed to have a vote, at least after the Civil War and the postwar amendments, and you claim that all men are created equal—can it work? And, if it does, might it be the salvation of all of us?

BRUCE SPRINGSTEEN: I like that.

PRESIDENT OBAMA: Sometimes people may be skeptical, but in the back of their minds what they're also thinking is, "If they could get it right, that would be a good thing. The recognition and the dignity of all people, everybody having opportunity and every child being able to become president and anybody being able to make it if they try—if that were true, man, that would be great." You know, every so often we'll actually be who we say we are, and when that happens, the world feels just a little bit more hopeful. And the converse is, when we don't . . .

BRUCE SPRINGSTEEN: It gets dark.

PRESIDENT OBAMA: Well, because then people say, "Yeah, you know what? The world is what it is. America is acting just like China," or "It's acting just like Russia," or "It's acting just like the old European empires," or "It turns out that we're still trapped in this pattern of 'might makes right' and the powerful exploiting the less powerful." And then people suddenly say, "I guess I can't hope for much more in my country either."

But when it's right, it's right. And that's why, for all the times we've made mistakes, you have always seen us able to recover, and that is why, by the way, our culture lives on even during dark times. That's why the French can have 80 percent disapproval of the Iraq invasion and still—

BRUCE SPRINGSTEEN: Fifty thousand of them—

PRESIDENT OBAMA: —crowd into a Bruce Springsteen concert singing "Born in the U.S.A."

BRUCE SPRINGSTEEN: I think even with something as small and insignificant as a rock 'n' roll band, we go over there and we do

present those ideals, we represent that promise. And we built a body of work that does that. We never overlook the flaws. Like I say, we are critical patriots. That's what makes it real. That's what makes it honest. But we always bring some transcendence and we present the promise of the country. And that idea—that sacred idea like, "Hey, what if it works?"— that possibility is not dead yet. It's still alive and it rings in people's hearts all across the globe.

I have dedicated part of my life to having a voice in the conversation about bringing us closer to our country's stated ideals through the vehicle of my music and my work. We've consistently fallen too short for too many years, for too many of our citizens, and that inequality, social and economic, is a stain on our social contract. It's up to each and every citizen and our government to strive to bring us closer to our stated ideals.

PRESIDENT OBAMA: So how do you think we can bridge those divides?

BRUCE SPRINGSTEEN: Well, there are some practical things that would seem just common sense: politically connecting across party lines; rediscovering common experience, the love of the country, a new national identity that includes a multicultural picture of the United States that's real today, rooted in common ideals and just seeing each other as Americans again, whether it's blue, red, Black, white. Those are hard, hard things to do, and any way we cut it, it's a long walk home.

PRESIDENT OBAMA: Earlier we were talking about how, after World War II, you have this sense that the middle class is coming, everybody's unified, you know what it means to be an American. And then you got these big ruptures, and one of the big ruptures is Vietnam. You were also describing how Nixon's idea of the "silent majority"—what internally they called the Southern Strategy—was the first time you saw a president specifically, explicitly, distinctively try to divide America.

> EVERY SO OFTEN WE'LL ACTUALLY BE WHO WE SAY WE ARE, AND WHEN THAT HAPPENS, THE WORLD FEELS JUST A LITTLE BIT MORE HOPEFUL.
>
> —PRESIDENT OBAMA

OPPOSITE: Ron Kovic entered military service with a desire to serve his country but was left angry, disillusioned, and committed to peace and nonviolence. He sustained his life-changing injury during a 1968 battle in a Vietnamese village. Shot in the foot and shoulder, he was paralyzed and left for dead. When he returned home he quickly became a leading antiwar activist, giving impassioned speeches to young people, leading fellow veterans on hunger strikes, confronting draft board representatives, and speaking at high-profile events like the 1976 Democratic National Convention. **FOLLOWING:** Bruce, touring overseas, circa 1984.

BRUCE SPRINGSTEEN: You saw the division immediately. The town split in two. There were men and women in the fifties and folks of the sixties. My lovely brother-in-law who married my lovely sister in 1968, one the hottest years of the civil rights movement, was always a man of the fifties.

He would've been a part of the "silent majority," and, of course, I fell on the other side. But it was the first time those sorts of strict divisions were deeply noticeable in society and were totally tied to the civil rights movement and an increasing role of Black voices in society.

PRESIDENT OBAMA: Yeah, you've got race, and relationships between men and women are changing, too. And to some extent, that fifties guy, that "silent majority," solidifies. And it continues to characterize our politics. I mean, Nixon sets the blueprint. Although Nixon himself had gotten some of that from Goldwater—

BRUCE SPRINGSTEEN: But he pushes it hard. The Southern Strategy, Lee Atwater. They take that to the bank as the way that they're going to hold on to power and make the country work for them.

PRESIDENT OBAMA: Now, part of the reason it works is that there was an American culture that we shared. The monoculture brought people together, except it excluded a big chunk of the country. A chunk of the country was invisible.

And then what happens is that part of the country that had been invisible, restricted to maids and porters, suddenly says, "You know what . . . we're here. We want to be at the center of the story."

And that's when all heck breaks loose. That's when the "silent majority" says, "Well, hold on a second. We were feeling pretty good about this shared American story. We understood what it meant to define ourselves as Americans. You're saying you want to be a part of that. . . . That's confusing to us." The reason it's important to recognize the importance of that cultural element is it's also reflected in the news. If there's a Fox News when Watergate happens, it's not at all clear that Richard Nixon ends up resigning.

One of my favorite stories happened fairly late in my presidency, so there's already been this polarization. We go up to one of the Dakotas, where I am going to do a commencement for a community college that does outstanding work training young people for immediate jobs. It's a small town, clearly not my demographic; this is not a county that I'm probably winning, I'm probably losing it by a substantial margin. But it's still a big deal for the president to show up, so everybody's

out on the road watching the motorcade go by and we get to the auditorium and it's filled.

Usually the White House press pool would just stay with me instead of going to explore this community that we're visiting. But, this time, one enterprising reporter went to a local tavern to see what the reaction of this town would be to me giving the commencement. And he's sitting there between a couple of guys in flannel shirts and caps and they're drinking their beer. The Fox newscasts carry the event live because I'm in their town. These guys are watching and they are sitting quietly. Then they turn to the reporter and they say, "Is this how Obama usually sounds?" And the reporter says, "Yeah, that's pretty standard Obama-speak." They say, "Huh, not really what we expected." Now, keep in mind, at that point I had probably been president for the last five or six years. The filter was so thick that I, as president of the United States, could not reach those guys unless I actually went to their town so that they would actually cover it. And that is part of what's changed.

So it's hard to figure out how we reconstruct that sense of a common bond that you were talking about. That sense of, it's not blue or red, it's not Black or white, it's America. How do you re-create that if you have a splintered culture? The reason at some point somebody says the Beatles are bigger than God or bigger than Jesus . . . is because they were on *The Ed Sullivan Show*. Elvis is on *The Ed Sullivan Show*. That was part of that common culture.

BRUCE SPRINGSTEEN: Absolutely. And I know there's been some debate over Elvis recently, as far as cultural appropriation. But—

PRESIDENT OBAMA: Go ahead, give me your Elvis take right now. And I should say, by the way . . . big Elvis fan.

BRUCE SPRINGSTEEN: Okay! Well, Elvis, you know, Elvis was part of my childhood. I was seven when I saw him on *The Ed Sullivan Show*.

You forget Elvis appeared as a novelty act initially. He challenged images of masculinity. Dyed his hair, wore makeup, moved, some said, like a stripper. And so, to a child, he appeared like a cartoon figure. He captured your imagination. And so I immediately went to the mirror and started to shake

---

OPPOSITE, TOP: Waiting for the motorcade at Lake Area Technical College in Watertown, SD, on May 8, 2015. **OPPOSITE, BOTTOM:** At the Cattleman's Casino and Bar in Watertown, SD, all eyes were on President Obama as he gave a speech in a local civic arena. In visiting South Dakota on this trip, President Obama had visited all fifty states as president.

Last night I stood at your doorstep / Trying to figure out what went wrong / You just slipped somethin' into my palm / Then you were gone / I could smell the same deep green of summer / Above me the same night sky was glowin' / In the distance I could see the town where I was born / It's gonna be a long walk home / Hey pretty Darling, don't wait up for me / Gonna be a long walk home / A long walk home / In town I passed Sal's grocery / The barbershop on South Street / I looked into their faces / They were all rank strangers to me / The veterans' hall high up on the hill / Stood silent and alone / The diner was shuttered and boarded / With a sign that just said "gone" / It's gonna be a long walk home / Hey pretty Darling, don't wait up for me / Gonna be a long walk home / Hey pretty Darling, don't wait up for me / Gonna be a long walk home / It's gonna be a long walk home / Here everybody has a neighbor / Everybody has a friend / Everybody has a reason to begin again / My father said "Son, we're lucky in this town / It's a beautiful place to be born / It just wraps its arms around you / Nobody crowds you, nobody goes it alone. / You know that flag flying over the courthouse / Means certain things are set in stone / Who we are, what we'll do and what we won't." / It's gonna be a long walk home / Hey pretty Darling, don't wait up for me / Gonna be a long walk home / Hey pretty Darling, don't wait up for me / Gonna be a long walk home / It's gonna be a long walk home / It's gonna be a long walk home / Hey pretty Darling, don't wait up for me / Gonna be a long walk home / Hey pretty Darling, don't wait up for me / Gonna be a long walk home / It's gonna be a long walk home / It's gonna be a long walk home

—FROM MAGIC (2007)

all around, grabbed the broom and started to strum the broom, and then I said, "Mom, I want that guitar." And I had that guitar for two weeks and realized it was real and needed to be played. And that was that until the Beatles hit the shore.

Later I learned that all of the music, particularly the earlier music of the Beatles and the Stones that I'd listened to, came from Black artists. Chuck Berry, Arthur Alexander, just too many to mention. So I was sent backward like that into the African American roots of rock music.

PRESIDENT OBAMA: This whole issue of cultural appropriation—I have to say I'm not a believer in narrowly defining who gets to do what.

BRUCE SPRINGSTEEN: I'm with you on that.

PRESIDENT OBAMA: I think we steal from—

BOTH: Everybody, everywhere.

PRESIDENT OBAMA: That's the nature of humanity. That is the nature of culture. That is how ideas migrate. That's how music gets created. That's how food gets created. I don't want us to be thinking that there's this way for that person, and that way is for the other person.

BRUCE SPRINGSTEEN: I agree.

PRESIDENT OBAMA: I think what's always been relevant about cultural appropriation is if the Black person who writes the song and who performs it better can't also perform it and can't get the record deal, that's the problem. I've got no problem with white artists doing Black music because I don't think there's such a thing as simply, exclusively Black music or white music or Hispanic music. It's the economics and the power dynamics underneath it, which obviously Elvis was part of. He didn't create it. But the fact was that you had Black songs being written that the Black performers could not cash in on.

BRUCE SPRINGSTEEN: Now, the only thing that could change my mind on this is Pat Boone doing Little Richard.

PRESIDENT OBAMA: That's a problem.

Elvis Presley made his first appearance on the wildly popular *Ed Sullivan Show* on September 9, 1956, when he was just twenty-one years old. Sullivan had previously refused to allow Presley on the show, as he considered him "not his cup of tea." After Presley's appearances on other TV shows drew big ratings, Sullivan changed his mind. Sixty million people (82 percent of TV viewers at the time!) tuned in to see the most-watched TV broadcast of the 1950s.

BRUCE SPRINGSTEEN: It's brutal. . . . I got a few other questions. Can I go?

PRESIDENT OBAMA: You are allowed!

BRUCE SPRINGSTEEN: All right, one was, who are our American heroes? Want me to start?

PRESIDENT OBAMA: Yeah, go ahead. What do you got?

BRUCE SPRINGSTEEN: Muhammad Ali.

PRESIDENT OBAMA: That's solid.

BRUCE SPRINGSTEEN: He's way at the top.

PRESIDENT OBAMA: If we are working off sports initially, you got to go with Jackie Robinson. Not only does Jackie Robinson make all of Black America proud to see him compete and excel in the face of the most vicious treatment and threats, but he also changes the hearts and minds of white America through the process. The number of white guys of a certain generation who will tell me how that changed them or their dads, and what it meant for an eight-year-old white kid in the stands to be rooting for a Black guy . . .

BRUCE SPRINGSTEEN: Music. You ready?

PRESIDENT OBAMA: What do you got?

BRUCE SPRINGSTEEN: All right. I got my man Bob Dylan.

PRESIDENT OBAMA: Dude, you can't argue with Dylan. And he keeps on going! He's a little bit like Picasso in the sense that he will just come up with different phases, and he just keeps on cranking out innovation. He seems to do it for himself as much as for anybody else.

BRUCE SPRINGSTEEN: He's an artist. He's doing what he got to do. That's all.

PRESIDENT OBAMA: He's this font of creativity.

BRUCE SPRINGSTEEN: I got James Brown. No hip-hop without James Brown. Musically, who do you got?

PRESIDENT OBAMA: Ray Charles.

BRUCE SPRINGSTEEN: Without a doubt.

PRESIDENT OBAMA: "America the Beautiful" is actually the national anthem.

BRUCE SPRINGSTEEN: I believe you're right.

PRESIDENT OBAMA: No offense to the other one, particularly Whitney Houston's version! I don't wanna suddenly be getting a bunch of email. . . .
Another is Aretha Franklin.

BRUCE SPRINGSTEEN: Boom. Huge hero.

PRESIDENT OBAMA: If I think about American music that could not come from anyplace else, when I listen to anything Aretha is singing, I feel America. You know who I love, just as an American artist? Frank Sinatra.

BRUCE SPRINGSTEEN: Way up there, encapsulates the entire age.

PRESIDENT OBAMA: That kind of casualness but precision, the sort of studied cool that he projects. It is a very specific American style to me.

BRUCE SPRINGSTEEN: The forties, the romantic cynicism.

PRESIDENT OBAMA: Yeah, exactly, it's like Bogart. Deep down you're a romantic.

BRUCE SPRINGSTEEN: Conversational blues, life is beautiful, life is shit, all in one shot, man.

PRESIDENT OBAMA: Stevie Wonder.

OPPOSITE: President Obama and Bruce Springsteen's American heroes: Muhammad Ali (top left) is not only considered the greatest heavyweight boxer of all time, his actions as a conscientious objector made him an icon to the Vietnam War generation. Ray Charles's (top inset) untreated glaucoma caused him to go blind by age seven, but he learned to read Braille and play piano, and by the mid-fifties he was pioneering the soul genre, combining gospel, R & B, jazz, and blues. Jackie Robinson (top right) became the first Black player to break the color line and integrate baseball when he started at first base for the Brooklyn Dodgers on April 15, 1947. Bob Dylan's (bottom right) innovative singer-songwriter career has spanned 6 decades, 39 studio albums, and more than 500 songs, including "Mr. Tambourine Man" and "Like a Rolling Stone." As the "Godfather of Soul," James Brown (bottom inset) introduced funk music to the masses, recording such legendary songs as "I Got You (I Feel Good)," and "Get Up (I Feel Like Being a) Sex Machine." Stevie Wonder (bottom left) was born six weeks premature and placed in an incubator that likely saved his life—but also took his sight. He loved playing music from an early age, and by age thirteen he became the youngest artist to have a Billboard hit single. "The Queen of Soul," Aretha Franklin (center inset), began her career singing gospel in a church choir in Detroit, MI. At age eighteen she signed with Atlantic Records, quickly becoming one of the best-selling music artists of all time. She won a total of eighteen Grammys and was an outspoken activist who donated money and time to numerous social justice causes.

OFTENTIMES THE FOLKS
THAT INSPIRE ME MOST WERE
THE LESS FAMOUS ONES.
NOT JUST JOHN LEWIS
BUT DIANE NASH AND
BOB MOSES AND ELLA BAKER,
FANNIE LOU HAMER,
JOSEPH LOWERY, C. T. VIVIAN,
FRED SHUTTLESWORTH.

—PRESIDENT OBAMA

BRUCE SPRINGSTEEN: Made the seventies decade's historical records.

PRESIDENT OBAMA: Five albums in a row that will match up with anybody else's five albums in history.

BRUCE SPRINGSTEEN: Who were some of the other Americans that inspire you?

PRESIDENT OBAMA: So not surprisingly what comes to mind first for me is Dr. King and Malcolm X, the yin and yang of the liberation movement in this country that helped shape me so much.

But sometimes those feel like larger-than-life figures, and oftentimes the folks that inspire me most were the less famous ones. Not just John Lewis but Diane Nash and Bob Moses and Ella Baker, Fannie Lou Hamer, Joseph Lowery, C. T. Vivian, Fred Shuttlesworth. People who never achieved that same kind of fame, might not have had those same extraordinary gifts, and yet, because of their doggedness and courage, achieved extraordinary things. They're heroes on a human scale.

BRUCE SPRINGSTEEN: I wanted to mention Ruby Bridges. Six years old. First Black child to desegregate the William Frantz Elementary School in Louisiana. Federal marshals take her to school alone.

PRESIDENT OBAMA: As part of the White House collection, we were given the opportunity to hang the Norman Rockwell painting of Ruby just outside the Oval Office. So I'd see it all the time.

This painting depicts Ruby, this tiny little thing with pigtails and white socks, and all you see is the huge bodies of these federal marshals, and in the background you can see faintly this graffiti scrawled with the N-word on the wall.

Ruby came by the White House. She's about my age now. We stood next to the painting and she kind of described the scene, and how she had felt. She was a great representative of that kind of quiet heroism that happened so frequently during that era. The absolute grace; you could still see it!

BRUCE SPRINGSTEEN: That's incredible. At six years old.

PRESIDENT OBAMA: As we broaden it, Lincoln still is at the center of what I think about as America. The log cabin stuff is not a myth. He is a broke-ass kid, growing up in very meager, limited circumstances, rough-hewn, not much formal schooling. Teaches himself essentially by reading the King James Bible and Shakespeare to become one of the greatest American

writers of all time. Has an entire career before anybody knows who he is. Teaches himself enough to pass the bar, become a lawyer. He's riding around Illinois making jokes and telling stories and doing business and making money. And yet somehow there is this deep morality and melancholy and depth that emerges out of him.

Finally he is at the crossroads of this central question about America, which is, "Are we going to be a truly free nation or not?"

He grapples with that in the most profound way. He never wavers in his hopes, but he never takes his eye off the truth, including the truth about himself, even amidst the bitterness of war and the uncertainties and the doubts. And what I'm always struck by is the fact that he did not break under that strain. And it was an enormous strain.

My reverence for him does not mean that I ignore the fact that he didn't necessarily think Black people were equal. He just thought, "I shouldn't be taking bread out of that Black man's mouth who's doing all the work. I should do the work and be responsible for my own bread." So I don't overromanticize Lincoln—

BRUCE SPRINGSTEEN: Yeah.

PRESIDENT OBAMA: I think that one of the hardest things, whether it's as an adult in our own individual lives or as a nation, is figuring out if it is possible for you to see the wrong in people without negating everything about them.

THE INAUGURAL ADDRESS

OF PRESIDENT

ABRAHAM LINCOLN,

DELIVERED AT THE NATIONAL CAPITOL,

MARCH 4th, 1865.

Fellow Countrymen:

At this second appearing to take the oath of the Presidential Office, there is less occasion for an extended address than there was at the first. Then a statement somewhat in detail of a course to be pursued seemed very fitting and proper. Now, at the expiration of four years, during which public declarations have been constantly called forth on every point and phase of the great contest which still absorbs the attention and engrosses the energies of the nation, little that is new could be presented.

The progress of our arms—upon which all else chiefly depends—is as well known to the public as to myself; and it is, I trust, reasonably satisfactory and encouraging to all. With high hope for the future, no prediction in regard to it is ventured.

On the occasion corresponding to this four years ago, all thoughts were anxiously directed to an impending civil war. All dreaded it; all sought to avoid it. While the inaugural address was being delivered from this place, devoted altogether to saving the Union without war, insurgent agents were in the city seeking to destroy it without war—seeking to dissolve the Union and divide the effects by negotiation.

Both parties deprecated war; but one of them would make war rather than let the nation survive, and the other would accept war rather than let it perish, and the war came.

One-eighth of the whole population were colored slaves, not distributed generally over the Union, but localized in the Southern part of it. These slaves constituted a peculiar and powerful interest. All knew that this interest was somehow the cause of the war. To strengthen, perpetuate and extend this interest was the object for which the insurgents would rend the Union by war, while the Government claimed no right to do more than to restrict the territorial enlargement of it.

Neither party expected for the war the magnitude or the duration which it has already attained. Neither anticipated that the cause of the conflict might cease, even before the conflict itself should cease. Each looked for an easier triumph and a result less fundamental and astounding.

Both read the same Bible, and pray to the same God, and each invokes His aid against the other. It may seem strange that any men should dare to ask a just God's assistance in wringing their bread from the sweat of other men's faces; but let us judge not, that we be not judged. The prayers of both should not be answered. That of neither has been answered fully. The Almighty has His own purposes. Woe unto the world because of offences, for it must needs be that offences come; but woe to that man by whom the offence cometh. If we shall suppose that American Slavery is one of these offences—which, in the providence of God, must needs come, but which, having continued through His appointed time, He now wills to remove, and that He gives to both North and South this terrible war as the woe due to those by whom the offence came—shall we discern there is any departure from those Divine attributes which the believers in a living God always ascribe to Him? Fondly do we hope, fervently do we pray, that this mighty scourge of war may speedily pass away. Yet, if God wills that it continue until all the wealth piled by the bondman's two hundred and fifty years of unrequited toil shall be sunk, and until every drop of blood drawn with the lash shall be paid by another drawn with the sword, as was said three thousand years ago, so still it must be said that the judgments of the Lord are true and righteous altogether.

With malice toward none, with charity for all, with firmness in the right, as God gives us to see the right, let us strive on to finish the work we are in, to bind up the nation's wound, to care for him who shall have borne the battle, and for his widow and orphans; to do all which may achieve and cherish a just and a lasting peace among ourselves and with all nations.

It's possible to look at our Founding Fathers and say, "Yeah, they were slaveholders," and then also say, "But man, that Declaration of Independence is something."

I am not of the view that by virtue of him having owned slaves, George Washington is less of the father of this country and an extraordinary historical figure. I am of the view that people are the people of their times, with the sins of their times often embodied in them. If you have a person of less character than George Washington, the country may not hold together, may not win the Revolutionary War, and afterward you may get a failed experiment, as opposed to a successful experiment.

In the same way, I want to be able to appropriate any kind of music I want or any tradition I want or any cuisine I want—if it's good, I want it. I also want to be able to appropriate and claim for myself the example of the good things that other people have done even if they weren't perfect.

BRUCE SPRINGSTEEN: I like that.

PRESIDENT OBAMA: I want to be able to read Lincoln's Second Inaugural and just revel in its majesty. I'll bet that sticks. . . . Here's what makes me optimistic, and see if you agree with me on that, because, you know, I'm the hope guy—

BRUCE SPRINGSTEEN: You are. I thought I was, but you're better than me.

PRESIDENT OBAMA: Come on, man. You're the "Rising" guy.

The question is, what makes us think that we can get to an America that is whole and is true and is better than where we're at right now? And what makes me optimistic is this generation coming up. You saw this even in this election. Overwhelmingly, the thirty-five–and–under crowd, they believe in a unifying story of America. Our kids, their peer group across the country, they believe, almost as second nature, that people are equal.

They do not believe in discriminating on the basis of someone's skin or their sexual orientation or their gender or their ethnicity or their faith. They do not believe in an economic order that is so grossly unequal that you can have a handful of people worth more than millions of their fellow citizens. They do not believe in a society that ignores the desecration of the planet. They reject the idea that we have no responsibility at all to future generations when it comes to issues like climate change. The good news is those are the folks coming up. The question is, can we hold this thing together long enough, so that when they are old enough to be in charge—

BRUCE SPRINGSTEEN: Waiting for the cavalry!

PRESIDENT OBAMA: —we haven't screwed things up so bad that it's too late? I have to believe that we can do that. Our job is to help create that bridge for that next generation.

And your songs and my speeches or books or this conversation, I think their purpose is to let that next generation know, "You're on the right track."

BRUCE SPRINGSTEEN: You gotta keep the lantern lit, my friend.

PRESIDENT OBAMA: Yes! Exactly.

BRUCE SPRINGSTEEN: That's the bottom line.

PRESIDENT OBAMA: Right. That America is true and real and available to you. I know it doesn't feel like it right now, but it's there.

BRUCE SPRINGSTEEN: I agree. It's corny, but your children force you to be optimistic, you know. It's their world that you're handing over now. I don't want to know a pessimistic parent. If that's who you are, you've done it wrong. My children, I say with God's thanks, are solid citizens whose character at barely the thirty-year mark far outstrips my own. They humble me, and Patti and I, we live in their grace and are thankful.

PRESIDENT OBAMA: I think we've done some good work today, brother.

BRUCE SPRINGSTEEN: We did, yeah. Thank you, brother.

PRESIDENT OBAMA: I learned something.

BRUCE SPRINGSTEEN: So did I.

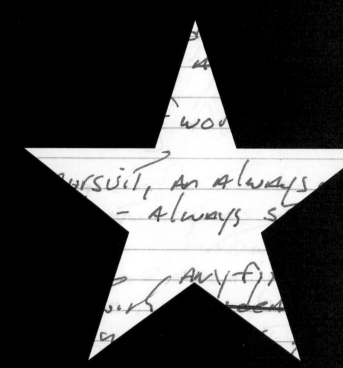

APPENDIXES
. . . .

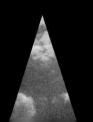

PRESIDENT
OBAMA'S
ANNOTATED
EULOGY FOR
JOHN LEWIS

DRAFT 7/30/20 1200pm
Keenan
202-550-6902

Remarks of President Barack Obama
Eulogy for John Lewis
Ebenezer Baptist Church, Atlanta, Georgia
July 30, 2020

"Consider it pure joy, my brothers and sisters, whenever you face trials of many kinds – because you know that the testing of your faith produces perseverance. Let perseverance finish its work so that you may be mature and complete, lacking nothing." *cite.*

With those words of scripture, let me say what an honor it is to be back in Ebenezer Baptist Church, in the pulpit of its great pastor, Dr. King, to pay my respects to perhaps his finest disciple – an American whose faith was tested again and again to produce a man of pure joy and unbreakable perseverance – John Robert Lewis.

President Bush, President Clinton, Madam Speaker, Reverend Warnock, Reverend King, John's family, friends, and staff – I've come here today because I, like so many Americans, owe a debt to John Lewis and his forceful vision of freedom.

This country of ours is a constant work in progress. We were born with instructions: to form a more perfect union. Explicit in those words is the idea that we are imperfect; that what gives each new generation purpose is to take up the unfinished work of the last and carry it further than they thought possible.

John Lewis – first of the Freedom Riders, head of the Student Nonviolent Coordinating Committee, youngest speaker at the March on Washington, leader of the march from Selma to Montgomery, Member of Congress representing the people of this state for 33 years, mentor to young people up until his final day on this Earth – he not only embraced that responsibility, he made it his life's work.

Not bad for the boy from Troy. John was born into modest means in the heart of the Jim Crow South to parents who picked somebody else's cotton. But he didn't take to farm work – on days when he was supposed to help his brothers and sisters with their labor, he'd hide under the porch and make a break for the school bus when it appeared. His mother, Willie Mae Lewis, nurtured that curiosity in her shy, serious child. "Once you learn something," she told her son, "once you get something inside your head, no one can take it away from you."

As a boy, John listened through the door after bedtime as his father's friends complained about the Klan. One Sunday as a teenager, he heard Dr. King preach on the radio. As a college student in Tennessee, he signed up for Jim Lawson's[1] workshops on the tactics of nonviolent civil disobedience. John Lewis was getting something inside his head, an idea he couldn't shake – that nonviolent resistance and civil disobedience were the means to change laws, hearts, minds, and ultimately, a nation.

---

[1] Jim Lawson will be there and speak before you.

He helped organize the Nashville campaign in 1960. He and other well-dressed, straight-backed young men and women sat at segregated lunch counters, refusing to let a milkshake poured on their heads, or a cigarette extinguished on their backs, or a foot aimed at their ribs dent their dignity. They persevered. And after a few months, the Nashville campaign achieved the first successful desegregation of public facilities in the South.

John got a taste of jail for the first, second, third…well, several times. But he also got a taste of victory. It consumed him with righteous purpose. And he took the battle deeper into the South.

That same year, just weeks after the Supreme Court ruled that segregation of interstate bus facilities was unconstitutional, John and Bernard Lafayette bought two tickets, climbed aboard a Greyhound, sat up front, and refused to move. Their trip was unsanctioned. Few knew what they were up to. At every stop, the angry driver disappeared inside the bus station. They didn't know who he'd come back with. Nobody was there to protect them. And while he made it through that trip unharmed, he was attacked on the first official Freedom Ride the next year, beaten for entering a whites-only waiting room.

John was only twenty years old. But he pushed all twenty of those years into the center of the table, betting everything, all of it, that his example could challenge centuries of convention, generations of brutal violence, and countless daily indignities for Black Americans.

Like John the Baptist preparing the way, or those Old Testament prophets speaking truth before kings, John Lewis never hesitated to get in the way. He climbed aboard again and again, got his mugshot taken again and again, marched again and again on a mission to change America.

He spoke to 250,000 people at the March on Washington when he was just 23.

He helped organize the Freedom Summer in Mississippi, registering thousands of Black Americans, when he was just 24.

And at the ripe old age of 25, John was asked to lead the march from Selma to Montgomery. He was warned that Wallace had ordered his troopers to use violence. But he and Hosea Williams led them across that bridge anyway. We see him on film, trench coat buttoned up, knapsack stocked with a book to read, an apple to eat, a toothbrush and toothpaste because jail wasn't big on creature comforts. Small in stature. But full of purpose. Looking every bit that serious child *his mother had talked about*

Their bones were cracked by billy clubs, their eyes and lungs choked with tear gas. As they knelt to pray, their heads even easier targets, John was struck in the skull. He thought he was going to die, surrounded by the sight of young Americans gagging, bleeding, victims of state-sponsored violence in their own country.

The troopers thought they'd won the battle; that they'd turned the protesters back over the bridge; that they'd kept those young men and women roped off from the political process. But this time, there were cameras there. This time, the world saw what happened to Black Americans on a regular basis. They saw Americans who weren't seeking special treatment, just the <u>equal</u> treatment promised to them a century before, and almost another century before that.

As the Lord instructed Paul, "Do not be afraid, go on speaking; do not be silent, for I am with you, and no one will attack you to harm you, for I have many in this city who are my people."

When John woke up, and checked himself out of the hospital, he would make sure the world saw a movement that was, as Scripture tells us, "hard pressed on every side, but not crushed; perplexed but not in despair; persecuted, but not abandoned; struck down, but not destroyed." He returned to Brown Chapel, a battered prophet, bandages around his head, and said more marchers will come now. He was right; they did. The troopers parted. The marchers reached Montgomery. Their words reached the White House – and the President signed a Voting Rights Act into law.

The life of John Lewis was, in so many ways, exceptional. It vindicates the faith of our founding; that most American idea; the idea that ordinary people without rank or wealth or title or fame can point out our imperfections, come together, push against convention, and decide that it is in our power to remake this country we love until it more closely aligns with our highest ideals.

John's whole life was about sacrificing himself in service of a country bound by those ideals. He understood that the only way to do that was to live and act as though those ideals were sacred, and incontrovertible. On the battlefield of justice, Americans like John, Americans like the Reverends Joseph Lowery and C.T. Vivian, two other patriots we lost this year, liberated us all in ways that many Americans came to take for granted.

America was built by people like them. America was built by John Lewises. He as much as anyone in our history brought this country closer to a true democracy. And someday, when we do finish that long journey toward freedom; when we do form a more perfect union – whether it's years, decades, even if it's another two centuries from now – John Lewis will be a founding father of that fuller, fairer, better America.

But here's the thing: John never believed that what he did was more than what any citizen of this country might do. He believed that in all of us, there exists the capacity for great courage, a longing to do what's right, a willingness to love all people, and to extend to them their God-given rights to dignity and respect. He saw the best in us. And he never gave up, never stopped speaking out. As a Congressman, he didn't rest; he kept getting himself arrested. As an old man, he didn't sit out any fight; he sat in, all night long, on the floor of the United States Capitol.

The testing of his faith produced perseverance. He knew that the march is not yet over, that the race is not yet won, that we have not yet reached that blessed destination where we are judged by the content of our character. He knew from his own life that progress is fragile; that we have to be eternally vigilant against the darker currents of this country's history, with their whirlpools of violence and despair rising again.

some of those in power are doing their darndest to discourage discourage voting — boy

Bull Connor may be gone. But today we can see with our own eyes police officers kneeling on the necks of Black Americans. George Wallace may be gone. But today we can see with our own eyes a government sending federal agents to use tear gas and batons against its own citizens. We may no longer have to guess the number of jellybeans in a jar before we can vote. But we can see with our own eyes that ~~Republican politicians~~ are closing polling locations, targeting minorities and students with restrictive voter ID laws, attacking our voting rights with surgical precision, even undermining the postal service in the runup to an election dependent on mailed-in ballots.

Now, I know this is a celebration of John's life. That's exactly why I'm talking about this. Because he devoted his time on this Earth to fighting these attacks on the very idea of America.

He knew, ~~this man raised in the humblest circumstances~~, that every single one of us has power. And that the fate of this democracy depends on how we use it – on whether we can summon a measure of John's moral courage to question right and wrong and call things what they are. He said that as long as he had breath in his body, he would do everything he could to preserve this democracy. As long as we have breath in ours, we must continue his cause. If we want our children to grow up in a democracy – in a big-hearted, tolerant, vibrant, inclusive America of perpetual self-creation – then we have to be more like John.

Like John, we have to keep getting into good trouble. He knew that protest is patriotic; a way to raise public awareness, put a spotlight on injustice, and make the powers that be uncomfortable.

Like John, we don't have to choose between protest and politics, but engage in both, aware that our aspirations, no matter how passionate, have to be translated into laws and practices. That's why John ran for Congress thirty-four years ago, and kept protesting anyway.

Like John, we have to fight even harder for the most powerful tool we have: the right to vote. The Voting Rights Act is one of the crowning achievements of our democracy. It's why John crossed that bridge. It's why he spilled his blood. But once the Supreme Court gutted it, ~~Republican~~ legislatures unleashed a flood of laws designed to make voting harder, especially in the states with the highest minority turnout or population growth. This isn't a mystery. It's an attack on our democratic freedoms. And we should treat it as such.

If politicians want to honor John, there's a better way than a statement calling him a hero. Summon one ounce of his courage and restore the law he was willing to die for. In fact, I think the John Lewis Voting Rights Act should go further than protecting the rights we already have.

~~Now, I don't hold public office anymore. I'm just a constituent. But as a constituent, I have some opinions. I think The John Lewis Voting Rights Act should finish the work of his Freedom Summer~~ By making sure every single American is automatically registered to vote, including former inmates who've earned their second chance. I ~~think it should make sure nobody else has to risk their job, their health, or their life to vote,~~ By adding polling places, expanding early voting, making Election Day a national holiday, and allowing every single American to cast their ballot by mail. It should guarantee that every American citizen has equal representation in our government, including the American citizens who live in Washington, D.C. and Puerto Rico. It should put an end to partisan gerrymandering once and for all – so that all voters have the power to choose their politicians, and not the other way around. And if it takes eliminating the filibuster – another Jim Crow relic – in order to secure our God-given rights, that's what we should do.

And yet, even if we do all this – even if every bogus voter ID law was struck from the books tomorrow – we have to be honest that too many of us choose not to exercise our franchise; that too many of our citizens believe their vote won't make a difference, buying into the cynicism that is central to the strategy of voter suppression.

So we must also remember John's words: "If you don't do everything you can to change things, then they remain the same. You only pass this way once. You have to give it all you have." As long as young people are protesting in the streets, hoping real change takes hold, we cannot so casually abandon them at the ballot box. Not when few elections have been as urgent, on so many levels, as this one. We cannot treat voting as an errand to run if we have time. We have to treat it as the most important action we can take for democracy. Like John, we have to give it all we have.

It's fitting that the last time John and I shared a public forum was at a virtual town hall with a gathering of young activists who were helping to lead this summer's demonstrations in the wake of George Floyd's death. Afterwards, I spoke to John privately, and he could not have been prouder to see a new generation standing up for freedom and equality; a new generation intent on voting and protecting the right to vote; a new generation running for political office.

I told him that all those young people – of every race, from every background and gender and sexual orientation – they were his children. They had learned from his example, even if they didn't know it. They had understood, through him, what American citizenship requires, even if they had heard of his courage only through history books.

"By the thousands, faceless, anonymous, relentless young people, black and white...have taken our whole nation back to those great wells of democracy which were dug deep by the founding fathers in the formulation of the Constitution and the Declaration of Independence."

Dr. King said that in the 1960s. It came true again this summer.

We see it outside our windows, in big cities and rural towns, in men and women, young and old, gay and straight and trans Americans, Blacks who long for equal treatment and whites who can no longer accept freedom for themselves while witnessing the subjugation of their fellow Americans. We see it in everybody doing the hard work of overcoming our own complacency, our own fears and prejudices, and trying to become a better, truer version of ourselves. That's where real courage comes from – not from turning on each other, but towards one another, with joy and ~~perseverance~~, and discovering that in our beloved community, we do not walk alone.

determination

Perseverance finished its work with John. He was complete. And I will finish today with some of his final words of advice to the young people who've led us all summer long.

"Give it all you got. Do not get weary. Be hopeful. Be optimistic...you cannot give up. You cannot give in. You will make it. [You] will lead us."

God bless you all. God bless America – and this gentle soul who pulled it closer to its promise.

We are ~~lucky~~ all so lucky to have had John walker with us for awhile. His job is now done, and God has taken him home. and show us the way.

American Heroes

Muhamad Ali – An "only in America"
                 character
         the violent skills employed so with
such precision   To
         the absurdist humor
the force of character + personality
              the dedication To his own values
regardless of the price he'd pay
              A great 20th century
historical figure

Bob Dylan – he follow his muse wherever
         it takes him. He is True To himself
the scope and brilliance of his writing
         he has the balls and fire
To Take on his Times.
              To believe he has the rights
And ability To call his country to accounts
              in his early protest music
And then A delve so deeply into it's
              character on his later work
An American Hero for me

the Astronauts, Neil Armstrong, Buzz
              Aldwin + Colins
         the men of Appollo 11 who went to
the moon, the coolness and steely grit
              To let loose the earths Atmosphere
And To cast yourself in A Tin can
              into the void frontiersmen
icons of American can do spirit
              I love 'em

As Symbols of "Americaness"

I have no daily regimen

I continue to try to write as
meaningfully, as sharply, as critically, sharply
as thoughtful as well observed
as I can about my country
And my countrymen
I let the rest of the chips fall
where they may

Imprint - I'd like to be looked back
on just as a guy who did his job well.
brought some fun and entertainment into
folks lives
while informing them a little about
the world and country around them

maybe if someone was interested
in America during it's post industrial period
of the 2nd half of the century
reflected in music
I might be somebody
worth giving a listen to.
but I have no expectations
of leaving any kind of "lasting"
footprint (that's yn sdm. well)
I'll be on my merry way back from where
I came
smiling the whole way

America Idea

American Idea — democracy, rights,
liberty, opportunity and equality

the right to your own definition of the
"American idea" and the freedom
to pursue it.

practical things — college education, a decent job
meaningful work, health care, freedom from burdensome
the liberty to define   depr.
                    and pursue happiness

the meaningfulness of work, of family life

          a noble pursuit, an always unfinished ideal
"We" the people — always striving
                    to be we.

    *
                              any fixed notion
I did not start out with ~~an idea~~ of the American idea
          I started working as a process to
define and pursue what that idea
                    might be for me... and for my
                              eventually
Born to Run — personal liberty   neighbors
Darkness — communal consciousness

    From the cacaphony of democracy
I wanted to make one blinding noise
    that would pierce you to the bone
+ make you ~~feel that idea~~
the American idea sits somewhere at
          the nexus of personal liberty + license
and communal conciousness. An always
          shifting and argued over imaginary
                              line

American Idea

Our story, the American story is
far messier than the arc of history
bending toward justice

Americans have never agreed on when
to prioritize the individual
and when the collective project
should come first

dangers
1. folks don't vote
2. income inequality
3. intergenerational economic
   mobility

Systemic Racism
4. disillusioned youth
5. complacence

lack of a national identity grounded in a shared set
of ideals
ideals that served as a source
of national pride and
promise for the future
thin & outdated

Trump - Arid nationalism of blood & soil
Anemic
universalism of the left
cultural nationalism of the right
battery the American sense
of national purpose

the nations shared identity
is crumbling

prosperity and justice flow from
each other
enlarging opportunity, restoring rights, pursuing
equality

BRUCE SPRINGSTEEN STUDIO ALBUM DISCOGRAPHY

1973

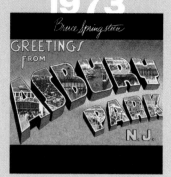

GREETINGS FROM ASBURY PARK, N.J.

1973

THE WILD, THE INNOCENT & THE E STREET SHUFFLE

1982

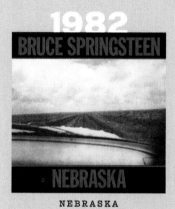

NEBRASKA

1984

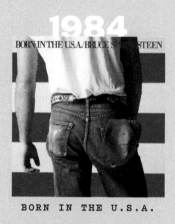

BORN IN THE U.S.A.

1987

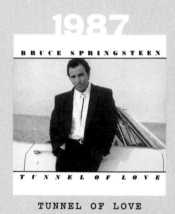

TUNNEL OF LOVE

1999

18 TRACKS

2002

THE RISING

2005

DEVILS & DUST

2010

THE PROMISE

2012

WRECKING BALL

2014

HIGH HOPES

1975

BORN TO RUN

1978

DARKNESS ON THE EDGE
OF TOWN

1980

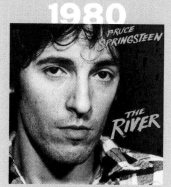

THE RIVER

1992

LUCKY TOWN

1992

HUMAN TOUCH

1995

THE GHOST OF TOM
JOAD

2006

WE SHALL OVERCOME:
THE SEEGER SESSIONS

2007

MAGIC

2009

WORKING ON A DREAM

2019

WESTERN STARS

2020

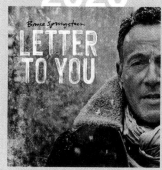

LETTER TO YOU

ACKNOWLEDGMENTS

FROM PRESIDENT OBAMA:

My gratitude to Michelle, Malia, and Sasha, for the endless joy they've granted me.

Thank you to the Higher Ground team, including Joe Paulsen, Dan Fierman, Anna Holmes, Mukta Mohan, and Janae Marable, for your tireless efforts in creating the podcast that inspired this book.

FROM BRUCE SPRINGSTEEN:

A special thanks to Patti Scialfa for her encouragement and inspiration. And to Evan, Jess, and Sam Springsteen.

Thanks to Michelle Holme, Thom Zimny, Rob DeMartin, Jonathan Erhlich, Don Friedman, Jon Landau, Barbara Carr, Jan Stabile, and Alison Oscar.

FROM PRESIDENT OBAMA AND BRUCE SPRINGSTEEN:

Thank you, also, to the Penguin Random House team, for helping us share this book with the world. At PRH, special thanks to Markus Dohle and Madeline McIntosh, for your enthusiasm for this project; to Gina Centrello, David Drake, Aaron Wehner, and Annsley Rosner, for your continued partnership; to Chris Brand, for your design vision, which brought this book to life so beautifully on the page; to Gillian Blake, Lorena Jones, Rachel Klayman, Matt Inman, Madison Jacobs, and Alonzo Vereen, for your editorial guidance; and to Lizzie Allen, Todd Berman, Denise Cronin, Skip Dye, Sally Franklin, Lisa Gonzalez, Derek Gullino, Anna Kochman, Ebony LaDelle, Cynthia Lasky, Matthew Martin, Annette Melvin, Dyana Messina, Jenny Poeuch, Matt Schwartz, Patricia Shaw, Holly Smith, Anke Steinecke, Chris Tanigawa, Jaci Updike, Claire von Schilling, Daniel Wikey, and Stacey Witcraft, for your valuable contributions. And to Deneen Howell at Williams & Connolly and Kate Schatz.

Misha Euceph, Arwen Nicks, Mary Knauf, Andrew Eapen, and the team at Dustlight, thank you for bringing our conversations to life.

BRUCE SPRINGSTEEN

has been inducted into the Rock and Roll Hall of Fame
and the Songwriters Hall of Fame. He is the recipient
of twenty Grammy Awards, an Academy Award, a Tony
Award, and a Kennedy Center Honor. He is the author
of the *New York Times* bestseller *Born to Run* and was
awarded the Presidential Medal of Freedom in 2016. He
lives in New Jersey with his family.

BARACK OBAMA was the forty-fourth president of the United States, elected in November 2008 and holding office for two terms. He is the author of three *New York Times* bestselling books, *Dreams from My Father*, *The Audacity of Hope*, and *A Promised Land*, and is the recipient of the 2009 Nobel Peace Prize. He lives in Washington, DC, with his wife, Michelle. They have two daughters, Malia and Sasha.

ART CREDITS